END OF THE DEADLINE

First published in South Africa in 2018 by Print Matters Heritage an imprint of
Publishing Print Matters (Pty) Ltd
6 Opal Way, San Michel, Noordhoek 7979
Western Cape, South Africa
www.printmatters.co.za
www.facebook.com/PublishingPrintMatters
info@printmatters.co.za

Text Copyright © 2018 Harvey Tyson (www.writinginc.co.za)

The moral right of the author has been asserted.

All rights reserved.

No part of this publication may be reproduced, stored in a retrieval system, or transmitted, in any form or by any means, without the prior permission in writing of the publishers or author, nor be otherwise circulated in any form of binding or cover other than that in which it is published and without a similar condition including this condition being imposed on the subsequent purchaser.

ISBN: 978-0-6399378-0-9

Publisher: Robin Stuart-Clark
Editorial Panel: Nicholas Yell, Craig Tyson, Vanessa Swanepoel
Project management: Vanessa Swanepoel
Design: Publishing Print Matters (Pty) Ltd
Formatting: Michelle de Almeida, The Design Drawer
Printed and Bound by Novus Print Solutions

Publishing Print Matters (Pty) Ltd advocates freedom of speech and the expression of views and opinions however diverse; the views and opinions expressed here are therefore those of the author and do not necessarily represent those of Publishing Print Matters (Pty) Ltd.

As far as we are aware all images are either in the public domain or belong to the author. Should, by some chance, this not be the case please contact the project manager at info@writinginc.co.za

Harvey Tyson
END OF THE DEADLINE
Behind the news 2

Memoirs are written by people who have lost their memories.

I have published that view many times, and now it seems true in my own case. However, I believe that a witness's wandering personal recollections may add truth, relevance, insights and some balance to the countless versions of world and South African history over the last 150 years.

heritage

Other books by Harvey Tyson

Editors Under Fire, Random House 1993 (with end-of-book contributions from Nelson Mandela, Helen Suzman and Lord McGregor, chairman of International Press Institute). "Awesome reminder that nothing like the events in this balanced, chilling account should ever be allowed to happen again" William C. Faure, film producer, head of Combined Artists and founder of TV's *Carte Blanche*.

A Walk on the Wild Side, Struik's Zebra Press 1995, and *Itch of the Twitch*, Struik's Zebra Press 1996. "As South African as Oom Schalk but ... more polished. Harvey Tyson is rapidly becoming a national institution" Jennifer Crwys-Williams, leading literary critic.

Have Wings, Will Fly, Editors Inc 1998. "A natural history classic, like 'The Plains of Camdeboo'." *The Star*.

Birders of a Feather, Editors Inc 1998 "A magnificent book to have on one's shelf, to read and read again!" poet Tatumkhulu Afrika.

Laugh the Beloved Country, Double Storey Books. Juta. 2003, compiled, edited by James Clarke and Harvey Tyson. "I couldn't stop laughing ..." Archbishop Desmond Tutu.

Blood on the Path. A Saga of the founding of South Africa, Springbok Press 2009. "... it puts the story back into history ..." Dr Guy Willoughby, playwright and professor of history.

The Other Side. Behind the news 1 – Print Matters Heritage, 2017. A personal account of the struggles of the past that have divided one nation since a century before it began – and as it continues to do so today.

Asking Questions.

*News 'begins with a man and a woman in a garden.
It ends in Revelations ...
It is always the unreadable that occurs.'*

Oscar Wilde, more than a century ago.

KEEP IN MIND THIS SIMPLE, yet exciting fact of life: You and your family are already living in the "4th Revolution" – and the biggest change in human communications that mankind has ever known. We may all be aware of this, but, after some deep reflection, our minds may boggle at the opportunities this offers, and at the reckless, unprecedented speed of change which is occurring.

To understand that future we need to understand our own perceptions of it and get some perspective of the fate that is staring us in the face. We live in a world where, for the first time in the history of mankind, people are *scientifically* aware of the presence of 'similar' possible life-sustaining planets 'nearby' in our universe. We listen to the leaders in astronomy warning us, for life-and-death reasons, to seek ways of colonising other suitable planets 'nearby' – and to do so *within 50 years*.

In any case, we live in a culturally moribund age which is about to end. It is an age that has been dominated for a hundred years by Western free nations – and their precious free press; an age disrupted by terrorists and dictators and disturbed by Trumpism and speeding global change.

What's next?
One of the next predictable changes – just starting as you read this – is the upwelling social revolution of gender equality. This current, vast new gender 'revolution' is changing, not only the way mankind has instinctively behaved throughout history, but is beginning to create genuine equality for womankind, and should leave females in civilised countries confident enough to assume, *unchallenged*, all the rights, privileges and advantages afforded males from birth.

An even greater fundamental change may be the officially announced Artificial Intelligence programme of China which aims one day to communicate all news and information in a universally available form to all global language groups and to both educated and illiterate people. Think what this could do to our lives; our beliefs; our values!

Amid the great changes about to occur, the world's printed press must plan its own demise and the end of the deadline as we know it. Precious values may be lost in the giant-striding progress of technology. Yet history might not be able to define the precise moment of its death and record it.

It is time then for many of us to recount the tale of the modern press, told in its own formula when reporting events of: "How, What, Who, Why?"

It is also timely for questions to be asked by you, the newspaper reader or journalist, about the press itself in order to explain:
- *How do editorially independent newspapers operate and offer accountability?*
- *What makes news and good reporting? And what the definition of a newspaper is?*
- *Who the great leaders of newspapers are – in this historically brief era of universal education and popular readership? Who its larger-than-life characters are? And who are its villains - the men who have devalued the role of the watchdogs of the Fourth Estate?*
- *More important is the question: "Who will replace them?"*
- *Why is the deadline so significant in news reporting?*
- *The final question is a fundamental one of "Why?"*

The Deadline – the moment when a newspaper's final page must be locked up and printed has, for generations of journalists, been the thrilling, exciting, ominous edge between triumph and disaster. Miss the deadline, then all your efforts are jeopardised. Charles Dickens and Rudyard Kipling knew this, better than anyone. A major story with a potentially vital headline, if its deadline is not met, might scar a good professional journalist for life.

But what matters is that the deadline not only concentrates effort, it provides both discipline and precise accountability. This is because all news reporting exists within the river of time. Floating on the current and merely changing published facts intermittently, as news broadcast stations and blogs are inclined to do, avoids a great deal of accountability.

Newspapers, on the other hand, have had to stand by their printed news and their public apologies for all of time.

The daily deadline, especially on an afternoon paper where every last minute on every page counts every single day on every edition, also provides the measure, the desperation, the challenge and the adrenaline on which news journalists live. It has been so for about 300 years. Until yesterday, people believed that printed papers, with their mechanisms of accountable news-gathering and of disciplined deadlines, were an intrinsic part of civilisation and democracy. They believed that 'the press' would last a thousand years.

So, why is the press – the printed press, with its crucial role in democracy – dying without making adequate arrangements for the next generation? ☐

Contents

PART 1 – THE NATURE OF THE BEAST   1

1. Setting the scene   2
2. Press mogul pisses on the people   16
3. Profile of a journalist   24
4. Household names in the writing trade   30
5. Mischievous misprints   44
6. Dangerous misprints   50
7. Best writing: fiction or non-fiction?   58
8. Reports from a green and pleasant land   64

PART 2 – TELLING IT LIKE IT IS   73

9. A fearful spectacle, defying censorship   74
10. Journalists' eyewitness accounts   82
11. The Dead Hand   92
12. The Berlin Wall   98
13. In the fog: Wat ye Tyler and other Stirring Tales   112
14. Africa's greatest war   122
15. Master spy and global murders   136
16. 'The bravest editor in the cemetery'   150
17. The Times vs. 'Jack the Ripper'   160

PART 3 – PAST AND FUTURE OF THE PRESS   177

18. Pulitzer and the birth of 'popular' newspapers	178
19. The Press Barons who wanted to be Emperors	188
20. US Champions of press freedom	200
21. The man who saved South Africa's 'black' press	212
22. The price of true and constant independence	220
23. Beware the disguised enemy within	228
24. Murdoch the mighty media manager ... Mmmm	236
25. It depends how you use 'Independence'	246
26. When 'independence' becomes a fake	258
27. How the Past could affect the world's Future	266
28. Online investigators bring down the President	272
29. In search of a place to talk freely	290
30. Conflict and the Press	298
31. The end of mainstream newspapers	312
32. The future of journalism	322

INDEX   334

ACKNOWLEDGEMENTS   342

1

The nature of the beast.

1. Setting the scene.

Burke said that there were Three Estates in Parliament, but in the Reporters' Gallery yonder, there sat a Fourth Estate more important far than they all.

Carlyle

Edmund Burke, the source quoted above by Carlyle, was an Irishman and "the greatest political thinker since Francis Bacon who has ever devoted himself to the practice of English politics", according to one historian.

That was why his words and values were accepted without explanation in the British Parliament in the 1870s, and are still quoted everywhere today. But there is another politician, Stanley Baldwin, also internationally quoted today, who had a different view of the press – or rather of the 'press barons' who first came to power in his era of government a hundred years ago.

The press moguls had been normal young men who shot to fame simply by catering to a new class of literate 'commoners' who, for the first time in history, became aware of the opportunities life offered them. Newspapers exploded in circulation by providing information to this first generation of newly literate males keen to explore skilled careers.

(The first British Education Act had come into effect in 1870, providing compulsory free education mainly for males. It was this comprehensive, initially gender-discriminating legislation that by 1930 produced a generation of young men eager to gain skills as well as knowledge. These literate, educated students were among the first in the world to break through most social and political barriers. They were the first readers of 'popular' newspapers designed specifically for

Stanley Baldwin, three times Conservative prime minister of Britain under three different kings with three future PMs working under him.

them. They were perhaps the first voters to be armed with sufficient information to choose their parliamentary representatives with knowledgeable discrimination. The pattern of free and independently absorbed general education, which is so necessary to instil values and strengthen democracy, is only now beginning to reach millions of young people across three continents in our digital world. In the 1930s, the threat of abuse of this literacy by the media became apparent and is likely to be experienced again in digital forms in Asia, Africa and South America in the 2030s.)

In Britain in the last century, Prime Minister Baldwin castigated two newspaper owners with the famous words:

"What the proprietorship of these papers is aiming at is power without responsibility – the prerogative of the harlot through the ages."

Stanley Baldwin was speaking of Lord Beaverbrook and Lord Rothermere. The eternal irony of this famous quote is that it came originally, in those precise words, from a friend of his, famous author and journalist, Rudyard Kipling, addressed to his friend Max Aitken, who became newspaper publisher Lord Beaverbrook! But Prime Minister Baldwin went on to say:

"The newspapers attacking me are not newspapers in the ordinary sense. They are engines of propaganda for the constantly changing policies, desires, personal vices, personal likes and dislikes of the two men. What are their methods? Their methods are direct falsehoods, misrepresentation, half-truths, the alteration of the speaker's meaning by publishing a sentence apart from the context ...."

Baldwin, as leader of the British government was rejecting the assumptions of two over-ambitious press barons, who believed their public influence was sufficient for them to be recognised and rewarded personally and politically by the government for whom their readers voted. It was overweening and stupid of the two newly-made 'lordships'. However, their sins were not as irresponsible as those of the tabloids of today.

We shall meet Lord Rothermere and a number of other ruthlessly ambitious newspaper magnates later. But first let us go right back in newspaper history to examine one of the earliest court reports ever recorded.

PRINTED NEWS may be traced to its beginnings in a court report in Europe nearly five centuries ago, before the concept of regular daily or weekly newspapers was ever considered.

This famous bulletin published in 1587 was interesting – well, sensational – but not very encouraging. Today it would not be tolerated, for it concerned a legal case involving a personage whose existence was not even proven. It involved 'The Devil himself'.

However, Walpurga Haussmannin, according to a news report filed in Vienna in that year, was accused of the most startling series of evil crimes that mankind could commit. It began, the packed court was told, when she "enticed with lewd speeches and gestures" a fellow worker "to indulge in lustful intercourse".

That, in itself, is not as ghastly an event of horror as some might think ... merely a preliminary perhaps to a court case that the *News of the World* might have carried in a few paragraphs before it closed down not long ago. But according to the court, in Haussmannin's case, there were aggravating circumstances. She confessed that, while "awaiting him and thinking evil and fleshly thoughts", it was not he who turned up, but rather a dirty devil, who, in the guise and raiment of her fellow worker, "proceeded to indulge in fornication with her".

The court report continues:
"After the act of fornication, she saw and felt the cloven foot of her whoremonger and observed that his hand appeared to be made of wood ... The very next night the Evil Spirit visited her again in the same shape and whored with her. He made her many promises for which she yielded herself up to him body and soul" ... literally according to the evidence.

Furthermore, Haussmannin "often rode on a pitchfork by night with her paramour ... She ate, drank and slept with the Great Devil who beat her cruelly. For food she often had a good roast or an innocent child, also well roasted, or a suckling pig, with red and white wine, but no salt". (It was common knowledge that the Devil could not abide salt.)

What kind of court could entertain such evidence?

It sounds like an episode from one of the 21st-century vampire film serials ... except that the 16th-century news report quotes reassuring source and detail: Walpurga Hausmannin was tried in the town of Dillegen by a judge and jury appointed by the Bishop of Augsburg, no less. She was convicted, by unanimous vote, under common law and under the criminal code of the Emperor Charles V of the Holy Roman Empire.

Walpurga, if we may be less formal with her name after 400 years, was the willing victim of a hoax by a dubious demon named Federlin, who promised to save her from poverty if she would swear allegiance to, and affirm a contract between herself and the devil. According to her evidence, Federlin then flew her (on his pitch-fork, of course) to visit Satan.

She described Satan as "a big man with a grey beard, richly attired and sitting in a chair like a great prince". He confirmed her contract, after which they drank wine, ate roasted babies and had sex.

Hausmannin claimed that the demon Federlin had given her an ointment which she had used to hurt people, children, animals and harvests; and had often visited her for sex, even in the streets at night and in prison. She was alleged to have murdered 40 children before they were baptised. She was accused of killing them during her work as a midwife, and allegedly sucking their blood like a vampire. She had joined with other witches in 'festing' on children and using their hair and bones.

But how on earth could such evidence be accepted?

Simple: The "evil and wretched woman, now imprisoned and in chains, has, under solicitous questioning as well as torture, confessed her witchcraft and made ... the admissions."

Her enforced confessions were so heinous (a Germanic word) that not only was she sentenced to burn at the stake, but ordered to be taken first on a long route in a cart where, outside the town hall and four other public points, her body was to be "torn five times with red-hot irons, first her right breast, then the other, then the left arm, then the other and finally her right hand to be chopped off before she reached the marketplace where she would be tied to a stake and burned in front of the populace."

The case was of such grave public import that a bulletin covering the trial and sentence needed to be published soon after the event in 1587. A copy of the original publication is housed in the National Museum of Vienna. It is, of course, a wonderful example of entirely accurate, judicious, reporting of a formal trial – written even before the printing press was properly operating – and tells us more vividly about the history and mores, beliefs, superstitions and educational standards of medieval Europe than any academic volume you are ever likely to read.

That is the virtue of contemporaneous news reporting.

The Vienna report, summarised here, was selected by two excellent professors of journalism, Louis L Snyder and Richard B Morris, of New York, for their *Treasury of Great Reporting*.

The Walpurga trial, staged well over 400 years ago, is perhaps the earliest landmark in the history of newspapers – and a basic lesson in why journalistic ethics are essential. The news in this case was a report – without comment – on a trial. The falsities were in the mouths of those who gave evidence which was built on ill-informed religious belief and liturgical invention.

Today, if a United States President speaks of "false news" that is news; even if his statement was false. But let's not go there.

FORTUNATELY, modern tabloid journalism is unable to match the sensationalism emanating from the Bishop of Augburg's court in the Middle Ages – though not through lack of trying. For instance, a headline in an unethical tabloid today might read:

MAN RAPES MAID IN DEATH-BED

"At dawn, with The Sun under her arm, the mini-skirted maid carried a tray of tea upstairs and entered Room 6 without knocking. She placed her burden beside the satin-sheeted bed. The lodger, very apparently, was wide-awake. At sight of him, her partly exposed breasts heaved, though whether from surprise, fear or passion, cannot be established."

The above is a fictitious report – slick, sick and gross – which might have been carried in a tabloid after a court verdict on rape and murder. The headline would have been huge. If it were not the pretty maid, but the landlord of the B&B who had been attacked then a smaller headline, only slightly bigger than the *New York Times* main lead, might have appeared in crisp Cockney slang: LODGER ROGERS CODGER.

A strange symptom of tabloid journalism is its allegiance to alliteration in all its allocutions, leading licentious illiterates into loads of linguistic leachate. (*Touché!* The Tasteless Tabloids' Technique is Twisted, Tested and Terminated in Two Ticks! ... In the time it takes to type this tripe in fact.)

However, this is the story of real newspapers and real life which, unfortunately for purists, seeks no difference of legal recognition between the tabloids and the mainstream 'Press'. Some might argue, though, that it is only the tabloids who revel in 'real life'.

Yet the starting point here is that the tabloids are more like adult comics, for they amuse and encourage the semi-literate to read. They are duplicitous, of course, when they lie and cheat and recklessly or *illegally* print scandal that damages the lives of popular 'celebrities' (a term applied to almost anyone these days, often of little reputation, who has managed to garner or been exposed to a little pop publicity).

The tabloid scandal sheets are at their worst when they bully and bribe. But they are at their most dangerous to society, as dangerous as the press barons were when they tried to be power brokers by personally influencing politicians and swaying popular opinion. And there lies the problem for the mainstream press. Some tabloid-size publications *are* newspapers. And some serious newspapers are tablet-size, but call themselves compacts. And a few broadsheet papers are really tabloids, disguising their degeneration in the traditional broadsheet format.

The first of the grotty, downmarket newspapers in the world were launched as a chain of tabloids, not necessarily in shape, but in the sense of their tawdry content. Conversely, the first major tabloid in Britain, *The Daily Mirror,* was once an influential socio-political newspaper, as we shall see. But then came Rupert Murdoch, who linked the ownership of the legendary London newspaper, *The Times,* to two notorious tabloids seen by many as whores: *The Sun* and the *News of the World,* which carried the scandal sheets down to their two lowest common denominators.

The mainstream or 'popular' press – sometimes called more precisely and correctly by some academics, the 'accountable press' – does not belong there.

However, as the tabloids insist on being called newspapers, it might distinguish them best if one were to use the term 'downmarket press'.

I intend to refer as little as possible to the eccentric tabloids, even in chapters on America's notorious Yellow Press, and in a brief history of the extraordinary, sometimes scandalous rule in Britain of the press barons. Celebrity scandal should remain in magazines and in TV shows devoted to the subject in a context where gossip and online speculation about the antics of well-known figures can be seen, not as news, but for what they are.

Established metropolitan newspapers were designed to carry news (never random scandal and gossip) and were meant to be set out in a style and specific page position and sequence that were known and accepted by their readers so that they understood each report's context and recognised each newspaper story's *professionally weighed significance*. None would accept a bit of local scandal as a front-page lead in place of the most significant – rather than popular – news story of the moment.

It is these newspapers which allowed the world's mainstream press to be summed up in a conundrum which was once fashionable across the English-speaking world: "What is black and white and re(a)d all over?"

Newspaper readers posed this spoken riddle to the ignorant or less literate of their acquaintances, decades before cable and pay-television; before full-colour mass printing was invented and before the famous *La Prensa* was attacked and closed down in Buenos Aires and *The World* was gagged and murdered in 1977 in Soweto, South Africa.

It was before journalists around the globe were being killed at the rate of two a week. It was before 'killing the messenger' became a crime that threatened to affect all mankind. On the 400th anniversary of its birth, the printed daily press finally reached its peak in the year 2005 ... when many circulations began to decline.

THERE ARE MANY dates appropriate for commemorating the start of newspaper history. The British would settle for 1601 when the Star Chamber ceased its total censorship. But 1605 is the date recognised in the 21st century by the World Association of Newspapers. During that summer in the 16th century, Johann Carolus was earning his living by producing handwritten newsletters with reports provided by a network of paid correspondents.

Mechanised printing replaces copying by hand.

His newsletter, entitled Relation, sold only to rich literate subscribers at very high prices. He found it took him "too much time" and he calculated he could earn a lot more money that year by using the new technology of mechanical printing to publish "a higher circulation for a lower price".

(People were pretty smart and independent in those early days, for they printed increasing numbers of papers at lower cost and sold them at a profit. Nowadays many newspapers frantically chase circulation by selling below cost! Or give them away to please or sometimes to delude their advertisers.)

The modern popular press came to life more than 300 years after machine printing began. It was prompted in technically advanced countries by the introduction of compulsory school education for all. As noted earlier, the British education legislation of the 1870s produced for the first time (as late as the 20th century!) a generation of readers who demanded, directly and personally, current knowledge about business and government, about job opportunities, training and self-improvement courses. They were also interested in less restrained reports of crime and scandals. Womankind in these advanced countries had to fight for similar rights until the 1930s – and struggle for the rest of the century for other rights.

The first cylinder flat-bed press was built by Friedrich Koenig of Germany and used by The Times of London in 1814.

However, instead of describing all this in an unavoidably boring, chronological history of the modern press, I will cover the story of the world's modern newspapers – their life and looming death – in chapters that hopefully will remind us all of what good journalism is all about. And of the many threats it has faced. These stories should remind us, too, of the thrills – not so much of the scoops – but of the discovery of interesting, useful and empowering, as well as powerful information. And, yes, also the thrills of the occasional excellent writing uncovered along the way.

Most of all, the story needs to be told of the overwhelmingly ambitious men who were corrupted by their own success as press proprietors.

A pressing story

The newspaper mechanical press itself has a story that needs re-telling. Some of it will be recounted in the first person because I suddenly realised that I am one of very few left who have worked beside newspaper presses ranging from an old-world flatbed to the latest giant rotaries. I remember with nostalgia working as a kid reporter beside venerable typographers on the *Diamond Field Advertiser*'s ancient flat-bed press in Kimberley, South Africa. This flat-bed was built in the mid-1800s and became one of the very last in the world to be used by an urban daily newspaper. It was still turning out a fully-fledged morning paper in the 1940s.

Also, my memory holds fast to a daily feel of the shake of a modern, pounding press, and the almost undetectable shiver upstairs during the basement-roar of various rotary presses of different kinds of newspapers on three continents. And finally, of being privileged to watch, almost daily, the last of the giant automated, full-colour Goss Metroliner printers on the Johannesburg goldfields. These presses were a combination of machines capable of producing 50,000 newspapers or up to 500,000 broadsheet pages an hour. Such combinations still roar day-and-night in a few major cities across the world, printing thousands of newspapers per minute. But their multi-million dollar costs are likely to discourage the replacement of similar giant presses in any major independent newspaper ever again.

Today more than a billion people across the planet read a daily newspaper in print. The Paris-based World Association of Newspapers represented in that anniversary year of 2005, more than 18,000 newspapers. Its membership included 72 national newspaper associations, individual newspaper executives in 102 countries, 10 news agencies and 10 regional and world-wide press groups. By 2014 all of them were facing the threat of digital news coverage and a foreboding, unknown future.

OF ALL THE TRAGEDIES that will be touched on among the newspaper comedies here, the greatest of all is the fate of 'the press' itself. It is, I believe, a cause for deep sadness that even the most solid and best of the mainstream papers are already dying. The metropolitan daily press will vanish, I believe, probably within a decade, but certainly after the demise of the current mid-life generation of readers who were the last to be weaned on a daily diet of press-printed information.

What will remain will be the constant struggle to report news accurately at all levels and to protect your right to information. These tasks will continue in less palpable, yet more powerful and flexible electronic forms. The shape, style, economic sustainability and professional accountability of the 21st-century 'press' have yet to be properly recognised and formalised. I am confident that these independent and competitive electronic newspapers without deadlines will require, and can get from the best of the existing mainstream press, better standards of journalism than before. Their first challenge is to overcome the torrent of rumour, gossip and multiplied lies that swamp the ether and confuse voters with "fake news" ... a term which President Trump made instantly famous in one of his countless ironies. "Fake News", he told his supporters, was what the famous free press of the United States was spreading about *him*. (President Donald Trump said in October, 2017: *"Really ... I think one of the greatest of all terms I have come up with ... is 'fake'."*)

On New Year's Eve, 1917, a review was broadcast on the status of journalists being held in custody around the world. The numbers were far higher than in previous years, yet did not include the dozens who had already been held in Turkey for ten months by then. More editors, reporters and foreign correspondents were being held without trial; particularly in Africa where a spokesman advocating freedom of expression and freedom of the press told the South African Broadcasting Corporation: "What concerns us is that African nations are so non-committal on the increasing numbers of journalists in custody."

She said that the shibboleth 'Fake News' seemed to be the excuse for locking up writers and commentators who were critical of politicians. And that the absence of the definition of 'fake news' not only encouraged more *arrests* in Africa, the Middle-East and China, it also discouraged *protest* at the jailing without trial of so many more journalists.

Leaving aside President Trump's irrelevant and false view, the question for today's newspapers is: will production of a mainstream digital 'press' have widespread readership? Will it be adequately heard in an era of increasing mass twittering, flash-messaging; instant commentary and dumbing down of language? The other contradictory phrase that accompanies 'Fake News' is 'Alternate Facts', a sinister and dishonest concept that needs to be countered by all journalists in search of the truth and nothing but the truth.

(However, language is in any case already changing faster than any master of grammar can cope with. This overrules their laws against sentences without a verb, and those ending with a preposition; as in my previous sentence.)

There are also countless competitive threats to traditional newspapers. Minute-by-minute video bulletins for instance – and the trend, arriving only in recent years, of 24-hour continuous coverage and comment on a single major event by top TV news channels – already demonstrate TV's total dominance of global, 'runningnews' coverage. Even TV *analyses* of these crises are suddenly outpacing and outweighing the editorial comment and coverage of top newspapers and top individual online commentators. The current TV blanket coverage of major running international news is another small example of how change is occurring so fast it is difficult to predict where it will lead. Will it ever render *The New York Times,* for instance, irrelevant?

Even if trustworthy, comprehensive in-context 'press' coverage increasingly dominates online, it seems inappropriate, as well as sad, that the physical press will be dispatched to rest in peace while the struggle still goes on to win or maintain your freedoms.

Until now, that struggle has been the constant and most significant role of the world's mainstream press. Sadly, the decades-awaited moment is coming when, at least so far as your 'accountable' printed newspaper is concerned, you will finally have to say: "God-bless you Gutenberg, and goodbye."

However, before this happens; before tears of nostalgia arise, it is worth taking a clear-eyed look at the phenomenon of the press barons who have led, and often plagued, the press. You are about to meet one "baron" who was decorated with the highest honour for bravery in war, and despised for his bravado and dishonesty in business. He was a pauper who made billions ... and died penniless. He was certainly one of the most flamboyant press proprietors in history. ☐

2.
Press mogul pisses on the people.

Principles never come 'atween him and his purse.

James Hogg 1820s

The press barons of Britain provide a gallery of portraits of the most extraordinary men; nearly all of them with overweening ambitions and supreme over-confidence. They have dominated most of the English-speaking world for the past century. Each might be a worthy subject for a Shakespearean drama or a sharply-drawn Dickensian character profile. Each appeared to become corrupted by intangible power. Each directly influenced English-language culture in various subtle and not so subtle ways.

Yet, as it happens, many of them were not British. It is an Australian who has been the most dominant in the world media; while the most interesting example is Robert Maxwell.

He was born Jan Ludvik Hoch as a Czech – with perhaps the most chequered career recorded anywhere in the 20th century. He dominates the press barons' gallery as the most flamboyant, and enigmatic, of them all. His life and death remain unsolved mysteries enacted in real-life in the style of a James Bond movie.

Indeed, he was featured in a James Bond movie.

If it is possible to sum up his life through his different careers, the list would include: Businessman. Philanthropist. Politician. Hero of the State of Israel. Arms dealer. Songwriter. Air force officer. Blackmailer. Harpist. Newspaper tycoon. Embezzler. International spy.

Robert Maxwell, man of many conflicting parts.

Let's start with the good stuff first: In World War II he so impressed General Montgomery that he was awarded the Military Cross. After the war his benevolence in helping the homeless was so widespread it could never be fully recorded. Later he was recognised as a benefactor of the new State of Israel,

The young warrior who ended the war against Hitler by winning an MC.

and honoured as such at his death. He was a harpist and songwriter, who wrote the world-acclaimed music for two well-known productions: *Ebb Tide* and *Shangri-La*. He was a patron of classical dance.

I saw him several times, but only at professional meetings where he showed a puzzling absence of the arrogance Fleet Street gossip said he displayed. He owned in the 1980s, among many other things, *The Daily Mirror* where he used to land by helicopter on the newspaper building's roof, and journalists would tell each other: "The Ego has landed."

So I was puzzled to observe him at one or two functions where he was not needed, where he sat, a small lonely figure, seemingly to appear to be hoping for recognition and some attention where he was unable to command it. His dejected manner in this context evoked sympathy rather than the fear and anger that his life produced.

However, a carefully researched BBC biopic presented him as the ebullient character that was his trademark. For instance, he is portrayed while entertaining two bankers on his Mirror Group rooftop and, after much champagne, invites them to join in his attempt to empty his bladder over the parapet onto pedestrians far below.

David Suchet, the actor who portrayed Maxwell, said this 'true-life' portrayal symbolised the tycoon's habit of treating people with disdain by pissing on them from a great height. An apt comparison perhaps; though some might have thought it to be the act of a somewhat inebriated host behaving like a mischievous kid.

But Suchet told *The Telegraph:*

"Playing him, I felt the sheer power of the man ... a dangerously intoxicating feeling for anyone. If you know that when you click fingers people will instantly jump ... you click your fingers. (Maxwell) was driven by a sense of being ostracised from the mainstream. He constantly said he didn't care about being accepted, but I think ... he wanted to be part of society, but society didn't want him. In fact, the more he tried to fit in with the establishment, the less they let him in. He became a media tycoon, because he was desperate to have influence and a voice."

Others believe Maxwell (his officially adopted English name) was driven by the poverty of his childhood – he claimed he did not own a pair of shoes until the age of seven – or by the fact that many of his family in Czechoslovakia and Hungary had died in Hitler's Holocaust. His Orthodox Jewish parents were also victims, and by his account, he only just managed to escape the concentration camps by fleeing to Britain in 1940. Whatever it was that drove him, Maxwell took every opportunity from every contact he made. He took reckless shortcuts whenever he thought it worthwhile.

By 1964 he had acquired sufficient wealth (through his contacts with German publishers) to win a Labour seat in Westminster, where his Prime Minister, Harold Wilson, referred to him when he left Parliament later as "the bouncing Czech". It was an obvious nickname, yet an insightful one, and ominous, because he possessed an obsession with being top dog.

He was obsessed with beating the Australian, Rupert Murdoch, who had already moved into Britain and bought newspapers.

In 1984 Maxwell seized his chance by raising the funds to buy the biggest of all, the Mirror Group of Newspapers, from Reed International. However, in 1988, like many of the press barons before him, Maxwell over-extended himself. He did so by scooping up the American interests in Macmillan publishers. His repayments on the deal at one point reached £3-million a day.

Inevitably, Maxwell's empire started to topple. At this critical moment he 'borrowed' £1-billion from his own companies' pension funds. It was one of the biggest frauds on record at that time.

His launch of *The European*, a serious upmarket newspaper, was among his finest achievements. That newspaper was one of the first in Britain to carry full colour and it covered the European continent as if all its peoples were his readers.

But like every media project he launched, it did not last.

Maxwell's death proved as spectacular as his colourful life. Having deprived his thousands of staff of their pensions, he set off on his private, four-deck, high-powered yacht and vanished from the public gaze. Later he was reported "lost at sea". The mystery of his disappearance made world headlines for three days before his body was found floating in the Atlantic near the Canary Islands. It was concluded that he must have stepped off the lowest deck of his luxury vessel in the early hours while most of the people on board were fast asleep.

His death in November 1991 at the age of 68 prompted the Labour Party to say of their long-term supporter: "Mr Maxwell was a man with a zest for life (who) ... attracted controversy, envy and loyalty in great measure throughout his rumbustious life."

In Britain uproar followed the discovery of Maxwell's theft of the Mirror Group's pension fund and sharp remembrance of earlier financial misdemeanours. (The growing habit of press proprietors to plunder their staffs' pension funds demonstrated early on that the anger of a journalist whose pension is stolen is twice that of a woman scorned.)

Britain read great outpourings of hate in the popular press, once readers had recovered from the shock of his supposed choice of death ... stepping quietly and alone into the ocean far out in the Atlantic at dead of night.

In Israel it was claimed that Maxwell in his bold younger days had secretly helped save the Jewish State during their 1948 War of Independence. He played a major part in smuggling aircraft parts out of Britain and ensuring Israel had air supremacy in that crisis. It was also claimed that Maxwell's contacts with Mikhail Gorbachev had helped hundreds of thousands of Russians to reach the Holy Land.

At his death, his newspaper, *The Daily Mirror,* published further claims, hotly denied, that he was assassinated by the Israeli Mossad because he had attempted to blackmail them. Maxwell's funeral took place on the Mount of Olives in Jerusalem, with all of Israel's government and opposition leaders and successive heads of the Israeli intelligence attending. Prime Minister Yitzhak Shamir said in the main oration: "He has done more for Israel than can today be said."

It would have made Robert Maxwell smile, at last.

Though hated by his employees, it is said that (like media moguls Rupert Murdoch and Tony O'Reilly) Maxwell could be immensely charming when he wished, and did a vast amount of work for the charities around him. His family life was marred by sadness, yet appeared impeccable. His death was still making waves (if I may use that macabre metaphor) in this century. For instance, in 2002 his old paper *The Daily Mirror* reiterated its original claim that Maxwell didn't jump ship but was pushed ... or, one is expected to conclude, was murdered in some way on board. The report read:

British Publisher Robert Maxwell Was Mossad Spy
New Claim On Tycoon's Mystery Death

After two and a half years of investigative journalism, we believe we have unearthed the true story of Maxwell's death and can reveal how he was murdered by the Israeli secret service, Mossad.

Our work, supported by documents, including FBI reports and secret intelligence files from behind the Iron Curtain, shows Maxwell had worked as a secret super spy for Mossad for six years.

The Jewish millionaire and former Labour MP died the way he had lived – threatening. He had threatened his wife. Threatened his children.Threatened the staff of this newspaper.

But finally he issued one threat too many – he threatened Mossad.

He told them that unless they gave him £400-million to save his crumbling empire, he would expose all he had done for them.

In that time, he had free access to Margaret Thatcher's Downing Street, to Ronald Reagan's White House, to the Kremlin and to the corridors of power throughout Europe.

On top of that he had built himself a position of power within the crime families of Eastern Europe, teaching them how to funnel their vast wealth from drugs, arms smuggling and prostitution to banks in safe havens around the globe.

Maxwell passed on all the secrets he learned to Mossad in Tel Aviv. In turn, they tolerated his excesses, vanities and insatiable appetite for a luxurious lifestyle and women.

Such is the flamboyant and flawed character of many a media mogul or press baron. We shall see these traits repeated a number of times in this account of the modern press. Their true stories – which, unsurprisingly, they succeeded partly in suppressing while in power – sometimes seem more incredible than anything you might read in the tabloid press. Which is saying a great deal.

Does this reflect on journalism?

Of course it does.

We've seen proof of this in the scandals surrounding Rupert Murdoch's *Sun,* which mirrored (pun intended) the very worst of Yellow Journalism – despite the objections of most of the journalists they employed.

But, as you will see from the records of many media moguls whose shenanigans will be examined later in this account of the press, it is usually the moneyed owners who are directly responsible for corrupt journalism. Their presence is the very reason why editorial independence needs to be protected; first from big business proprietors and then from politicians and corrupt governments. Most journalists spurn big money. And they have considerably more value for that. □

BEHIND THE NEWS 2

3.
Profile of a journalist.

Journalism will kill you, but it will keep you alive while you are at it.

Horace Greeley (founder & editor,
New-York Tribune, died 1872).

"How can I become a journalist?" That's the question I have been asked most often in the past 50 years. Usually it is from a parent enquiring resignedly on behalf of an eager student wishing to become a hot-shot reporter or scintillating columnist, with a website journal of his/her own in ten years' time. The question leads to a predictable conversation, beginning with my counter-question:

"Why does your child *want* to get into journalism?"

"Heaven knows! I've tried to dissuade her/him. I want my child to take up a respectable and useful career like mine – but the idiot refuses to consider anything except writing ... even when I point out that there's no money in it."

"Bad luck," I say. "It seems you have a very promising journalistic candidate in your family."

The most erudite, eloquent journalist I ever knew did not attend a day at high school, ever. Poliomyelitis crippled him for life and kept him in bed throughout his youth. Instead of formal learning, he read, over several years of his childhood, hundreds of books in bed. Percy Baneshik grew up to be a famous commentator on theatre, the arts and music and a literary critic in print and in broadcasting.

All my children, despite my strenuous efforts at dissuasion, went into journalism one way or another. Each has different talents, different skills and even different educations. One has a degree in computer accountancy – when most journalists pride themselves in finding it difficult to add six and seven. Another kept me in awe for years by getting 100% in final exams for maths! Only the eldest had a degree in journalism. All three ended up being damn good at the job, especially in the different writing styles each adopted. It shows how infinitely varied journalism is, in each of its innumerable aspects. My stepson went first into law, then advertising, then sacrificed a good income in order to become a full-time freelance writer!

There is neither formal guidance nor general rule to determine who makes a fine journalist.

Yet there is one sure sign. It is the presence of two qualities: enthusiasm and curiosity. Enthusiasm most of all; even when suppressed. That's the test.

When looking for journalistic qualities in candidates you should search for those two, and if you see them, then question whether your budding candidate suffers from the writing *itch*. (If she or he has the itch, usually unknowingly, then it's almost certain your candidate has some kind of talent for the calling, because that's where the itch originated in the first place. My own experience teaches me that even an unremarkable talent can create a serious, impossible to resist, lifetime itch.)

That is one reason why I tried very hard to dissuade all my family from joining the ranks in which I was employed. I needed to test them. My other motive was that I would have wished that my kids might earn enough to support their, at one time, penniless journo father in his old age. For that goal, journalism is a very thin bet. Anyway, they took no notice of my advice, as I expected.

My eldest even disregarded the best advice one could give any journalistic candidate. It is this: if you *must* be a journalist/writer, place not all your faith in a journalism degree. Study some major subject that may enrich your life. Economics. Literature, perhaps. Politics. Law. Botany. Even Art.

For a budding all-round journalist, law and economics usually prove to be the most useful subjects in which to immerse oneself. But if candidates' interests are in specialised issues, then they should follow those particular interests, no matter how esoteric the subjects may be. It is where life tends to lead anyway.

The above thoughts are to encourage your children – if they have the journo/writing *itch* – to think outside the box.

How do you define a journalist? Well, you can't really. That's the point of free speech. Anyone can be a journalist.

The flattering concept of being ranked the Fourth Estate so enchanted the world's scribes that they applied it to themselves without discrimination – forgetting that it referred only to us rogues in the parliamentary gallery. A century later a journalist (Rudyard Kipling) restored balance by alluding to a colleague thus:

He hath sold his heart

To the old Black Art
They call the daily Press

The Press has been called many things in its time, very few of them sincerely good. Its detractors consist mainly of politicians, demagogues, white collar criminals, vile bodies (which is a reminder to read – please do so, if only for the laughs– Evelyn Waugh's old classic entitled *Scoop*). The detractors of journalism, of course, include journalists themselves.

Evelyn Waugh was one of the great satirists of the last century ... so wicked and funny and so prolific in finding targets (including journalism) that he was left with few friends and less of a writer's reputation than he deserved.

Journalists are indeed filled with human fallibility and there are many with decidedly nasty frailties. It must be conceded, however, that their idealism exceeds that of brothel keepers (usually), and invariably used car salesmen, politicians, bankers, businessmen, brokers, hoteliers, policemen, consultants and uncivil servants.

Who in that list, beside journos, can you count on to go to jail to protect an impalpable professional principle?

Who is least likely to be bribed? Remember Humbert Wolfe's famous tribute, now treasured by scribes across the world:
You cannot hope to bribe or twist
(Thank God) the British journalist
But seeing what the man will do
Unbribed, there's no occasion to

WHAT TYPE of personality; what qualities, make a good journalist?

It is a good question, but it has no answer. Successful journalists – like fine artists and great actors, no doubt – defy psychometrics, psychological probes and skills tests. The best journalists, whether shy or extrovert; articulate or silent; precise or disorganised, have one thing in common: they burn to write. They have a mission – even if it may be merely to spread the news – and they demand to do what they do best. Financial reward comes remarkably low in their priorities.

There are so many fine journalists. And there are so many weird characters. There must be three times as many eccentrics in journalism than in any other activity ... except, probably in the theatrical arts. Several eccentric journalists I have described elsewhere. Here are others whom I have known:

The court reporter of the *Natal Daily News* who tried to sue a dear old Zulu washerwoman for two shillings and sixpence (25 cents) because she 'ruined' one of his shirts.

The Star's chief sub-editor (in his younger days an Olympic hurdler) who, when a colleague called to see him in his luxurious apartment block, found him lying ill on a mattress on the floor of a bare room. He looked up from the telephone directory he was perusing to explain: "After reading so many thousands of words of bullshit every day, I prefer looking at this to reading books in my spare time."

The affable financial journo in Johannesburg who boasted of his ownership of a Thai brothel.

The Foreign Correspondent in New York, who used to demonstrate an irritating and uncomfortable obsequiousness when you visited his office in Times Square. This behaviour –"Yes sir, no sir, three bags full, sir" – would last until about the fifth drink at the famous bar down the road ... where he would suddenly glower at you as if you were his Mafia landlord. He would then turn on you with a verbal assault that threatened to become physical before he suddenly abandoned you to fend for your lonely self; lost with your luggage in the Big Apple. It was a ritual I came to expect and almost to admire.

The sub-editor (Jewish) who resigned from *The Star* because he could not stand the tension of living in South Africa's apartheid state any longer.

"Which country have you chosen for a peaceful life?" I asked.

"I'm off to Lebanon" (the land where any pro-Israeli journalist would be highly unpopular ... and at a time when Beirut was the most bombed city on Earth).

The journalistic 'characters' come in all forms, shapes and sizes, most of them harmless though ominously filled with good intentions. The high number of eccentrics in the professional ranks of journalism is as it should be.

Of course most journalists will contradict anything. The reporter who once tried to sue his wash-lady – and had the disconcerting habit of rattling a pencil between his teeth until the newsroom echoed with it – once announced:

"It's a pity there are just no *characters* left in journalism anymore."

The ones described below are less salutary, motivated it appears by politics and self-aggrandisement – and operate, mostly, outside of the organised, professional ranks.

But the principle of freedom of speech demands that anyone can indulge in journalism – and 21st-century technology, together with talents for blogging, is at last allowing this to happen.

In an article by staff writer Johanna Neuman, the *New York Times* once listed numbers of dubious representatives of dubious 'news' organisations – even imposters – who succeeded in joining the elite White House press corps to question the President and his spokesperson.

"I've made mistakes in my past," one such dubious character told the *Washington Post*'s media critic, Howard Kurtz. "Does my past mean I can't have a future? Does it disqualify me from being a journalist?"

Apparently not.

The White House press corps has since attracted an array of unusual personalities. There was Naomi Nover of the Nover News Service. No one ever saw her work published, but Nover – whose coif of white hair somewhat resembled George Washington's wig – got past a security cordon during a Reagan trip to China after a reporter showed guards a US dollar bill as evidence of how important she was, reported Johanna Neuman.

Clinton's White House Press Secretary, Mike McCurry, told her, "I've always thought it was dangerous for the White House to get into the business of defining who is and is not a member of the press corps ... That is better done by the news media."

Reporters, too, seem reluctant to join the fray.

"We wanted to err on the side of inclusion," said Steve Scully of C-SPAN, who serves on the executive board. "Once you start dictating who is a journalist, you go down a slippery slope." (My emphasis.)

Talent and honesty are two badges that immediately identify good journalists, as those I shall name in the next chapter instantly testify. ☐

4.
Household names in the writing trade.

"Goring," wrote Rebecca West at the Nuremberg trials, *"has the look of a brothel madam."*

Word images of that calibre are almost impossible to forget.

Generally, journalism is a respected – not respectable – profession. And if the 'indiscipline' sometimes associated with the calling infers insufficiently controlled, then thank goodness for that. But, if lack of discipline is taken to mean lack of specialist knowledge, of rules, of codes, of institutes of instruction, etcetera, let it be said that journalism is over-fed with these. In fact, from where I sit on another continent, the USA appears to possess more university schools, text guides and guidelines on ethics than most other careers.

Lack of respectability? There's a thought. The most respected journalists are inclined to be rebels. Certainly they question, criticise and make independent judgments about almost everything. Journos do not, or rather should not, seek respectability. Respect, yes. Let me offer at random a few examples of journalists who have gained more respect than a successful millionaire can imagine.

The journalists listed below attained:
- International respect above that of kings, presidents, prime ministers
- Greater admiration than multi-billionaire donors to charity, or victorious five-star generals
- Global acclaim as high as that received by any of the world's academics, financiers, lawyers and doctors.

This young reporter didn't really want to write – yet he did so throughout his life.

Take, for instance, the journalist who began his career as a second-stringer to the London *Morning Post*'s correspondent sent to cover the South African War in 1898. He outshone his senior partner, and became an unofficial roving correspondent, later going home to become a political commentator. Regrettably, he was distracted by politics and similar interests for much of his life – but never gave up writing. It was this practising of journalism, and a bit of journalistic oratory, that made him famous. And look at the glorious books he left the world.

Considering his mistakes in peace-time politics, Winston Churchill might have done better, during any peaceful environment, if he'd stuck to the writing trade.

Then there was that somewhat stuffy Africa correspondent who was dispatched, you will remember, to places where other reporters would not, or could not go. He designed his own tropic explorer's hat and single-handedly slogged it through *veld* and *vlei* until he encountered the subject of his interview and pronounced his famous greeting: "Dr Livingstone I presume?" HM Stanley wrote a tremendous book about it. He did much more than that. He wrote another (which I and many thousands of others still have in our libraries today). It is a book which opened up central Africa to the rest of the world. For he had followed the mighty Congo River from its source to its mouth. He wrote about its potential and the vast unmapped forests and resources each side of it. He triggered the 'Scramble for Africa' which changed the African continent for better, for worse, and forever.

What about Sam Clemens? Sam was a country boy with a modest education, but an instinct for rebellious journalism. He became a roving freelancer, covering unpopular issues such as poverty in mid-America and racism in San Francisco. He was among that rare group of scribes – the few who do not take themselves too seriously. His comic talent led him to adopt a new persona for his reporting *and* his writing. He became Mark Twain, the most popular man in America, popular even after he had dared to write a novel about a rebellious white orphan-kid who joined up with a runaway slave and sailed down the Mississippi, making fun of folks and defying the law by not turning in the slave as he was supposed to do.

Young Sam became a reporter who wanted to make people laugh.

Huck Finn was just a boy who knew no better. Mark Twain travelled round the world (once he caught a ride on a proved-to-be moving Swiss glacier, which proved too slow for him) and was hailed everywhere, even in South Africa, which boasted an *unthreatened* free press at the time. He became more famous than his President, Theodore Roosevelt.

Rudyard Kipling became so famous that he had to buy up all the properties around him in London to give himself privacy. He was a damned hard-working reporter and editor until the fame of his freelance writing, and Victorian patriotism, overwhelmed him. He not only won the Nobel Prize for literature, he did something many considered much better. He invented snow golf, using a red golf ball. Edgar Wallace, a boy from a lowly home with no money and little learning, forced his way up life's ladder to become a newspaper editor in South Africa and the author in London of *more than 40* crime thrillers. Sometimes he wrote several books at once.

Two other names that are the basis for any journalistic list are two 'icons' of the craft: Daniel Defoe, author of *Robinson Crusoe, Moll Flanders* and countless other books, pamphlets and reports under at least 198 pennames in the early 1700s. He is recognised in the English-speaking world as the 'father of journalism'. (He was one of the earliest journalists to be sent to jail, which helps establish his title.)

The other icon, of course, is the reporter who has been described often as "the greatest writer in the English language after Shakespeare". His freelance writing rose directly out of his reporting duties, and was done under deadline and published in instalments in the newspapers. He wrote under his own, ordinary name, Charles Dickens. He championed the poor, attacked the class-system, the skewed capitalist system and most other contemporary wrongs – and reached a level of popularity, through his breezy prose, greater than anyone before him. Respected? He was revered – especially by the Russian revolutionaries.

Young newshound Charlie, began to write light stuff – and heavy stuff.

The three journalists pictured above deserve full recognition. They are the faces of young Winston Churchill, of young Charlie Dickens, and of young Sam Clemens, who called himself Mark Twain.

However, there are many more household names in the writing trade –

END OF THE DEADLINE

You thought 'demos' were a 21st-century phenomenon? In mid-20th century, Americans wanted back their freedom – at a moment when the world's most democratic nation almost lost it. (See Alistair Cooke's Report from America, below.)

including the women reporters, who fought their way into journalism before they had a vote or a right to education, or even access to business and industrial premises.

Let us now look at more great names – including Clare Hollingworth, for instance, the first woman cadet reporter in Fleet Street who began her career by alerting the planet to one of the biggest moments in human history. She witnessed the very moment that World War II secretly started.

Journalists who gained respect, even admiration, in my day include some old-timers like Scotty Reston, Ernest Hemingway, Alistair Cooke, Hunter S. Thompson, Tom Wolfe, Clive James, John Simpson and a hundred others who became household names in the English-speaking world; and beyond.

Here's a random sample of other names among the hundreds who are internationally famous:
- **John Steinbeck** (1902-1968) of the *San Francisco News* reported on the poverty-stricken migrants of the Great Depression three years before he wrote about them in his classic, *The Grapes of Wrath*. Steinbeck also

visited and reported on Stalingrad, though not directly on that greatest armoured battle in history. His gift, though, was for writing brilliant novels, because they looked – almost simultaneously – at life and fun, and horror, and dramatic experience, from many unexpected, deeply relevant angles. He was dismissed by some of his contemporaries for appearing to flirt with 'the communists', (then associated with Stalin's dictatorship). Yet his novels, light or dark, remain today as rich in their multiple layers as anything you will find in literature.

- **Sefton Delmer** (1904-1979): Fleet Street byliner who stood beside Hitler, Chancellor of Germany, at the Reichstag fire and led his report with Hitler's involuntarily infamous quote:

    "... this (fire) is the handiwork of the communists! There is nothing that shall stop us now suppressing political opposition and seizing dictatorial power." Sefton Delmer's byline was a highlight in Fleet Street's memory for many years.

- **Walter Lippmann** (1889-1974) was hailed in the United States as the greatest journalist of the 20th century, and that claim might still be valid if his behind-the-scenes role in history can be sorted out. For more than 50 years he stood at the centre of American politics. He observed the US rise to dominate the world after World War II, and he reported on its gradual waning. Through his New Republic in the days of Woodrow Wilson before the First World War, Lippmann quickly built up an audience

The Reichstag fire, a Nazi plot that put blame on unnamed communist Jews and allowed Hitler to seize control of Germany. Sefton Delmer's report on it helped expose Hitler's lies.

of millions who relied on him for his judgement of the issues and their consequences. His famous newspaper column, "Today and Tomorrow" helped him become an arbiter of the 'American century' in which readers across North America regarded him as a spokesman, a moralist and a guru.

Founder of The New Republic in his youth; author of the term 'The Cold War' and 'press stereotyping'; winner of two Pulitzer Prizes and adviser to Presidents, Walter Lippman assumed disquieting power as a journalist.

A journalistic saint? That would be an oxymoron, and in any case, Lippmann traded his fame for an active place behind the scenes, according to one biographer, Ronald Steel. Lippmann's little-known second role was his unreported but *active* involvement with "presidents, politicians and powerbrokers in helping to shape events that changed the fate of nations".

He was instrumental in formulating Wilson's Fourteen Points. He conspired and fought with FD Roosevelt over his New Deal. He coached Wendell Willkie and Dwight Eisenhower for the White House, and counselled John Kennedy and Lyndon Johnson – though castigating President Johnson for his role in Vietnam. Lippmann supported the Marshall Plan for Europe, but he quarrelled with Truman over Korea. However, the praise and revelations of his behind-the-scenes role and the sweeping claims of his power and his influence have hurt rather than helped his great reputation as a journalist. In this capacity he was too close to too many conflicting interests; too close to 'power'.

For my era I would choose as 'the best' **Scotty Reston** of the *New York Times* or his good friend and fellow-Scot, Alistair Cooke, a superb columnist covering America for *The Guardian* and the BBC. **Alistair Cooke** made a huge impression on some of us. In 1978 I wrote a review of one of his books in which he spelled out the dilemma of the journalist striving to be objective, yet without being impaled in sitting position on the fence.

"Even a journalist conducts his life on certain assumptions of what is just, tolerable, obscene and so forth ..." I wrote as a rather earnest champion of objectivity in journalism. "And even the urbane Mr Cooke found it difficult to be temperate when it came to reporting on 'interference in personal liberty'."

The reference was to his reports on the United States' dangerously extremist, almost hysterical, anti-communist hearings and condemnation of hundreds of innocent public figures back in the 1950s.

McCarthyism, and the House Committee on un-American activities, split the nation with their aggressive persecution. America came close to abandoning its rules of free speech and justice ... but the political accusers were defeated by good men, both on Capitol Hill and in the press – including the 'foreign press' represented so well by Alistair Cooke.

President Eisenhower commented, with marked approval: "McCarthyism is now McCarthywasm."

Its death was due mainly to America's mainstream press; castigated by extreme right-wingers for being 'agents of the Left' – in the manner that the Donald Trump fan club attacked the media in 2016.

It is true that most of the great papers in the last century went on to support the struggle for Afro-American rights. They did so in their comment columns while reporting the facts dispassionately, but in depth.

Alistair Cooke, who reported all this, was educated at Cambridge and Harvard, and lived as an American and British national. He was a foreign correspondent for *The Guardian* before launching his BBC-broadcast "Letters from America" heard in about 30 countries – and lasting 58 years!

Reporters come in all shades

The list of great reporters who contributed to how people thought and the international debate, and a broader knowledge of their times, seems endless: Alan Moorehead, Ernest Hemingway, Wilfred Thesiger and 'Lawrence of Arabia' (adventure lovers reporting on their own exploits). Ben Hecht and HL Mencken, (the scourge of the narrow-minded Holy Rollers in the American Bible Belt). Stephen Crane of 'American Civil War' and 'Red Badge of Courage' fame. Edward R Murrow, the voice of CBS reporting to America nightly on Hitler's war. Robert Graves, English poet, soldier, journalist.

And what about Eric Arthur Blair?

The journalist named himself **George Orwell**, author of *1984,* and of *Animal Farm,* and the author who quietly uttered more wisdom about the follies of the West, the communists and rule in India, than perhaps any other politician or writer of his time.

One could go on and on with this roll of fine journos. Let me add just a couple more:

Herman Charles Bosman was a hugely talented writer whose fictional stories are yet to become familiar in the wider world. At home he has often been acclaimed as "the best satirist in southern Africa". (I think Athol Fugard is a better writer; and there are several local novelists, past and present, who are world renowned ... but how can you compare bananas and pineapples?)

Bernie Sachs, who was Bosman's colleague and contemporary, thought South Africa had produced only two truly great brains in his time: genius General Smuts and the reprobate/reporter/writer Bosman.

Bosman wrote lightly and brilliantly. His lifetime was blurred somewhat by his peculiar character – and the mind-focusing factor of being sentenced to death (later reprieved from the death cell) for killing his stepbrother.

Reporters come in all shades, as does genius, journalists might tell you, self-mockingly.

Lastly I must mention one of my favourite reporters/writers:

James Morris, who, among innumerable eyewitness accounts, wrote about the first conquest of Mount Everest. He was at 22,000 feet waiting to meet Hillary and Tenzing as they slowly descended that "crisp, sparkling" morning.

> "From the ridge of Lhotse a spiral of snow powder was driven upwards by the wind ... From time to time there was a sudden thrilling high-pitched whistle as a boulder screamed down from the heights. Everest itself, its rock ridge graceless against a blue sky, was as hard and enigmatical as ever."

Later, he was to use the feminine byline, Jan Morris. Her writing was often even better than his. She provides the bridge to a whole list of some of the greatest journalists of all time ... this is so partly because woman journalists for generations had to work twice as hard as their male counterparts to achieve fame; despite their excellence.

Heroism is a description that might be used in these cases, for all women had to struggle against huge odds to succeed in an exclusively man's world where chauvinistic prejudice was the easiest blanket-defence against their competitive talents.

Women's talents excel

It is dangerous to generalise in this matter, but my own experience of women journalists, even now when they have conquered and over-run almost all of the male barriers, thus needing to strive far less against unfair handicaps, is that they are likely to be more conscientious in their work; to be more interested in small yet telling details; to show more empathy for victims in most situations. They are likely to be more precise in editing, and therefore more effective in journalistic skills. That is not always so; but there is much inspiration to draw from.

Here are some examples:

Elizabeth Jane Cochran was one of Joseph Pulitzer's triumphant 'discoveries' in the late 1880s. Or rather she fought to get onto his famous newspaper, *The World,* by accepting, as a test, a near-impossible assignment while working under a silly *nom de plume,* Nellie Bly, which she had already used to get her first article published elsewhere.

'Nellie Bly', at the age of 23, was pioneering not only women's journalism, but a new way of investigative journalism — reporting from the inside. To gain entry to what were bluntly called 'lunatic asylums', she posed as a lunatic to do so.

Nellie Bly aka Elizabeth Jane Cochran, by H. J. Myers, photographer.

And she covered the issues from the point of view of the helpless inmates.

She joined strikes to report on poverty, protests and corruption. She wrote about world famous boxer John L. Sullivan, and on any issue on which any male might be able to match her.

She reached national and international fame when she accepted, in 1889, the challenge to go around the world in less than 80 days. She beat the achievement of Jules Verne's fictional hero, Phineas Fogg, by more than a week. The audacious, caring and intrepid 'lady', travelling "by ship, train and burro" across five continents, got back to New York in 72 days, 6 hours and 11 minutes; cheered by crowds of women – and many more men – for her daring achievement.

Flora Shaw, in the Victorian man's world of the 1890s, was no wide-eyed non-sophisticate seeking a wider career than housewife. She was a home-educated, highly intelligent woman who had started her career in her youth by writing children's books. She sought powerful literary contacts such as John Ruskin and George Meredith who helped her become a contributor to the *Pall Mall Gazette.*

In 1888, the *Gazette,* probably at her urging and on her purse, appointed her their correspondent in Cairo where she also represented the *Manchester Guardian* and got to know *The Times* correspondent. When he returned to London he found her a job, still further from London, as *The Times'* South African correspondent. She did some great work, even venturing into diamond and gold mines to get 'atmosphere' interviews.

She got to know Cecil John Rhodes – they probably had a mutual sympathy for their celibacy, and a shared enthusiasm for 'the benefits' of colonial expansion – especially expansion into the Transvaal gold reefs. Her work earned her the post in London of 'Colonial Editor' of *The Times,* the only female editorial executive in Britain. Her connivance on behalf of her newspaper in dealing with Rhodes and the unlawful Jameson Raid caused considerable embarrassment for both; but at the subsequent inquiry by the House of Commons, she acquitted herself truthfully and well.

BBC correspondent and author John Simpson makes the interesting point that, had the British press shown any instinct for investigative journalism – which neither the press proprietors nor their readers wanted in that era – the press might have uncovered a scandal within the Jameson Raid *fracas* which would have dissuaded the government and the British public from supporting a war against the Boer Republics.

Dame Flora Shaw continued to use influence as a 'Colonial Editor'. She gave Nigeria its name and supported the establishment of Hong Kong's university.

'Girl Gets Biggest Scoop in History'

No news reporter of any gender has beaten the achievement of a young woman, **Clare Hollingworth;** who within five days of becoming a journalist, pulled off possibly the biggest newspaper scoop in history. It was so big she could hardly take credit for it, but she did indeed alert the planet when World War II broke out one dark dawn.

The *Daily Telegraph* sent her off to eastern Germany on the inauspicious date of 31 August 1939, with the vague instruction to check for German reaction to Chamberlain and Hitler's latest peace pact.

She found Nazi armoured troops gathering. Her office thought there was nothing in this to get excited about; but instead of sitting around aimlessly interviewing the locals, she drove off and booked into a hotel on the main road right on the German border. Before dawn she was awakened by tanks rumbling past her window. Hitler's panzers, in breach of his peace pacts with Chamberlain, were invading Poland without declaring war! No one would believe her until she held her telephone receiver outside her window to capture the sounds of armoured convoys clanking by her room.

When she finally convinced *The Telegraph* of the immensity of her discovery, she was told to check first with the British embassy in Warsaw. The embassy was as incredulous as London, but soon confirmed her alerts in time for the story to be published immediately on 1st September. Britain went onto a war footing and formally declared war on 3rd September.

The novice's first news story was not mere luck. It was driven by an alert instinct, enthusiasm and determination that served her well for decades. Clare Hollingworth worked for the London *Telegraph*

for the next ten years; for *The Guardian* for the next 15 years; for *The Telegraph* and for *The Sunday Telegraph* thereafter as one of the world's best-known Foreign and Defence Correspondents.

Two unforgettable eyewitness accounts

However, the most famous and talented of all woman journalists in the last century was probably **Martha Gellhorn**. Her career could be summarised thus: Born in St Louis, Missouri. At the age of 21, she talked her way into a free passage to Europe in 1930, and arrived in Paris with only $75, and proved that she could earn a living as a foreign correspondent. She returned to America in 1934 and two years later published her first book on Depression-hit America; based on her own investigations and the official reports she had written.

She impressed Eleanor Roosevelt, the wife of the US President, and became her life-long friend.

In 1937 she returned to Europe as a war correspondent, and for the next nine years she reported on the civil war in Spain, the Russian invasion of Finland, the Japanese invasion of China and South-East Asia (Singapore would not be able to defend itself against a rat, she correctly prophesied) and finally she returned to Europe to report the European view of World War II.

After 1946, she left fulltime journalism to become a freelancer, reporting on whatever engaged her interest or caused her concern, from Cuba to Vietnam, from Central America to the Middle-East. She also wrote five novels, six collections of stories and novellas and several works of non-fiction, including her autobiography *The View from the Ground* which prompted comment such as: "One of the most extraordinary women of her era", (*Philadelphia Inquirer*), and: "There is a hard, shining, almost cruel honesty to Gellhorn's work," (*The Guardian*).

She was, as the whole world knew, married for five years to another writer/reporter, Ernest Hemingway ... but she avoided mentioning him in her writing. She did not wish to be known as

"Hemingway's wife", let alone ex-wife.

What some of us will remember her for is her eyewitness account of the lynching of a 19-year-old black man named Hyacinth, when the 'silly sounds' of a car starting up and accelerating forwards  were the biggest – the only sounds – to be heard by anyone … because the next sound was of Hyacinth strangling as he fell off the moving car's roof and was hanging and kicking in front of a casual crowd until he was dead.

What I shall also remember – how could one forget? – was that she was one of the first to describe the skeleton-like figures emerging from a German concentration camp at war's end. (Her story appeared in *Collier's Weekly Magazine*, on June 23, 1945. *The New York Times* named her article about Dachau as "one of the 10 Magazine Articles that Shook the World.")

I'd quote some of her words, but I can't remember them. Like her, my memory has what she described as "black holes, deathless chasms, vast reaches of impenetrable fog."

Once you've written your report, you let it slip out of your head. You know it has been recorded … somewhere.

Gellhorn covered the Adolf Eichmann trial, but I don't think she (or I) would remember what she wrote, without looking it up.

However, what is impossible to forget are a newspaper's misprints. Especially mischievous misprints, which must be seen as crimes created for laughter that their makers cannot resist. Yes, the jokes are legendary and irresistible, making fun of royalty and dignitaries. But often they are no joke, and are the bane of editors. Oh the costs; the trouble; the harm they can cause! Yet you will see that seeming 'misprints' were deliberately used at least once to defy apartheid's censors and Secret Police. □

5.
Mischievous misprints.

How can you explain to an aggrieved socialite that she will be remembered as a "battered hore"?

The first misprint in newspapers to impress itself on my mind was one that appeared in a Johannesburg newspaper shortly before I entered journalism in 1947.

I like to think it occurred, not in the paper I was about to join, *The Star,* but in the *Rand Daily Mail.* It certainly wasn't in the Nationalist Party newspaper *Die Transvaler,* because its editor, later Prime Minister Dr Hendrik Verwoerd, boycotted the occasion. He did so as the rest of the South African media of all persuasions devoted endless, boring, upfront stories and pages of pictures to the post-war Royal Visit of King George VI, his consort Queen Elizabeth, and the two princesses.

Die Transvaler gave 'the Royal Visit' a single paragraph in an inside page social column; noting merely that a leading British family would be here for a short stay.

The royal family visits Johannesburg. Queen Elizabeth (centre) consort of King George VI, with the princesses Elizabeth (right) and Margaret beside her father. The Queen was insulted in print at the Rand Easter Show, where a decade later Dr Verwoerd was shot by a would-be assassin.

It was a surprisingly neat touch, for a humourless, blindly bigoted political party paper. Other newspapers went wildly overboard and more than made up for Verwoerd's silence on the matter of *die vreemde Engelse* (alien English).

One paper really put its foot in it. The mistake I'm referring to occurred at Easter, 1947. I was on the staff of *The Star* newspaper, but not yet a full-fledged journalist, and in the constantly embarrassing stage of being the only male wimp learning typing and shorthand in an all-girl stenographers' class – a hurdle that had to be jumped in order to meet the newspaper company's qualifications to become a reporter. (There were no academic 'cadet' journalism schools in those halcyon days, and *The Star* was yet to have a 'practical journalism' course in its own building.)

I know it was Easter at that time, because a Johannesburg newspaper carried two memorable front-page Easter pictures.

One was of the prize cow of the Rand Easter Show. The other was of Her Majesty the Queen visiting the same Easter Show.

The mistake was that the captions to the pictures were swapped. This 'mistake' was probably made by some mischievous typesetter who probably lived on the tale all his days thereafter. His crime was *lese majeste* – fortunately no longer punishable by death.

He was following a long history of such crimes. The famous misprint of the report stating that Queen Victoria passed over Edinburgh's Firth of Forth Bridge – with an 'i' where an 'a' should be in 'passed'– is a classic of two centuries ago; still revered for its capability to shock in terms of gross indecency in those times.

Queen Victoria bridges time and suffers lese majeste, but no longer wants people hanged for insulting her.

Thus it was that in my day we used to take great care to ensure that a sub-editor or a copy-reader could produce a full record of every hand that had touched every story from the moment it entered the sub-editors' room until it appeared in the paper in the publishing dispatch room. That process stopped many errors and deliberate humorous mistakes. But no one could prevent all misprints.

The irony of another swapped photo caption

The irony for me of the 'swapped picture captions' syndrome is that, during my last years as a chief editor, I was the victim of my own newspaper's version of this mistake.

It happened during our deliberate challenge to the apartheid government's Police Act and its Prisons' Act – both of which banned publication of pictures of police stations and prisons. *The Star* had already been punished for publishing a well-known aerial photograph of central Johannesburg (which automatically included central landmarks – now authoritarian Key Points – such as the notorious police HQ of John Vorster Square and the jail in the historic Old Fort). Worse, the two laws forbade not only pictures of such buildings with prison cells, but also pictures of arrested citizens and prisoners. This ban left political prisoners in limbo and prey to prison assault and possibly undetectable torture.

We were always on the lookout for opportunities to challenge such unjust laws, so dangerous to prisoners without trial. (The Key Points' 'security' legislation, though, still exists under SA's current democratic government!)

When a fallen hero of apartheid, Secretary for Information, Eschel Rhoodie, fled his country after the Infogate scandal and was brought back under arrest by his own government, *The Star* deliberately published six different pictures of the arrested apartheid Government officer after he stepped onto South African soil. Each such published photo was a felony. We made it clear that the published pictures might be in contravention of at least two recent dubious laws concerning prisoners ... laws designed to keep from the public eye any illegal actions by police and jailers. When the expected summons came for picturing arch-nationalist Rhoodie under arrest, we refused to pay the fine. I went into the dock to face the charges and to challenge the laws – laws being used mainly to hide all information, not about political powerbrokers, but about detained political prisoners.

"The restrictions imposed on photographs were not found necessary before these new laws were introduced," I reminded the magistrate. And I asked: "Why are they necessary now? All they do is create confusion and raise suspicions and anomalies ... These photographs (of Eschel Rhoodie under police guard) illustrate a confusing, ominous and absurd situation."

Our lawyers questioned the magistrate: "Which law overrules which law? We need a ruling from the Bench."

The magistrate, unfortunately, was up to the impossible challenge: "Cautioned and discharged," he said, dismissing me and the case.

Most media did report the trial, however, and spelt out the challenge.

Only my own paper, *The Star,* got it wrong. It re-published the picture of Eschel Rhoodie, as we intended to do, but with the caption: *The editor, Mr Tyson ... declined to pay admission of guilt.*

And under a picture not allowed in the newspaper in normal circumstances, was a face-shot of me, under the caption: "*Dr Eschel Rhoodie ... when may he be photographed?*"

It showed how confusing things could get, I suppose.

Correcting the corrections

Countless people around the world continued to build albums of printed errors. Especially treasured were the 'double errors'; the much-quoted mistakes creeping into the published apologies and corrections. Classic example: "We apologise for describing police officer Smith as a member of the 'Defective Force'. He is of course a member of the Detective Farce."

We were acutely aware, in the editorial mahogany row, of the proven statistic showing that the corrections themselves were vulnerable to a 10% chance of introducing new errors. For instance, when the Argus Printing & Publishing Company published its annual financial report back in the 1960s, head office sent a message to our editor on *The Argus* newspaper, very tactfully reminding him that his paper had carried errors in its report of the company's annual financial statistics for three *successive* years – and could he now please ensure it would not happen again?

Our editor commanded the entire 'mahogany row' to read already corrected proofs, and sign them before printing. The 'Stone Sub' overseeing dispatch of the page in 'the Works', as well as the whole of the printing department, laboured under dire threat to ensure no error crept in. All of us were fully relaxed when copies of the approved edition were rushed to our desks. The text 'proofs' was precisely correct and virginally pure. But, when the paper was printed, it was immediately apparent that one lowercase 'm' and a zero had suddenly and mysteriously disappeared from the headline.

Instead of proclaiming the then grand sum of R40m, the headline now read: "Argus Co announces excellent R4 profit."

A battered 'hore'

My personal favourite – because I spent much time back in the early 1960s galloping around trying to correct it – was the caption in the Natal *Daily News* reading: "Well-known hore-woman wins jumps at gymkhana." As a lowly assistant editor responsible for final proofs, I phoned 'the Works' and instructed that (as there was no time to add the 's' to 'horse-woman') they should batter the type.

Even if misspelt, the word 'whore' simply never appeared in respectable newspapers in those days, while the name of the lady horse-rider appeared often, for she was very well-known indeed. I strolled through to the editor to inform him of the amusing misprint. Fortunately, instead of congratulating me on my acumen, he shouted: "Go straight to the Stone (where the hot-metal type, now lying cold in lead columns, was composed into pages) and check that the correction has been made. Then go to Dispatch and ensure that not a single copy of the paper with the misprint leaves this building."

I knew I had caught the misprint in time, but I went, anyway. Sure enough, by the time I got to the Stone, my order had been carried out, and now the corrected newspapers were pouring off the presses.

"Look for yourself," said the Works' foreman, gesturing at the corrected page-form. One glance at the typefaces in their backward, reversed mirror image revealed that the offending misprint 'hore-woman' was indeed battered. All that was visible, and now in print, was the phrase 'well-known hore-xxxxx.'

One could write whole books on the mischief that (usually deliberate) manual misprints used to make. But they've been written already. What is rare is the danger in misprints.

In reality they are no joke – especially a dangerous misprint deliberately made in order to challenge censorship. It is indescribably tiring having to skirt the law, or make oneself challenge the law every day. All one can say of running a legal and independent newspaper in an illegal state before freedom came to South Africa is that it was a bad dream; a nightmare that seemed to have no ending. It is difficult sometimes even to think about that era of our past. The joke I'm about to tell you was that I was belatedly sued by a judge, even after the era ended and after I had retired! □

6.
Dangerous misprints.

Of course I was biased, but wouldn't you also have seethed at the perceived injustice at this particular judgement against you – given by Justices in favour of a fellow Justice accused by you of injustice? It's enough to make one think – irrelevantly and irreverently and irrationally and, I suppose rather nautically – of a rigged jury.

An active editor's career is filled with litigation. But sometimes, and often in 'bad times', and in publicly unjust circumstances, he may deliberately invite prosecution.

Most of us manage to avoid dramatically expensive damages – though I remember the proprietor of the slanderous, constantly-sued, London *Private Eye* informing us one day with undisguised pride:

"My current editor is brilliant. He's being sued for *a million pounds* – our record demand for damages! It makes me feel quite envious. When I was editor no one ever sued us for more than £750 000".

(The record figures quoted may be slightly inaccurate, but no matter, because *Private Eye* never ever had enough money to pay those who successfully sued it.)

A bench of judges in the South African Constitutional Court symbolising solidarity, wisdom and justice. Say no more. Irrespective of race, age and gender, the Bench is truly your best guarantee of individual rights and a free press.

In my years as an editor I was involved in litigation more modestly and more cautiously, but far more often. Ours was a sober-sided, necessarily profitable organisation which kept lawyers occupied fulltime in protecting us from litigation involving heavy fines and jail without the option of a fine, and worse, jail without trial. But that was because the State itself had become lawless.

As mentioned earlier, I was sued even after I had retired. The experience occurred when a judge of the Supreme Court continued to dispute an article *The Star* had carried during my tenure. The article expressed the view that the judge had shown racial prejudice in some of his judgments. The courts had to decide whether this accusation was justified. I was travelling overseas, and unaware of the case until my return when I saw my name in the headlines. How pleasant it was to read the details while appreciating how academic and unimportant they had become in my life.

But the verdict against me was disturbing. Of course, I was biased, but wouldn't you have been seething at the perceived injustice at this particular judgment against you – given by Justices in favour of a fellow Justice accused of injustice?

It's enough to make one think – irreverently and irrationally, and I suppose nautically – of a jury rig. The original accusation of the judge's racial bias was made in *The Star* – not by us, but in an 'Op-Ed' bylined feature written by a very learned member of the legal profession ... but not a judge. As editor I lost my case without being in court to give or hear any evidence.

This was an aberration on the eve of political transformation of the State, however. Through both eras, the press has depended heavily on the courts to protect freedom of expression – and the courts do occasionally have to rely on the support of the press to maintain their independence. This symbiosis is vital to any democracy. It kept the press alive and independent even under apartheid and its Emergency Regulations, even when judges, in terms of the Constitution, were appointed by the State. It was rare indeed that we felt compelled to challenge any judge. Racist bias by the High Courts, too, was extremely rare.

Risks lie even in the adverts

The courts were usually our only hope in the illegally administered apartheid era. On one occasion we placed our faith and fortunes entirely in the hands of a court still to be called. Our fate would depend on the wisdom and independence of a judge not yet named, yet we were able to risk everything by deliberately creating a misprint in an advertisement – knowing justice was on our side.

Although threats were huge and could involve sums running into millions, I felt we were honour-bound to risk, carefully and deliberately, two other politically-charged cases which might jeopardise the very life of the newspaper itself.

The keys to both cases were a few harmless words that we deliberately changed in an already banned advertisement. It was a risk that simply had to be taken because it involved not merely justice, but the lives and liberty of hundreds of young people who simply disappeared without trace. Our surety was the trust I placed in a single individual, Max Coleman, leader of the Detainees' Parents Support Committee (DPSC). The issue was one which we were going to publish anyway; but overnight its relevance turned on an advertisement paid for by the DPSC.

The advert did not use names. It called for the release of all political detainees and observance of a National Detainees Day. The advertisement had appeared in the then small, exclusively 'black' newspaper, *City Press*. The police formally notified every major publication in the land that the advertisement should never be published again. To do so would mean confiscation of the newspaper, they warned.

I had never come across this strange, radical form of pre-censorship before. I was wondering what could be done when Max Coleman, whom I had come to know and respect for his courage and honest reliability, came to me somewhat disconsolately for advice.

Max Coleman

"Well, we cannot publish *this* advertisement," I told him. "We have been specifically warned that it is forbidden under the Emergency Regulations." (Violation of this particular press curb was punishable by 10 years in prison, without need for proper trial. Much worse, it might entail closing down the newspaper.) "But if we change a couple of words it will be a *different* advertisement," I suggested.

"I believe that if we get either of these versions into court, we can successfully challenge the police ruling, and at least publicly attack any Emergency Regulation that prevents anyone calling for release of detainees."

The stakes were huge, but I hoped to minimise the risk. On 10 March 1987, with our two media lawyers, Peter Reynolds and Paul Jenkins standing by, we published the advertisement (same headline, same shape, same content, same message. Just a few amended words which altered neither the meaning nor impact). Even before the paper finished its first run of the first edition, plainclothes police were in the building – which says a lot for their inside informers.

A senior officer showed me a notice authorising them to confiscate every copy of *The Star* which carried the advertisement they had warned against.

"Check with your headquarters again, I said, handing them a letter to the Commissioner of Police which I had already hurriedly written and signed. It read:

> *... I refer to the drastic action which you intend to take against The Star by seizing it in terms of Regulation 6 of the Media Regulations. Before your representative acts on your order ... consider the following:*
>
> *2.1. The DPSC advertisement has been scrutinised by our legal advisers who are perfectly satisfied it does not break the law.*
>
> *2.2. If your order is directed at the Page One editorial (supporting the call to release political detainees) ... they are likewise satisfied it does not break any law.*
>
> *2.3. If you proceed, The Star will suffer hundreds of thousands of rands loss and the proprietor will obviously seek to recover its damages from the State ...*

One officer went off to his superiors with my warning of legal action. The other stayed as the presses rolled, then read the advertisement inside the newspaper and the editorial (leader) which was placed – against all normal practice – as a front-page statement with a byline: The Editor.

My Page One leading article observed that for more than 700

years, since the drafting of Magna Carta, Western civilisation had accepted the principle that no person should be incarcerated indefinitely without a trial by his peers. The editorial continued:

> ... But suddenly in our country even the right to question imprisonment without trial is now threatened. How can we have reached this kind of totalitarian action? How can any fair-minded person, even during a state of emergency – even in a state of war – support the idea that no one can call for the release of detainees? To what depths have some so-called representatives of Nationalism sunk?

The policeman again read the advertisement and the front page editorial with great care. He made no comment, but we could see he had not detected how the advertisement differed from the already banned advertisement.

As for our front-page editorial, our disingenuous defence would be that it did not break the ban on appealing for the release of detainees. It merely posed some questions. (We always contrived a legal defence, however preposterous, and defined our motive before deliberately breaking censorship laws.)

I have to confess I was becoming nervous. I had already worked out the 'worst case' cost of this exercise. It was appalling. I had not asked anyone's permission to take this risk – management (and our company head office) were standing by, trusting my judgement and not even asking questions about my decision to ignore the police warning and publish the advertisement. (While, by law, an editor is responsible for *all* content, normally business and advertising in our company was handled by management. This was done in the cause of transparent editorial and commercial independence.)

Deep down I knew, however, that the risk I was taking included more than the usual penalties of a fine or an individual jail sentence. It involved the confiscation of the paper and a fall in circulation. The worst-case financial loss might lead to the closure of *The Star*, the loss of thousands of jobs – the possible closure also of several others of our metropolitan newspapers across the country if the flagship went down.

An hour later I was telling an urgent sitting of the Supreme Court that arbitrary confiscation of the print-run that day would cost half a million rand (perhaps 10 or 20 times that in today's terms). The court granted a temporary interdict preventing confiscation without the police showing just cause. The police called off its mission, claiming it had done so before the interdict.

Anxious staff of The Star, caught by cameras and microphones of the international media at the moment of crisis. The government called it "a publicity stunt". It was everything but that.

We celebrated in the knowledge that we had torn open the security blanket that hid all information about people whom police locked away without explanation and without any kind of trial.

Months later *The Star* faced almost the same issue all over again. This time, the paper printed, side by side at the same length, its reasons for publishing statistics, and the censor's reasons for warning us not to publish the fact that no less than 8,000 youths and children were held in prison without trial – about 40% of all political prisoners.

Later, when my friend Rex Gibson (formerly editor of the *Rand Daily Mail,* which its owners had closed down) was acting editor-in-chief of *The Star* in my absence, he phoned me about another request from Max Coleman of the DPSC. Coleman had painstakingly collected all the names of the detainees! Could we publish them? *The Star* published column after column of names of South Africans who had disappeared behind bars. Nothing happened. But later, on 14 February 1988, the fourth wave of regulations hit us. The Detainees Parents' Committee was banned (its work secretly passed on to the Black Sash), while 33 other organisations that had sprung up during this time of extreme oppression were also banned. New pro-government 'media vigilance' organisations automatically began to burgeon like mushrooms.

It was all downhill for anyone interested in democracy, until Senator FW de Klerk took over from PW Botha as President of SA, and Nelson Mandela, the world's best-known political prisoner, was released ... and we could see his photograph for the first time in decades. In the celebrations that have occurred ever since, and in the honours awarded to the heroes of 'The Struggle', I believe there are many individuals who have never received adequate recognition for what they did.

Among the foremost, I believe, is Max Coleman, the quiet, gentle, man of steel who cared ceaselessly for his own and everyone else's young men, women and especially children who went to prison without trial. ☐

7. Best writing: fiction or non-fiction?

*I always write a good first line,
but I have trouble in writing the others.*

Molière (In the 1660s)

*I do most of my work sitting down,
that's where I shine.*

Robert Benchley (In the 1940s)

Good writing has many faces. One of them is the taut face of a reporter who witnesses an unforgettable event; the public assassination, say, of a world leader. Or a giant hurricane smashing homes and lives in front of the reporter's eyes.

The event might inspire great writing and an experience burnt forever into the consciousness of any journalist. But would *you* believe this dramatic headline material, even brilliantly described in the heat of the moment, to be 'the best' form of newspaper writing?

Instead, 'the best' was once regarded to be the writing of a newspaper's leading article, now known as the leader or editorial. Yet the first priority of a 'leader' has been – not to express individual writing talent – but to express the considered view of the newspaper in addressing its community or the nation. And to do so in that particular paper's leader column's accepted style ... very different to that which broadcast and digital news commentaries offer you. Very different from descriptive, emotional prose.

The traditional process of producing newspaper editorials is arcane and remains a mystery even to most journalists.

What really does go on behind those closed doors? Who reads those editorials? Certainly not the mythical 'man-in-the-street', or woman. Newspaper editorials are written for all those public leaders, academics, economists, lawyers, business people, politicians, analysts, diplomats from other lands and ordinary folk who follow current affairs seriously. Newspapers know that their comment on any issue will be read very carefully by the members of society who are being criticised, encouraged, or are affected by the issue addressed in an editorial. Again, this significance, in easily-challenged print, has – or used to have – far more weight than broadcast comment or opinions circulating on the web.

As I have had the exceedingly rare privilege of being invited – you could never *ask* – to attend the leader conference behind closed doors of a number of newspapers, including some of the best in the English-speaking world, I can safely affirm that the process is roughly similar in most *large* mainstream newspapers in the free world.

So I can provide here a specific example of how the leader conference works in a big metropolitan daily.

Bear in mind again that the constant business of writing editorials in newspapers is quite different even from the columnist's work of producing socio-political opinion pieces, or the cheap way of doing so in blogs. At its height, *The Star* could call upon as many as six to a dozen senior specialist journalists within the building to write on national, continental or world socio-economics and politics; and many local or arcane subjects – and do so under the editor's direction, in order to reflect the recognisable voice of a newspaper speaking to a specific group of readers from different cultures and languages.

Proposed leader topics were subjected in most cases to serious debate *and counter-argument* by perhaps half a dozen other leader-writers. They too were specialists – in leader-writing. They were experts in research and presentation. They knew how to research instantly the decades of 'backgrounders', news stories, comment pieces and myriad leaders on countless subjects in the newspaper's century-old library.

Trying not 'to lead'
What professional, fulltime leader-writers seemed to be most adept at in a crowded leader conference, was dodging their job.

They would often offer topics of the day for consideration, of course – but topics better suited to their colleagues' expertise, in the hopes of avoiding having to undertake the onerous daily task themselves. It was always a fascinating game, evoking both wit and laughter as well as serious debate and introspection.

That is one formula – though the style of leader conference debates depended on the issues of the day and, of course, on the mood and personality of the editor.

In heated times and national crises, an editorial might be written on the back of an envelope. For instance, on *The Star,* several written in the last convulsive days of apartheid were published without debate and deliberation, but as an instant deliberately angry voice on Page One.

None of this encourages fine writing. What did encourage individual style was the Third Leader which many major newspapers adopted from the original Fourth Leader introduced by *The Times* in London long ago. Much later, in the 1950s, *The Times*' daily Fourth Leader ran to more than 500 words; but with no specific limits either way. It was designed to entertain, in the form of an essay covering subjects at whim, and ranging from *"THE JOYS OF APOLOGY"* to the riddle of *"PURE FLUKES"*. My favourite, in those days, was *The Times*' Fourth Leader that analysed the feats of the U.K. Meteorological Bureau in predicting England's notoriously fickle and varied weather. With a 56 percent pure success rate, said *The Times*, they might as well save the Bureau's annual budget by spinning a coin, heads or tails, each morning.

MORE THAN A CENTURY ago, the Fourth leader was emulated in upmarket newspapers across the English-speaking world. It became, usually, "The Third Leader", offering the same mood and style of *The Times*, but with a shorter, heavily disciplined length. To describe the once popular Third Leader is difficult, as the following attempts will show.

The Third Leader used to be where potential writers were instructed to employ – not their art – but a finely disciplined talent. It was a school for leader-writers. Good writing may lie in rigorous, astute analysis. It must do so in quality of style. It will require considerable practice to broach, in a few words, some intricate, inane or ineffable subject.

The challenge is this:
Produce an editorial, a Third Leader, on a topical subject, and compose it within an evening paper's deadline of 30 minutes. The result which you are required to reach, possibly four days a week, must meet at least one, preferably all, of the following conditions:
- *It makes a succinct, sharp point*
- *It lightens the day and produces a smile*
- *It provokes a moment of philosophy*
- *It punctures pomposity*

Every attempt should contain fewer words than the maximum 150 which I should reach immediately before this grammatical full-point.

So, my deliberate 151 words in italics, above, deliberately fails the 150-word challenge on two counts ... three if you penalise puns. But it matters not. Regrettably, the challenge of the 150-word Third Leader is itself no more. Even the lengthier Fourth Leader of the London *Times* exists no longer.

My 151-word sample above illustrates merely *the length* of a Last Leader, whether Third or Fourth. The purpose of the "little last leader" was profound, but never explained. Here is a second attempt at Profiling a 'perfect' Third leader:

As it hesitantly existed, nostalgia suggests that its essence might be described in several ways.
It was a gentle jibe or a delicious drop of acid on the tongue.
A subtle twist of logic or a soupcon of phrases worth savouring.
It was a quick-witted sally, and essentially unexpected.
Surprise was its salty icing.
Unpredictability was the Third Leader's badge.
Sarcasm, irascibility and narrow point-scoring were beneath its contempt; as were political point-scoring or personal insult.
Leader writers remember a Third or Fourth as the creation of a few moments of intense, concentrated mental energy. Something that striving could not produce.
But I am remembering an ideal. There is no perfect example. No composition of words; no expression of wit, love or irony, could ever be perfect.
Ah memory ... how distorted it becomes concerning things lost over the years. I am left in despair – with a word to spare.

(Yes, the word count this time is: 149)

Writing in the real world

Can *reportage* produce writing that is good enough to rival *literature?*

The question may be unanswerable, but I turn to an unbiased authority who offers a divergent view. Prof John Carey, Merton Professor of English, Oxford University, says:

"The advantages of reportage over imaginative literature are clear. Literature habitually depends for its effect on a 'willing suspension of disbelief' ... or collusion or self-deception on the part of the audience or reader. Reportage, by contrast, lays claim directly to the power of the real, which imaginative

literature can approach only through make-believe.

"It would be foolish, of course, to belittle imaginative literature on this score. The fact that it is not real – that its griefs, loves and deaths are all a pretence – is one reason why it can sustain us ... It gives us ... a precious illusion of freedom. It allows us to use for pleasure passions and sympathies (anger, fear, pity, etc.) which in normal circumstances would arise only in situations of pain or distress. In this way it frees and extends our emotional life.

"It seems probable that much – or most – reportage is read as if it were fiction by a majority of its readers. Its panics and disasters do not affect them as real, but as belonging to a shadow world distinct from their own concerns, and without their pressing actuality.

"Because of this, reportage has been able to take the place of imaginative literature in the lives of most people. They read newspapers rather than books ...

"However enjoyable this is, it represents a flight from the real, as does imaginative literature, and good reportage is designed to make that flight impossible.

"... (Fiction) exiles us from the sharp terrain of truth. All the great realistic novelists of the nineteenth century – Balzac, Dickens, Tolstoy, Zola – drew on the techniques of reportage, and even built eyewitness accounts and newspaper stories into their fictions, so as to give them heightened realism. But the goal they struggled towards always lay beyond their reach. They (lacked) the vital ingredient of reportage which is the simple fact that the reader knows all this actually happened."

If you want an example of compulsive 'reality reading', you might weigh up this next report from a green and pleasant land where its people were slaughtering each other almost daily. The newspapers on either side of the great divide were trying to calm down their own readers and supporters. □

8.
Reports from a green and pleasant land.

Why do moderates put up with this senseless violence? Well, just when they can't stand their own bullies any more, the other side does something unspeakable in the name of revenge. The war starts all over again.

The Editor, *Belfast Telegraph*, 1985

The propeller-driven passenger plane spluttered, coughed, and squealed its tyres on the runway before coming to a halt in what seemed to be a bucolic idyll. There were bunnies hopping in the grass beside the aircraft. The double-storey air terminal looked like a great country house about to welcome guests. No crowding. No fuss.

From its portals a taxi carried me through a picturesque pastoral scene of hedgerows, meadows dotted with fat sheep, sleek cows, and a loch shimmering on the horizon. After puttering along 'o'er hill and dale', the scenery gradually fused into a vivid green-blue image of startlingly lush fields bounded by a cobalt sea and sky. Suddenly, over the rise, was Belfast with its Edwardian architectural city centre looking as staid and peaceful as the more recently established city of Cape Town.

At breakfast the next morning, in a hotel overlooking a scene reminiscent of upper Adderley Street in the Cape of Good Hope, I came upon another familiar, but ominous comparison. It appeared in two single-paragraph reports on an inside page of the *Belfast Telegraph* – a respected newspaper rather like *The Cape Times* of that era.

I was riveted by the brief report of a 10-year-old boy injured in a motor accident. And by a single paragraph about an 18-year-old girl who had won a scholarship. The reports referred to "a Protestant" boy and "a Catholic" girl. The labels leapt at me from the page, labels as unnecessary – but as meaningful to the northern Irish – as reports at home of a "White" boy and a "Coloured" girl; an "Indian" South African and a "Zulu" tribesman, a "European" woman and a "Bantu" male.

Those Irish news reports labelling separately Catholics and Protestants were the main memory of my first visit. The year was 1960, and I had arrived in Northern Ireland after the protests – and killings – at Sharpeville, and the mobilisation of naval units and armed troops at Cape Town where we'd witnessed a giant, peaceful protest march as well as burnings and killings.

People in Belfast had been amused or offended by the small, vague comparison of 'racial labels' that I had associated with South African violence and their Northern Ireland peace in 1960.

IN 1985 – a quarter of a century later – I was back in their beautiful territory where violence had come in 1968 and had grown into a senseless 'civil war' of incredible inhumanity. The editors of the *Belfast Telegraph* (non-sectarian/Protestant) and the *Irish News* (Catholic) were interested when I told them, at different meetings, that I had introduced during the last decade at Johannesburg's *The Star,* a rule that said no racial labels should be used unless these were relevant and essential to a news report. We had persevered, although readers of all races appeared to think that, for different reasons, race identity was always essential. The Irish editors said they were familiar with this blinkered reader reaction. And hostage to it.

My first discovery on this return visit was that, after 17 years of industrial growth and human slaughter in Northern Ireland, there were still bunnies in the grass at Belfast's airport. However, when visitors drove over the rise at the entrance to the city the first thing they now saw were square, flat-topped factories wearing thorny crowns of barbed wire

– to prevent people firing weapons or hurling missiles into the streets below.

This time, in those staid streets I had remembered, were British troops and less visible NIR police, nearly all of them helmeted and in protective suits and heavily armed. Public buildings deeper in the city were locked and barred. There were huge corrugated-iron shutters over banks' windows and heavy grilles protecting McGinty's bar and its neighbours opposite the now famous Forum Hotel; a favourite with political visitors and the world's visiting news media.

For one who was accustomed to the casual treatment of bomb threats and occasional street violence in South Africa – where few police and no military were ever likely to be seen on the streets – the security measures in Belfast seemed at first glance to be hugely excessive. You couldn't get into the hotel grounds without your car being thoroughly searched. Once parked, you had to return to the street to enter a pre-fabricated guardhouse to join a queue in which you were ordered to open your luggage for searching and to empty your pockets for inspection – and only then step onto a wire-protected walkway to reach the foyer of the hotel where your documentation would again be studied.

For journalists, it was worth the walk. Over the years all the sad stories of Northern Ireland's incomparable 'troubles' were retold there by old hands, or more likely, the barmen who had heard it all. A really lazy journalist from a far-off country might get all the 'news' he needed from them, without ever leaving the bar. The first thing I learned, when complaining about all the security, was that the hotel had already been bombed *26 times*. Another attempt was about due, said the barman.

Later he might tell the old, apocryphal tale of the two men in Belfast Prison's condemned cell. "What are you in for?" asks the newcomer.

"Shopliftin'," says Paddy.

The newcomer is astounded. "The death penalty for shoplifting!"

And Paddy says, "To be sure, it was Wolford's shop that we lifted you see, but some people were inside it."

The tale probably ends with the word, "Begorrah".

But the story does have relevance.

'Masked men gunned him down'

On my first night I slipped through the pedestrian and traffic checkpoints of Donegal Street where the main shops stood. Several great stores stood as blackened ruins; monuments to unspeakable and illogical violence.

McGinty's pub was a puzzle. It too had been bombed in the past, of course. I visited it on a busy Sunday eve, and my notes at that time record the scene thus:

> "Outside the pub are small groups of young women, seemingly unconcerned about bomb threats or security. They are dressed in Sunday-socialising-in-the-pub gear: tight leather skirts, stockings, long ear-rings and longer high heels, with artful differences in make-up accessories. Few of the girls enter the pub immediately. They stand on the far corner of the street re-arranging their little groups, bending towards one another intermittently to share a cigarette – and waiting ...
>
> "In the gathering dusk two trucks arrive and unload troops in battle camouflage. Casually slinging their automatic rifles, the young soldiers scatter into a long-spaced patrol. The young women observe them intently, pretending not to. In the dusk I cannot tell whether they are signalling flirtation, or aggression. The soldiers, studiously, almost pretentiously unaware, move off. Their audience swivels on high heels and undulates in small waves into the pub – a battered building with boarded-up windows and scars of explosive assault."

The pub's recent history was hard to credit in the uninhibited atmosphere of the saloon. The packed, smoke-choked room throbbed with noise, laughter and a sense of momentary happiness; like most pubs all over peaceful Britain on any weekend evening. I stepped outside, but within the length of an empty city block, I nearly snagged my nose on the barrel of an up-thrust firearm held by a helmeted, padded-uniformed member of the Royal Ulster Constabulary who stood around the corner, silently and alone in the dark.

Next day I walked up notorious Falls Road in the Catholic Quarter where violence was so quickly and so easily triggered. Long lines of soldiers with weapons at the ready were patrolling the area. They covered both sides of the busy main road. Their parallel lines stretched as far as the eye could see, just off the busy pavements. Each soldier marched alone, 30m from the next, his rifle covering the back of the man in front of him. How abnormal could daily city life get? And what on earth could such elaborate patrols achieve? Nothing, in the end, it transpired. Violence had become a way of life. It was used, not only by Protestant on Catholic and vice versa, but by Catholic terrorist on Catholic terrorist. It was bitterness turning in on itself, as it was to do later in Bosnia at the other end of Europe.

An example of life under terrorism made headlines while I was in Belfast. A well-known and popular entertainer was murdered in his own home in The Falls by a terrorist group calling itself the Irish Freedom Fighters.

"He died when three masked men entered his home and gunned him down in broad daylight yesterday morning ... His 21-year-old daughter, speaking on behalf of her mother and younger sisters, said: 'We are all shattered. My mother had us out of the room, but we heard the noise ... My father was going to give me a party at the theatre where he performed. Instead we are preparing for his funeral tomorrow.'

"A brother of the victim said he was dumbfounded by the claim made by the Irish Freedom Fighters. He challenged the terrorists to produce evidence of the allegation that (his brother) was an informer. Meanwhile a massive security operation, coordinated at Security headquarters, is trying to track down the killers. It is understood from security sources that the 'Irish Freedom Fighters' is a group of renegade Provisional IRA members."

Violence-ridden Northern Ireland, which had been propelled into a horrifying blind alley by the Protestant Paisley demagogues on the one hand and the IRA fanatics on the other, has failed to be a lesson for the rest of the world. I left Belfast feeling uneasy and saddened. Yet, in one small way, the experience was uplifting (though not in the sense an Irish bomber might use the word) and very sobering (though not in the sense that an Irish barman might employ the phrase).

It came about through my discussions with the editor of the eminently sober *Belfast Telegraph* and the editor of the optimistically hopeful *Irish News*. Their views were uplifting because both were trying to get their opposing readers to see reason ... and their opposing political spokespeople to reason together. Both were acting with honesty and dedicated newspaper professionalism in a society more divided, more bitter and more prejudiced and fearful than ours in South Africa.

"Most of the people here are moderates. They abhor this senseless violence. Even many extreme nationalists and unionists dislike violence. But they are driven," said the editor of the *Belfast Telegraph*. "They are driven," he repeated.

"Why do they put up with it? Well, just when they can't stand their own bullies any more, the other side does something unspeakable in the name of revenge. The war starts all over again."

"How can the cycle of violence be broken?"

He throws up his arms. "If only we knew! All we can do as a newspaper is preach moderation, discourage incitement, and remain as balanced as possible."

The reaction was the same from the editor of the (Catholic) *Irish News*.

"I won't even publish the advertisements of the IRA because, though they are legal, they hint at violence," he told me.

I asked: "Are you not afraid of being attacked yourself by Irish terrorists?" He shrugged. "It's more likely to come from those weirdo Protestants."

In that year of the mid-1980s there seemed to be much in common among independent moderate newspapers in their city and mine in South Africa. We compared notes. The *Belfast Telegraph* had been attacked several times, with bombs set off in its basement, and at that stage the Johannesburg *Star* had already been hit by its first incendiary bomb at its street-level back door. The editor of the *Irish News* had received seriously believable death threats, and so had I, and probably other editors in South Africa. *The Star* had developed a system of one-to-five-star alarms to decide whether to ignore facetious and crackpot bomb threats – or to act instantly in evacuating the building. The Irish had taken similar steps.

In these circumstances, only the moderate press, it seemed to the three of us at that time, were constantly at risk; often from "their own" readers.

"How do you deal with incitement in your newspaper columns?" I asked the non-sectarian, pro-British *Telegraph* and the Catholic *Irish News*. Both editors, each interviewed alone, reacted with a sigh. Both found the option 'to publish or not publish' always difficult to decide. Photographs of violence created the most problems. We agreed that publishing them depended not only on the horror of the subject, but its timing in a situation of near-rioting. Our communities bore a tension that separated our concerns from much of the normal focuses of the world's media.

"You're damned if you publish, and you're damned if you don't," said the editor of the *Telegraph*, "but we need to think in terms of cost of lives. It seems editors in South Africa face untenable laws, so they publish information up to a point where they think they will be prosecuted. I'm sure they're right. But we have a different dilemma. We have to draw our line much further out on incitement. And of course the line shifts … depending on the prevailing violence and political climate."

It's hell being a moderate. Especially in our business.

So, how does the press cope in that stress?

Reporting news in Ireland's society, one in conflict with itself and plagued by political murders and massacres, was old hat to Douglas Gageby. He had been a reporter in Northern Ireland for a Dublin newspaper and, for 20 years, editor-in-chief of Dublin's *Irish Times*.

"We've had all the features of guerrilla warfare that the world knows: car bombs, ambushes … assassinations on a tit-for-tat basis … and a particularly vicious practice in which, if a Protestant marries a Catholic in Belfast, either that Protestant or that Catholic may be found afterwards dead in a ditch. There's religion for you."

Gageby added: "All in all, 2,600 people have been killed in ways like this in the north. Tens of thousands injured. Hundreds of thousands intimidated … All this in a population of only one and a half million."

The Irish newspapers on both sides constantly appealed to their supporters for peace, common sense and understanding, he said.

"We know that a tough rattling paper that gives hell to the opponents without thought for other views makes one feel good – but it doesn't shift a single person's thinking. It changes nothing."

Nevertheless, no newspaper reporting on Northern Ireland's vicious civil war agreed to 'tone down' the truth (or where feasible the whole truth) despite pressure from any government or paramilitary quarter.

"Reporting the details is better than argument and comment … and far, far better than rumour."

Gageby was speaking to us in Johannesburg in 1987, and pointing out that the 'straight' reporting he was describing was not at all the dubious, but innocuously named 'responsible reporting' which SA's apartheid regime was urging South African newspapers to do.

He congratulated our newspapers for doing a good job in covering conflict under extremely difficult circumstances. However, comparisons were not possible. No authority in Northern Ireland arrested journalists or threatened or closed down any independent newspaper during the horrendous Irish troubles. □

2

'Telling it like it is'.

9.
A fearful spectacle, defying censorship.

Some-one had blundered.
Theirs not to make reply,
Theirs not to reason why,
Theirs but to do and die:
Into the Valley of Death
Rode the six hundred.

Alfred Lord Tennyson

The first and perhaps the most famous news report of the last two centuries is the one that led to the poem of the Victorian poet laureate quoted above. The 'uninvited' journalist's coverage of war changed the concepts of military command and of the role of women at the war-front.

The other specimens of reporting that follow in this chapter are as deep or as shallow as the subjects they address. They are as varied as the natures of those who wrote them; as different as the circumstances under which each of the events occurred. The few carefully chosen examples in this and the next chapter are intended to mirror the broad sweep of good journalism.

The focus is on the era of modern popular journalism which began with the spread of literacy and education in the late 19th century. The era produced perhaps the greatest all-round, full-time news correspondent the English-speaking world has known. He rejected his title of 'war correspondent' and rightly so, for he was the top all-rounder in the business; in technique of news-gathering; in style of reporting, and in communicating with his readers.

William Howard Russell

Horsing around

William Howard Russell was an Irishman who 'fell into journalism by accident'. His great good fortune was that *The Times* in London sent him off to cover a dreary little war in the Crimea; wherever that was. A war with insufficient men and ill-equipped officers with seemingly nothing to gain and much to lose.

Russell, like the weary British army, was stuck there for almost two years. In all that time, the British never won a single encounter, except the last. Logistics and administration were appalling. Far more soldiers were dying from lack of facilities and medical attention than those killed in conflict. Russell, possibly for the first time in recorded history, reported to *The Times* and its influential readers back home all the army's shocking blunders. A high-ranked officer described him as "a vulgar low Irishman, [who] sings a good song, drinks anyone's brandy and water and ... is just the sort of chap to get information out of youngsters."

(There are lots of those 'sort of chaps' in modern journalism, fortunately.)

Russell was blacklisted by the British commander Lord Raglan who advised his officers to refuse to speak to the reporter. So Russell set out to report the war all on his own; without assistance – but without censorship.

A rare incident indeed.

As a direct result of his reporting, the government sacked many administrators, and the public heeded Russell's appeal for nurses to offer voluntary service in the Crimean war zone. Through this single reporter, legends came alive through the example he had in mind: The "Lady with the Lamp", Florence Nightingale, whose devotion and courage in war became a national inspiration in "caring".

Florence Nightingale, one of the first heroines of the modern press.

He also described a battle involving a regiment's "thin red line" tipped with steel, which withstood a major onslaught. Forced by lack of numbers to form a line two-deep instead of the customary four-deep or square, the men in red tunics repulsed a mass attack. Russell's account of it created the "thin red line" image used for the next 150 years throughout the English-speaking world.

The Battle of Balaklava – and the Light Brigade which was sent, by mistake, to face certain death because of a bungled, misunderstood military order – also came alive through William Russell's pen. Russell's permanent influence came, not merely from his writing style, but also from the excellent research and detail he gathered for his news reports. He filed a 4,000-word report that extraordinary day in November 1854; meticulously recording the statistics, the scenes of battle and the words of the army leaders involved. His report lists five squadrons of Light Dragoons and Hussars and Lancers and gives each of their precise numbers!

His report below contains this succinct summary of the famous – *and* infamous – cavalry charge:

"At 11.10 our Light Cavalry Brigade swept proudly past, glittering in the morning sun in all the pride and splendour of war. We could hardly believe the evidence of our senses! Surely that handful of men were (sic) not going to charge an army in position?

... They advanced in two lines, quickening their pace as they closed towards the enemy. A more fearful spectacle was never witnessed than by those who, without the power to aid, beheld their heroic countrymen rushing to the arms of death. At the distance of 1200 yards the whole line of the enemy belched forth, from 30 iron mouths, a flood of smoke and flame ... marked by dead men and horses, by steeds flying wounded or riderless across the plain.

With a halo of flashing steel above their heads ... sabres flashing ... and with a cheer which was many a noble fellow's death cry, they flew into the smoke of the batteries. [Soon] the plain was strewed (sic) with their bodies and with the carcasses of horses ...

At 11.35, not a British soldier, except the dead and the dying, was left in front of these bloody Muscovite guns. Our loss, as far as it could be ascertained at two o'clock today was: (out of 607 cavalrymen) 409 lost and 198 returned from action."

Those last two statistics that he somehow dug out and checked, during moments of chaos and tragedy, revealed the shocking ineptness of the generals in causing needless death on an unprecedented scale. It led to the public disciplining of senior officers.

However, as in all wars, the British public remembered, not the loss and defeat, but the gallantry of the fallen. Future generations may also remember the useless massacre of *hundreds* of faithful steeds.

Russell went on to pioneer some of the uses of cable and telegraph for faster reporting (most of the technology was still being installed across the world by his home country, Britain). He pioneered, too, the role of independent war correspondents while covering the Indian Mutiny, the American Civil War, the Franco-Prussian War and the Anglo-Zulu War between the British Empire and the Zulu Kingdom in 1879.

Russell wrote for that explosion of education in Britain which, within little more than a generation, ushered in the era of popular newspapers.

John Simpson, 21st-century TV war correspondent, has commented that, with the heightening of imperialism in the 19th century, the attitudes of newspaper correspondents hardened.

"By the mid-1860s new men were taking over from Russell and were setting a different tone: more opinionated, and increasingly more nationalistic," he wrote. By the time of the Anglo-Boer War, jingoism had seized the English newspaper correspondents, so much so that they reported shocking British defeats as if they were near victories. Most observers failed to report the results of Lord Kitchener's desperate anti-guerrilla move in rounding up the women and children of Boer families and placing them in what they termed concentration camps.

(Nor, it seems, did the press report sufficiently on the inept logistical arrangements by the British army which brought enteritis and other deadly infections into the concentrated barracks outside Kroonstad at the start of the war, killing *thousands* of their troops.)

Later, similarly poor logistics and care in the Boer concentration camps led to nearly 40,000 deaths of inmates, black as well as white ... and it wasn't the press, nor history's celebrated Emily Hobhouse, who insisted on putting things right. It was a group of six English women, inspired by press reports, yes, and led by the no-nonsense Mrs Millicent Fawcett, who toured the war zones as 'the Fawcett Commission' and then tackled Lord Kitchener.

Playing around

Here is a different sphere of reporting, illustrated by extracts from an unusual report on tennis by correspondent Martin Johnson for *The Telegraph,* London. It is a reminder of how good sportswriters have to be in chronicling events that are, by their very nature, highly repetitive. His coverage is in the form of what sports journalists (and court reporters) call 'a running report' scribbled as the action is happening on deadline. But the polish of this sample suggests Johnson had done some careful background preparation well in advance.

He met the final edition, with the 'update' filed at 3:21am GMT 17/01/2008. Here it is ... If you are not aware of the beauty and habits of Sharapova as a young, emerging world tennis champion, you are now about to find out.

Martin Johnson wrote:
"It was the kind of contest you would normally expect to see closer to the semi-finals of a grand slam event than the second round, between a 31-year-old who has only just come back after having a baby and a 20-year-old who sounds as if she is about to give birth to triplets. Not surprisingly, perhaps, the younger legs, not to mention the stronger tonsils, prevailed.

The glamorous Sharapova has some loud opinions. Pic by Charlie Cowins from Belmont, NC, USA.

Lindsay Davenport has won more prize money than any other female player, so it's probably safe to assume that she's not mounting a comeback because she's struggling to pay the bills.

But Maria Sharapova rakes in more loot from pouting and posing for photo shoots than Davenport ever made on court, and the nature of her 6-1, 6-3 victory was not far removed from another modelling contract. She even came on to court carrying a purple handbag.

The factory in the former Eastern bloc turning out women tennis players is still on a high enough production rate to have its workers, so to speak, on permanent Ova time, and there are no fewer than 20 of them (not to mention four Evas) in this year's women's draw. Sharapova is still the No 1 seed in the glamour-puss stakes, but she has slipped down to No 5 in the tennis rankings after an ordinary 2007. She is not even the No 1 'Ova' any more.

Maria, though, is now ranked three places below Svetlana Kuznetsova, who apparently makes just as much noise as Sharapova, albeit inside the locker room playing rock music. For this information we are indebted to the Serbian world No 3 Ana Ivanovic, who also reveals in her not-to-be-missed daily column in the Melbourne newspaper The Age that she spends a lot of her spare time "acting out scenes from TV shows" with her friend Daniela Hantuchova.

Do these girls know how to live it up on tour, or what?

Sharapova spends a lot of her time on court acting out scenes from wildlife programmes, especially ones featuring piglets fighting over a bucket of swill. She has been recorded making grunts of 101.2 decibels, which is roughly equivalent to a Harley-Davidson revving up at the traffic lights.

It is a wonder, Australia being such a nanny country, that the health and safety people allow anyone into a Sharapova match without issuing them with the kind of earplugs they will shortly be issuing to spectators at Melbourne's Formula One grand prix.

Listening to the noise coming from the other side of the net, Davenport must have thought she was back in the labour ward, but the one thing you can safely say about Sharapova's shrieking is that her groundstrokes are every bit as fierce as they sound.

Davenport was simply blown off court by the Russian girl's power, conceding the first set in 26 minutes and the match in barely more than an hour. It would have been considerably less than that, too, were it not for Sharapova's interminable routine of ball-bouncing and attending to her coiffure during service games."

TIME, THEN, to consider reporting that is contrastingly cold, silent and stripped of emotion – such as the single, sad report smuggled from the scene of the execution of a beautiful spy.

Also, a reporter's reaction as he watches his whole city burn down.

And a journalist's contemplation of classic war crimes.

And last, but not least, you should witness the brave correspondent being forced to expose himself in a nudist colony.

These are just a few of the type of hazards any reporter might be compelled to record in precisely accurate, plain words at any moment in his or her life-time. But reporting comes in 50 shades, as you will see in the differing styles of journalistic writing that follow. ☐

10. Journalists' eyewitness accounts.

*Reportage, by contrast, lays claim directly
to the power of the real,
which imaginative literature can approach
only through make-believe.*

Prof John Carey

BEHIND THE NEWS 2

Here are more news reports which I believe you will enjoy for the writing alone – and the vastly differing literary styles. The reporters include popular favourites such as Jack London (of *White Fang* fame) and Damon Runyon (of *Guys and Dolls* fame).

The subjects range from the Mata Hari spy scandal of the early 20th century to the War in Iraq scandal of the early 21st century.

Oh yes, and here too is a full exposure by an embarrassed veteran newsman in a nudist colony.

But first, the reluctant report by Jack London on an event he believed was too close to him and too sad to report.

Who said journalists have no hearts?

Watching a city convulse and burn to death

Jack London of San Francisco was a sailor, a mill-hand, a janitor, a prospector before becoming a newspaperman and novelist made world-

San Francisco's Great Fire breaks out. Its citizens have never been better behaved.

famous through his *White Fang* stories. He was once hired with other famous writers by millionaire Randolph Hearst to launch his chain of newspapers (though none of these top writers stayed long with Hearst's 'Yellow Press').

On 17 April 1906, Jack London watched his city burn down, and swore never to write about it. There weren't the words to describe it, he said. But he couldn't help himself. Within days he was penning a piece at the request of *Collier's Weekly*:

"San Francisco is gone! Nothing remains of it but memories ... Its residential section is wiped out.

"The factories and warehouses, the great stores and newspaper buildings, the hotels and the palaces of the nabobs, are all gone ...

"On Wednesday morning at 5.15 came the earthquake. A minute later the flames were leaping upward ... Within an hour the smoke of San Francisco's burning was a lurid tower visible a hundred miles away. And for three days and nights this lurid tower swayed in the sky, reddening the sun, darkening the day ...

"Within 12 hours half the city was gone ... Out on the Bay, not a flicker of wind stirred. Yet wind was pouring in upon the city from every side. The heated air rising made an enormous suck. Thus did the fire of itself build its own colossal chimney through the atmosphere ... There was no withstanding the onrush of the flames ...

"Remarkably ... there were no crowds, no shouting, no hysteria ... [Fleeing towns-people used] baby buggies, toy wagons and go-carts as trucks, while every other person was dragging a trunk. Everybody was gracious. Never in all San Francisco's history were her people so kind and courteous as on this night of terror ...

"Near City Hall ... creeping warily under the shadows of tottering walls, emerged occasional men and women. It was like the meeting of the handful of survivors after the day of the end of the world. ...

"San Francisco, at the present time, is like the crater of a volcano, around which are camped tens of thousands of refugees ... "

Man learns to fly

The first report of successful heavier-than-air flight by mankind went almost unnoticed by the world. It appeared without a byline on 18 December 1903, in a local paper named, with local shipping activity in mind, the *Virginian-Pilot*.

The 'world-shattering' story – seen by very few – read: "The problem of aerial navigation without the use of a balloon has been solved at last."

"Over the sand hills of the North Carolina coast yesterday, near Kittyhawk, two Ohio men proved that they could soar through the air in a flying machine of their own construction, with the power to steer and speed it at will ... Like a monster bird, the invention hovered above the breakers and circled over the rolling sand hills at the command of its navigator and, after soaring for three miles, it gracefully descended to earth again, and lightly rested upon a spot selected by the man in the car as a suitable landing place ..."

The report was a long one, demonstrating the local reporter's precise knowledge of the background and technical aims of Wilbur Wright, the inventor, and Orville his sandy-haired brother. But envious critics have claimed for years that the reporter 'got the facts wrong', as many reporters seem to do. The envious critics of the report point out that the first flight consisted of three, not one attempt, and it lasted, not three

Seconds into the first airplane flight, at Kitty Hawk, North Carolina; December 17, 1903. Photo first published in 1908.

miles, but *ten feet*, staying aloft *for twelve seconds*.

However, it is the critics who are wrong in this case, as critics so often are.

If you read carefully the reporter's opening paragraphs (above) and seek out his *full* account, you will see no claim of "first flight". The first flight was timed and measured, but kept strictly confidential to enable the Orville brothers to announce it when they were ready. However, they allowed a friendly scribe, whom they knew well, to break the *news* first ... but only when, after several attempts, there was meaningful *proof* of man-made flight. The final sentence of the momentous 'first report' gives the answer:

> "Their last appearance was on 1st September, and since then they have been actively engaged upon the construction of the machine which made yesterday's successful flight."

It is a reminder to critics of good journalism that the first rule in criticism should be to observe their own mantra: first check the facts ... as we should do about one of Europe's legendary double-spies ...

Death of a beautiful spy

Mata Hari was already famous as an exotic dancer. She was a 'lustrous-eyed, golden-skinned' Eurasian, born in Holland with the name Gertrude Margarete Zelle. She became a double spy, for the Germans and for the French, in The Great War of 1914-1918 ... the first 'war to end all wars'.

In October 1917, Henry G Wales of the *International News Service* described how Mata Hari was rushed to her death by a French firing squad soon after her dramatic capture.

Wales reported:

> " ... She drew on her stockings, black, silken, filmy things, grotesque in the circumstances ... high-heeled slippers ... long black velvet coat edged with fur and huge fur collar ... worn over the heavy silk kimono (and) over her nightdress ... She placed on her head a large, flapping black felt hat with silken ribbon and bow. Slowly and indifferently, it seemed, she pulled on a pair of black kid gloves. Then she said calmly:
> 'I am ready'.
> " ... (At her place of execution) Mata Hari was not bound. At her own wish, she was not blindfolded.

" ... The officer commanding the 12-man firing squad, who had been watching his men like a hawk that none might examine his rifle and try to find out whether he was destined to fire the blank cartridge which was in the breach of one rifle, seemed relieved that the business would soon be over ... each man gazed down his barrel at the breast of the woman which was their target.

"She did not move a muscle."

"... a volley rang out. Flame and a tiny puff of greyish smoke issued from the muzzle of each rifle ... Mata Hari fell dead. She did not die as actors and moving pictures would have us believe that people die when they are shot. She did not throw up her arms nor did she plunge straight forward or straight back.

"Slowly, inertly, she settled to her knees, her head up always, without the slightest change of expression on her face. For the fraction of a second it seemed she tottered there, on her knees, gazing directly at those who had taken her life.

"... Bending over her, an officer placed the muzzle of his revolver – almost but not quite – against the left temple of the spy. He pulled the trigger, and the bullet tore into the brain of the woman."

Mata Hari, posing here, was her stage name. The poor little Dutch girl had a Scottish surname (McLeod) and became world famous – too late. A newspaperman managed to beat martial law to report her fate.

Grotesquely, Henry Wales' famous dispatch was remembered not so much for its vivid picture of the brutality of execution. It was remembered mainly because his detailed report had killed a lascivious rumour that the beautiful and much-admired dancer was clad only in a fur coat which she flashed open at the last moment to reveal her naked body to the firing squad.

Shakespeare would love this guy

Damon Runyon first wrote for the Colorado *Adviser* when he was 13 years old. That was because he was the son of the printer/editor. But when he moved to the Big Apple, he became a sports writer, a court reporter, an author and a playwright of note. After his death his words became collectors' items and his works turned into music, as in the internationally acclaimed *Guys and Dolls* Broadway hit and Hollywood movie.

In speakeasies in New York it was often debated whether or not he was the best reporter in the world, and a hard time was had by any horse-head who said 'nay'.

A British critic wrote: "Seriously, though in a minor sphere, Runyon is comparable to Shakespeare and Milton as an improvisator (*!*) of language."

I agree. That's why Runyon appears here, though he is difficult to quote and impossible to appreciate until you have absorbed his language and his Runyonesque Broadway style.

Here is a small sample of his sports writing in 1925:

"What a football player – this man Red Grange! Say it again. He is melody, and symphony, on the football field. He is crashing sound. He is poetry. He is brute force."

Or of Runyon's court reporting, for example the trial of Al Capone for tax evasion in 1931:

"Capone was quietly dressed this morning, bar a hat of pearly white, emblematic, no doubt, of purity."

In 1927 Runyon covered the murder trial of Ruth Snyder, a chilly blonde and Judd Gray a 'corset-salesman cavalier' involved in a commonplace case that caught up the public imagination and "consumed more newsprint than any other *cause celebre* of the 20th century", outside of the kidnapping and murder of the famous Lindbergh baby, of course.

" ... She – she – she – she–she – she. Twas an echo from across the ages and an old familiar echo, at that. It was the same old 'squawk' of Brother Man whenever and wherever he is in a jam, that first framed the words: 'She gave me the tree, and I did eat'.
"It has been put in various forms since then, as Henry Judd Gray, for one notable instance close at hand, put in the form of

eleven long type-written pages yesterday, but in any form and in any language it remains a 'squawk'.
'She played me pretty hard ...
'She said, 'You're going to do it [kill him], aren't you?' ... .
'She kissed me.
'She did this ... She did that ... Always she–she–she–she–she, ran the confession of Henry Judd.
"And 'she' – the woman accused? (A chilly-looking blonde with frosty eyes, cold as an ice-cream cone; and with one of those marble, you-bet-you-will chins). How did she take this most gruesome squawk?
"Well, on the whole, better than you might expect ... "

The off-beat, oft-changing style and language of Damon Runyan is not something that can be captured in a paragraph or two. You need to read one of his books of short stories to appreciate what a great writer and journalist he was.

Journalism seeks to explore every political, social and emotional subject. The more emotional, the more divisive and the more unusual an issue is, the more dispassionate the reporting usually becomes. Exposure by an American reporter of atrocities by American troops at My Lai in Vietnam is a case in point. But there are more mundane exposures that also merit dispassionate treatment. Humorist H Allen Smith, when he was with *United Press*, 'uncovered' one such news assignment.

He reported:
"All arguments to the contrary, it is very embarrassing to have a young woman walk up to you stark naked and tell you nudism is going to sweep the nation. The shed-your-pants apostles at this particular nudist camp are serious about it. They appear to feel nudism will do wonders for this world. This is your correspondent's first visit to a nudist camp, and this one is operated by Miss Jane Gap, who apparently cuts her own hair ...

Your correspondent was stripped in 10 minutes ... and it all seemed perfectly natural walking back and forth without so much as a pair of shorts on.

Then round the corner came Miss Gronlin ... very blonde, very handsome. And she didn't even have shoes on. Your correspondent, a bird lover, became intensely interested in a thrush that was going into a power dive over Bear Mountain ... She laid a hand on my arm. 'Please come swimming. The lake is wonderful'.

Miss Gronlin, your correspondent told her firmly, 'I am not used to this business'. 'Oh, that's all right', she burst forth 'the water isn't so deep in places'.

Miss Emery, who is in charge of the dining room, came down to the pier and ripped off what little clothing she wore. (After complaining that some nutty people stray into the camp) she yawned and started off on a classical dance – one of those here-we-go-gathering-nuts-in-May dances ...

Standing on the dock, Miss Emery, still as naked as the day she was born (as was your correspondent) explained that the idea of this nudist camp is health.

The sun, she said, is good for one ... "

When the 'good guys' kill the innocent

Here is a very different example of 'telling-it-like-it-is' reporting: The great gadfly and humanist of war correspondents, Robert Fisk, sent the following dispatch to the *London Independent* from Baghdad during the Gulf War:

"In the smashed concrete and mud, there was a set of Bat Woman comics. On page 17, where the dirt splashed on the paper, Bat Woman was, oddly, rescuing Americans from a burning tower block ...

Not far from the crater ... on the wall of the sitting room, the clock still hung on its nail. It had stopped at exactly 7.55, which was when the missile smashed into numbers 10 and 10A of the laneway in the Zukah district of Baghdad on Saturday night ... There was a school at one end of the lane, but no obvious military target that I could see ... The missile crashed into No 10, burying a man and his wife and two children and punching a crater 20 feet into the ground ...

So why the missile? Why should the Americans target with their supposedly precision ordnance this little middle-class ghetto? (A witness told me:) 'On Friday night we had 15 missiles here. Fifteen?

They are trying to assassinate President Hussein, the vice-president said, 'What kind of state tries to assassinate another country's leader then says it is fighting a war on terror?'"

The same question was being asked in 2012, a decade later, in Afghanistan. Fisk was always a radical journalist, providing much-needed balance to the overwhelmingly 'patriotic' reporting of war correspondents, even in the free world.

The difference between reporters such as he and most bloggers on the web today is that he operates at the scene within the disciplines and accountability required of professional journalism.

'I was there' reporting is basic to accountable journalism, but of course much vital information is gathered in hindsight. A magnificent example of this is the story told by a journalist researching the extreme dangers of permitting news to be censored in the name of 'security'. The next story is one by a journalist who was awarded a Pulitzer Prize. Though it missed its vital deadline by several years, it was brilliantly researched and reported ten years after the chilling event. □

11.
The Dead Hand.

… Lt-Col Stanislav Petrov was sitting in a top-secret 'early warning' station near Moscow when the electronic panels in front of him flashed a red light: "LAUNCH". A siren screamed. It was alerting the entire underground crew – as if they needed it – to signals of an enemy nuclear missile attack that had been picked up by Russia's Satellite Five.

Journalist David E. Hoffman,
who won the Pulitzer Prize for this long-banned report.

BEHIND THE NEWS 2

It was only in 2008 that the cold, precise story of what the world had been almost unknowingly facing for the previous 25 years was publicly revealed.

Humanity was – as many feared or suspected – just a hair trigger away from nuclear war in which missiles could eliminate all life in large parts of Europe and America within an hour.

Perhaps the greatest event of the 20th century – overshadowed possibly by the Space Race occurring simultaneously – was the Cold War. It lasted 40 years and was a longer existing threat to humanity than both WWI and WWII. It threatened to mutilate or destroy the so-called civilised world.

Testing of nuclear weapons; the A-bomb, the H-bomb and the rocket warhead bombs, went on around the world for years. Those who created them and tested them made sure they polluted the atmosphere as far from their own territories as possible. And promised never to use them. But giant bombs were made ready to be blasted off in a crisis and at an instant's notice. And in the Cold War there were many crises; most

93

of them unreported, it appears now. Those hair-trigger threats were hard to exaggerate, and were sometimes closer than the general public ever knew.

Every US president in office, from Truman and Eisenhower, to Kennedy and Reagan, was forced to be within a moment's reach of the nuclear-bomb trigger during every hour of every day and every night. The 'trigger', requiring more than one key, was carried by a special aide who was said to be manacled to its portable case. What precautions other nuclear bomb-builders offered is not known.

The Cold War was the least reported event of its era. Yes, this was partly due to unquestioned and unprecedented 'security' measures involving intense secrecy and spying activity. But it was also because civil society was judged to be unable to entertain such awesome suspense *permanently*. Nations were led to trust in the theory of a balance of power that made nuclear war 'impossible'.

Yet, behind the Iron Curtain, the prospect of nuclear war and annihilation was dire. It led in the last stages to near panic among Russia's leadership and nearly reckless action by subordinates. Only recently has documentation been published of moments during the Cold War when the finger on the trigger of a nuclear warhead belonged to a nervous senior Russian army officer, not sure of what decision he was expected to make.

ON 26 SEPTEMBER 1983, as the Cold War began to heat up again, Lt-Col Stanislav Petrov was sitting in a top-secret 'early warning' station near Moscow when the electronic panels in front of him flashed a red light: "LAUNCH". A siren screamed. It was alerting the entire underground crew – as if they needed it – to signals of a US missile attack that had been picked up by Russia's Satellite Five.

This had never happened before. Men crowded behind the glass, watching their experienced leader's hand as he reached for the phone to inform his waiting seniors. Then he paused. He could sense his own doubts and a gut feeling about unreliability in the relatively untested system. But he must respond immediately to his waiting superiors. He read the panels again, clicked on his phone and said: "I am reporting a false alarm".

He took a deep breath; slumped back and felt his body flooding with relief.

This was at a height in international tension. The enemy's leader, U.S. President Ronald Reagan, had recently called Petrov's homeland "an evil empire". And a few weeks previously the Soviet Defences Forces had shot down – by mistake, he knew – a pro-American Korean airliner, killing 269 civilians. Now everyone was unusually tense. Worse; Russia had long ago become fearful of the West's supposed plans to annihilate the gloriously free Soviets. All of Russia was paranoid about this deadly, seemingly overwhelming threat.

Two minutes after the first satellite warning, the Russian watchers' panel flashed again.

Another missile launched. Another. And another. And another. Five nuclear missiles heading towards Moscow. The warning system had gone 'ballistic'. There were just minutes left for Petrov's leaders to react in the way they had been specifically trained. Then the additional signals triggered an additional, never seen before form of warning, spelling out the word MISSILE ATTACK on Petrov's screen as it sent automatically an electronic blip to the higher levels of the military. The satellite also signalled a message: "High reliability."

Petrov now had to make a second, doubly-hard decision. He knew the system had had glitches in the past. And he could detect no verification from any other of his monitoring sources ... only this frantic urgency from the 'frontline' observation satellite.

Forcing himself to action, he raised the phone and told the duty officer, again, in as calm a voice as he could muster: "This is a false alarm."

THE ABOVE ACCOUNT is an accurate one of a real event. It is also true that if, in those few moments, he had taken the easier route and made the call he was trained to make, the message would instantly have been sent up the military ladder to the chief of General Staff; to the two top Soviet leaders, and then probably to the 'Perimeter System' which would have triggered an automatic process of firing a total response, aimed at identified targets in the USA.

The Perimeter's automated system of nuclear weapon launching was devised to keep firing even if all Soviet command structures were incapacitated or destroyed by incoming nuclear missiles. The automated system was similar to the device in the hands of a dying train-driver whose grip slips from the controls. Only in this instance it was half the world's nuclear arms that were subject to 'The Dead Hand' ... leaving no consciousness, no conscience, no human being to deal with problems inherent in the deliberate delivery of mass death and destruction.

All this should have reminded us of what these ominous threats involve, because a similar crisis occurred not long ago – without the world knowing then about the incipient drama of a possible man-made melt-down on Earth.

There were at that moment 18,400 nuclear warheads poised to be launched by both sides, enough to destroy the two super-powers many times over. It has since been calculated that the two super powers were armed for a *ten times over-kill*. Enough to destroy the civilised world on the eve of the 21st century.

There was worse news in 2018. A Hydrogen Bomb was being mooted, perhaps being cuddled into existence by a mentally unstable dictatorship in North Korea. No matter what international agreements are made with Korea, there remains a remote possibility that a nuclear holocaust could still happen in the coming decade. The Federation of American Scientists warned recently that it estimates there are more than 17,000 nuclear warheads in the world. More than 4000 of them are "operational" and ready for use.

JOURNALIST DAVID E. HOFFMAN reported on the Petrov event, and many more, in fascinating sometimes horrifying detail in his book, *The Dead Hand*, published by Doubleday in New York in 2009 (and around the world by other publishers after 2011). He won a Pulitzer Prize for his work, but it deserves much more than that. His findings need to be better-known than any of Hollywood's and Bollywood's blockbusters.

I found his work only because my friend, George Trail, a retired ambassador in the US, brought it to my attention in 2011. I urge you to read it. It needs to be taken very seriously.

A *New York Times* review is quoted in the book's tributes as saying "*The Dead Hand* is deadly serious, but this story can verge on pitch-black comedy ... " That, in my view, is a misconception which many are under, to their own danger.

The reason why the entire Soviet Union citizenry suffered from paranoia – and bankrupted their empire trying to *defend* themselves against 'American imperialism'– was that they really believed they were going to be attacked at any moment with superior nuclear weapons; or with nerve gas, or with fatal forms of germs, delivered by missiles and artillery shells. They believed the US was bent on invasion and destruction of Mother Russia. Even Russia's KGB and military leaders believed their own propaganda!

The same phenomenon of believing your own propaganda led to the self-mutilation of the divisive cultures which were soon tearing apart Yugoslavia with bitterness and vast bloodshed.

There is evidence of danger in any country where its people are blindly misled and their right to freedom of information is denied

The Berlin Wall, for instance, which symbolised the bitter strife between West Germany's free society and East Germany's communists, caused confrontation between America and Russia that led to the nearest outbreak, so far, of World War III.

Only three newsmen reached both sides of The Wall that day. When the tanks and snipers and hidden troops backed away from each other, 'inside reporting' seemed to require some light relief. My unplanned *eye-witness* account in that vein follows. □

12.
The Berlin Wall.

In the moment of panic the other journalists looked at me as if I'd sold their mothers as specimens for a Russian torture chamber school.

To appreciate how threatening the power was behind what Winston Churchill called the Iron Curtain, one has to go back to Berlin itself. It was here that Stalin and the Western world faced off, with Germany divided after WWII into four parts under French, British, American and Russian rule. Berlin was well inside the Russian zone and behind the 'curtain', so the Russians occupied half of Berlin and all the territory around it. Only three small isolated enclaves of the metropolis were occupied by the Allies.

'I WAS ONLY LOOKING—I'M CHARLIE!'

The Kremlin decided unilaterally one day in 1961 to shut down West Berlin's trade and travel links with the West. All westward autobahn and rail routes were blocked 'until further notice'. West Berliners were left to starve, or capitulate to the East.

And thus began the greatest air armada in peacetime history. Cargo planes and disarmed bombers flew, almost in 'line of sight', day and night, to land, unload and hastily take off again to rejoin the conveyor belt of weary aircrew who provided West Berlin's lifeline. At great risk to their own lives, pilots delivered tons of fuel and machinery, toilet rolls and violins, bread and books to West Berliners. Finally the Kremlin backed down and Berlin's internationally agreed links with West Germany were restored.

For the remainder of the Cold War – even during the traumatic moments when The Wall suddenly sprang up and frantic residents died in trying to cross it – the neon lights of flourishing West Berlin shone as a tantalising beacon across subdued and ill-lit Eastern Europe.

"The most critical moment of the 20th Century"

The reporter should never become the story, but in this case he was trapped in it.

My innocent and insignificant role in the Cold War is a long story; so I shall repeat here merely the middle of it. The middle is a place still standing, and still known after half a century, as Checkpoint Charlie.

In the heady relief after a critical showdown that threatened a third world war, the scene was accurately captured in a cartoon in the London *Daily Mail*.(And by global newsreel cameras.) The Wall itself made world headlines all over again in 2014 when the 25th anniversary of its fall was celebrated.

But the preserved border post, and other memorials to the dead, can in no way describe the suffering of the times. They can only hint at the tension that existed for so long.

Nor were three journalists, one from *The Times of India*, one from *The Christchurch Press* in New Zealand and one from the *Natal Daily News* in South Africa, sufficiently aware of the reality when they found themselves at the hostile border. The Wall, a sudden, infamous and daunting barrier, was still in the process of being constructed, lengthened, mined and double-barricaded while we were there in 1962.

As 'neutral' foreigners, we had been trying to get into East Berlin after being turned back by the British at the Brandenburg Gate and by the French military further down, and were now feeling frustrated and irritable.

Finally we tried the American sector where, unknown to us, all the trouble had started the previous evening while we were beginning some private research into West Berlin's hyperactive nightlife.

During the evening, the politically-probing American ambassador, no less, was refused access by lowly East German guards to attend an opera in the Russian-occupied zone. It was seen in the West as the final, unprovoked and knife-edge breach of WWII peace treaty protocols.

The crisis came in the midst of arrests and murders on the Russian side of their wall where innocent citizens were being shot in cold blood as they tried to flee from the East.

They risked death to reach freedom by being smuggled across in the mock fuel tanks of cars; or leaping over barbed wire and the wall itself as the *Vopo*s (the *Volkspolizei* – East German People's Police) suddenly switched on their floodlights and shot them in the back. The West side of the wall was decorated at this point with a growing chain of fresh wreaths mourning the dead.

Preventing America's representative access to the Russian zone of Berlin at such a time more than dishonoured the 1945 peace treaties. It was the last straw and the ominous signal for a new war. Tanks and helicopters, troops and snipers began mobilising on both sides close to, but out of sight of the Wall.

We three newshounds had no inkling of this denouement. We were bent on seeing for ourselves the Russian zone in the guise of tourists or un-Western and irrelevant journos – whichever worked – on a sightseeing visit, escorted by a driver/guide. He was a young and somewhat nervous Lebanese student known to the normal border guards on both sides. He had been making such trips, in less tense times, to pay his way through university. It just happened that he was secretly on the payroll of West Berlin's administration, we learned much later. But he was a relatively innocent general observer. For all we knew, he may have been in the pay of the Russians as well.

He grew extremely uneasy when he saw the senior US military officers and the tension at Checkpoint Charlie as we tried in various practised newspaper ways, to talk our way across the border. After a flurry of telephone calls to US headquarters somewhere, we were suddenly waved through.

We had no inkling that we were to be the little fish allowed to test suddenly boiling political waters. Ours was the only vehicle to cross the border that critical day, and we were more than surprised at the big and blatantly ominous reception we received from the East German guards beyond the zigzag of tank-traps that stretched two or three city blocks through a cleared, military security zone of East Berlin.

At the *Vopos* checkpoint, several uniformed men simultaneously cross-examined each of us and pored over our passports. Telephone calls were made. Senior officers arrived. More telephone calls were made, and finally we were let through – after our vehicle had been searched, inside and out and underneath in the usual manner. We were given permission to drive to three specific areas (including a visit to East Berlin's Russian War Memorial!) and to get out of the Russian-occupied zone within six hours.

Only later did we appreciate that we were not only America's little fish permitted to test hot waters, we were now little Russian guinea pigs allowed some freedom in their backyard. But why should the American military use three journalists – without warning them – in so risky an experiment? Because we were expendable, we realised in hindsight. And the Russians? Why should they let us into East Berlin at the same time as they were massing snipers, troops, tanks and other armour on their side of the wall? Because, obviously, they were hoping the American occupying force would not shoot from the hip, but first test access to the zone.

But why three nosey journalists?

The explanation, it seemed to us, when at last we took the time to look for explanations, was that we came from the ends of the Earth: from India, ruled in some parts at the time by communists. From South Africa, run by mad segregationists and repudiated by the West. And from New Zealand; but who knew or cared where that was?

If all went well, the presence of visiting journalists should indicate to the outside world that access to East Berlin had been restored.

However, the moment when the Cold War could almost have turned into a hot one came when – in unfeigned innocence – I left our car and tried to take a photograph of Hitler's bunker. Our terrified guide muttered something about this being *verboten*, on the ridiculous grounds that under the ruins of the grass-covered bunker was a Russian "key strategic post".

This was confirmed, however, when guards suddenly popped out of the low, border-line mound of grass which my camera was focussed on, and shouted at me to halt or be shot.

There was no way I was going to halt, let alone be arrested.

I got away by retreating sideways and pretending not to hear.

Yet you quickly appreciate, from that prickly feeling in your back, that there are guns pointing at you as guards shout "Halt!" and other ugly unintelligible things; and because your driver has gone deathly pale.

"Drive on, very, very slowly," I told him as I climbed back into the revving car with great, innocent deliberation. My colleagues looked at me as if I had betrayed them as enemy spies. However, we were soon out of sight, gulping small sighs of relief.

But around another corner, our fleeing party was stopped by a line of heavily armed *Vopos* strung across the street. It seemed they had been signalled to stop us and confiscate my camera or photographs. I gave our gesturing interrogator a spool – but not this increasingly precious spool (on which were pictures, I discovered later that were meaningless and not publishable).

We drove off while I celebrated our second escape.

"What!" shouted my companions when I told them of my sleight of hand in giving the police a different spool.

"They'll know about that before we can get back to the checkpoint!"

In the moment of panic the other journalists looked at me as if I'd sold their mothers as specimens for a Russian torture chamber school.

Now what were we to do?

Sarkar suggested the least predictable move.

"We must go straight to East Berlin's Communist Party headquarters", he said.

Our driver almost swooned in horror.

But it made some sort of sense.

Sarkar, renowned journalist from India as he was, had once been a card-carrying member of the Indian Communist Party and believed he would be able to vouch for our innocence if not our foolhardiness.

We experienced a highly interesting two hours of the Russians, the *Vopos* commanders and Communist Party spokesmen talking, and waiting on yet more phone calls, before we were instructed to go back to the West, directly and immediately, and never to return. Our guide was ecstatic about this advice – after accusing me of trying to get killed to start a war!

After further unexpected travails our last fearful moment was to find an American tank, blocking the gate at Checkpoint Charlie, so that we could stare up its lowered gun barrel, while our Allies decided what to do.

The hot waters of the Cold Wars, and our nerves, were again thoroughly tested not once, but three more times during agonising moments and forced waits during our rush to return to safety.

Finally, against the background of the massed troops, tanks, guns and helicopters of Russia and America on each side of us, and in the atmosphere of international hair trigger suspense, our little escapade had become, indeed, of public interest.

It was part of the 'crisis news' published in Berlin, London, then round the world as main headlines in all media globally, and as front-page leads in our three little eye-witness accounts in our newspapers back home.

What really matters, though, is that America and Russia, after a week's confrontation at their mutual border in Berlin, withdrew their forces without a shot being fired.

The Cold War blew hot and cold until the Wall fell down 27 years later.

My part in it was a lesson on how not to be a temporary war correspondent.

However, to be deadly serious, I confess that we three un-briefed journalists were in awe and felt deeply privileged to be the only newsmen to be eyewitnesses – and unwitting participants – at the precise place and precise moment of the greatest news event in our lifetimes.

The latter was confirmed by the director of the famous BBC television series *The World at War* who also directed CNN's series, *The Cold War* – broadcast in late 2014 – which concluded that the moment before the two armed forces backed off a few yards from the Berlin Wall was the world's *"most critical moment of the 20th century"*.

The untold bigger story

Our three reporters' experiences at the climax of the East-West confrontation soon turned into a useful anecdote with its amusing memories, told originally at some length in my first book, *A Walk on the Wild Side* (Struik, 1995), where it was published with many other light stories about escaping from charging rhinos and the rest ... But in reality, like fleeing from a head-down charging rhino, it had been no joke, except in retrospect.

My instinctive choice of risking being shot in the back by trigger-happy border guards – rather than walk into their underground HQ – demonstrates how anxious I was in that war-like crisis. The tension was tangible – and extended far beyond our brief escapade. Later I discovered that it poisoned the life of every Berliner behind the Wall in ways almost impossible to describe unless one lived for years, trapped in that atmosphere. It represented the antithesis of the basic values of family and free society.

The fact is that we three senior foreign journalists, in our few hours there, missed the real story that was just beginning – the sad horror of the other side of the Berlin Wall and of its human victims on both sides of it.

THE DEATH-SPEWING Wall had suddenly appeared "in the middle of town" in the preliminary shape of a two-metre barbed-wire fence, cutting through family properties and marking the foundations of the brick and concrete frontier that followed – a ruthless path, slicing through occupied buildings as well as highways and railways and waterways.

As the wall went up, residents on its perilous border had started jumping from their windows to reach freedom. One day, while a gathering crowd of West Berliners watched, four fugitives made the leap from various levels, one after the other ... and died of their injuries. A six-year-old boy was dropped from a third-floor apartment and was caught in a sheet hurriedly stretched by volunteers below. He received internal injuries. His mother made a florid but safe landing on the same desperately held sheet. His father suffered serious spinal damage in the same sheet, and said later: "It was worth it. I would jump again."

One of the earliest and most notorious incidents at The Wall involved a lone youth, aged about 18, named Peter Fechter, who lay, wounded from gunshots, and dying on the barbed wire crest.

"... for 50 minutes without medical assistance or help from the guards, who remain in hiding," reads a caption below a photograph of the drama. "Risking their own lives, West Berlin police throw him bandages. He is too weak. He is finally carried away, dying."

When I returned, decades later, to the scene, Checkpoint Charlie had become a museum; exhibiting countless such stories and their photographic evidence of human courage, sacrifice, cruelty and cowardice. The evidence showed that *Vopos* guards had not all been heartless. Some had, in fact, risked their own lives to help, for instance, a child cross the border, or a refugee in pain. One West Berlin rescuer, having safely conducted a whole family over the dangerous No-Man's Land, turned and fired on the watching *Vopos* ... making sure he aimed high above them, in the knowledge that they had quietly refused to act. His bullet marks above their heads would be evidence they might need.

There is another kind of evidence still bitterly remembered. It is seen in a photograph, for instance, of a beautiful girl's face showing inexpressible, uncomprehending pain. She has asked a 20-year-old "escape helper", Dieter Wohifahrt, who had selflessly and repeatedly assisted no less than 50 people through the wire, to aid her mother's escape from the East. The drama unfolds thus:

Arrangements are secretly and satisfactorily agreed with her mother for a long-awaited reunion and joint freedom at last. The mother, already waiting near the Eastern border, gives an arranged signal, and Dieter cuts through the wire. He is ambushed and shot dead. A soldier, Heinz Kliem, fleeing across the border in disgust at this crime, reports that the mother *had appeared at the East German guard house two hours beforehand!* With the mother as their witness, the *Vopos* had simply waited to kill the young rescuer, he says.

You could have spent days, weeks, years – a generation – looking at photographic evidence of heart-rending or infamous behaviour by humans under the stress experienced 'behind the Wall'. But no one seemed to have the time or interest.

Babies being shown to their grandparents on the other side of the Berlin wall.

The media and the world grew tired of the spectacle ... despite its ever-changing drama. The political commentators, from Edinburgh to Los Angles, disregarded such ordinary human suffering and the UN wrung its hands in the usual way more than a few times. But the world and even the free media failed to be accountable. They turned their backs on several million citizens, involuntarily isolated by despots, and bullied until they lost their own humanity.

Most of us were unaware of the fate – their misfortune worse than death in many cases – which overcame East Berliners in the icy shadows of that era. The murder story told above of a mother's betrayal, did provide a clue. But it was only through a few persistently researched paperbacks, not published until this 21st century, that the world outside learned what ideology and failure of law and censorship can do to 'civilised' people.

Anna Funder, an Australian lawyer, researcher and TV presenter, explained in her first book in 2003, entitled *Stasiland** that the East German state had employed 97,000 Stasi (security staff) during the Cold War. But the new communist state also had on file 173,000 civilian informers "... one informer for every 6.5 citizens", the author points out ... This compared with Hitler's Third Reich which had one Gestapo agent for every 2,000 citizens and Stalin's USSR with one KGB agent for every 5830.

The relevant statistics don't matter. What matters is that, if there were an informer for every seven people in East Germany, it suggests almost every extended *family* in East Berlin might have someone spying on his or her relatives. This seemed likely because, when East Germany capitulated and the *Stasi* closed down, thousands of files were revealed. East Berliners rushed to inspect the security files, for they included notes listing things such as what books were read in some informer's or neighbour's home; why the husband was demoted by the *Stasi* government; why the eldest son had been refused a university education. East Berliners were stunned at the volume, nature and use of the dubious information on file.

The *Stasi* records revealed countless informants, many of them seeking approbation by providing whatever they could think of about their neighbours; their doctor; their friends; their spouses; their close relatives.

The same files listed what happened to some of the citizens who had been secretly reported. Life in prison? Death?

Records showed that some of these victims were fortunate enough to be freed. They were put up for auction in West Germany by the *Stasi* when the police were in search of funds! Small comfort no doubt for the registered, and now revealed, informers.

WHAT DID LIFE under strict state control do to many of the 17 million citizens of East Germany, or more pertinently, to the few million concentrated city-dwellers in the eastern side of Berlin?

Even Orwell would struggle to conceive of the personal consequences. Or determine what deductions could be made of circumstances in which most citizens were degraded and their lifestyles filed as items of gossip.

How soon, and how often, were families aware of spies among them? How much suspicion, hate and fear might arise from most of these tens of thousands of intimacies, rumours, spiteful lies placed in the 'secret' police files by friends or members of their own family?

This sounds beyond belief, but the statistics, the photographs and the piles of sworn evidence do not lie.

First of all, you must picture the desperation of the tens of thousands of those trying to escape – a total of about a million people; it was estimated when the Wall fell.

Escapers tunnelling their way to freedom were so many that, in one meticulously recorded case, two tunnels "collided" inside Eastern Berlin. Another case involved a father from Western Berlin, going in search of one of his children trying to tunnel his way out of the East. Their planned meeting caused a tunnel collapse and alerted the guards, who shot the father as he emerged.

But freedom-lovers always cherished hope from the dramatic accounts of successful escapees, such as the gas-propelled balloon, its tanks designed secretly by an engineer, launched one dark night with two adults and two children aboard, which landed safely and silently in a selected open space in West Berlin. Or the man, who designed himself a home-made 'submarine', and propelled it down-river beneath the surface until he reached the sea; then popped up and paddled to Denmark.

Betrayal was offset by bravery in countless cases. More than a thousand East German army guards defected to the West during the Cold War quarter century. Participants in the ceaseless 24-hour struggle have claimed that if the security guards had all been faithful to the instructions of the *Stasi,* the death-rate at the Wall would have been 20 times higher.

"Stasiland", quickly and apparently deeply buried in Berlin, should be preserved somewhere in the world, to remind us how crucial it is for all communities to ensure that real freedom exists; that authority must always be curbed and made accountable; that information should not be shackled by power-seekers. Or free speech stifled 'for the sake of national security'. Communists, whether in China or in Chippingdale UK, need to protect their ideals and ideology by freeing them of ideological chains. Perhaps the digital world will do it one day for all of us.

But never forget Stasiland, which had first to be rescued from hell by Breznev's Moscow, among other would-be reformers.

End of the Soviet Union

The brutal Berlin Wall was a symbol dividing East and West for nearly 30 years. Then, in a single, spontaneous, popular demonstration in Berlin one day in 1989, the trapped Berliners – including some from the oppressed Eastern half – pulled pieces of it down themselves.

When the Berlin Wall fell, as a result of the arms race, so did the Soviet Union, and this resulted in a large number of nations being set free. Political independence grew rapidly around the world. The fall of the Wall made the domino effect of the recent fall of a Tunisian dictatorship, and the resultant revolution throughout the Arab world, look insignificant by comparison. For instance, within five years South Africa was estimated by some to be the 48th nation member, returning to the UN as a fully democratic and independent state ... made politically feasible by the Soviet's collapse.

Fortunately for mankind, the myth of liberation movements, conquering their dictators all by themselves, lives on. It provides the propaganda and self-pride that allows, sometimes, a form of new government other than communist, totalitarian, militarist or colonial rule to assert itself.

But in mid-20th century the Russian Empire possessed territories that stretched unbroken across nearly half of earth's time zones. Russia had more nuclear bombs than it knew what to do with. Its armies were the biggest in the world. Its technologies, appropriated as well as invented, had rocketed the first man into orbit around the planet. It had squadrons of spies embedded in high places in many countries, and agents who carried poisoned-tipped umbrellas, and thought James Bond was the hero of a little fairy tale. Russian torturers and spies were unhindered by democratic checks on extremism. Unlike the London protests in 2018 at Russian-spy killings, the Russian State at that time was all-powerful and could afford to ignore global democratic protest.

Then, seemingly overnight, Russia went bankrupt.

Virtually all of Mother Russia's dictatorial, economic and geo-political structures collapsed after the arms race and the space race. The fall of the Wall and the end of the Cold War unsettled the balance of powers sufficiently for China to come out of the cold; for Islamic fundamentalism to rise; Cuba to shrink into the economically precarious little dictatorship it had previously been; for African politics to change ... and for new kinds of unmitigated wars to break out on three continents.

In all this upheaval, the fall of the Wall left one clear message: rule of law and freedom of expression – demonstrated in an independent judiciary and a free press – are critically important to any healthy society. ☐

* Anna Funder, Stasiland, Penguin Books 2003, deals directly with the Wall.

For context, Gitta Sereny, The German Trauma, Penguin Books, 2001, surveys the results of Nazism.

13.
In the fog: Wat ye Tyler and other stirring tales.

The cloud resembled a silent, black-coated highwayman lurking in the gloom, waiting for an opportunity to kill.

The ancient town of Dartford stands on the Roman road that runs from the Londinium of yore to Dover, beside the white cliffs. Still standing on that ancient Roman route, on a section later named Watling Street, is a miraculously preserved medieval, timbered pub, Wat Ye Tyler; named after the man who led the Peasants' Revolt in 1381.

Dartford became my temporary home when I retreated to the provinces, joined the *Kentish Times*, and was assigned to one of its half-dozen weekly newspaper editions, the *Dartford Chronicle,* beside the Thames close to London. The place is redolent with history. For instance, you can learn in Wat Ye Tyler what a Dog's Nose is (when it isn't on a dog). It is a beverage made up of a pint of good Kentish bitters with a

Wat Tyler, leading his protest march to demand freedom and justice from teenager King Richard II.

big tot of gin dropped into it, invented long ago by some ailing citizen in urgent need of a tonic, no doubt.

On the 5th of December 1952, I was there when history was made once more in the old town as we walked out of Wat ye Tyler into the dark. We found ourselves groping about in a 'pea-souper' that would have been familiar to Charles Dickens, Sherlock Holmes and Jack the Ripper – a blanket of smog so thick you couldn't see the pavement below your feet. You couldn't see your feet. You couldn't even see your hands stretched out in front of you. Traffic had come to a standstill (and, of course, disappeared before our eyes). All I could hear in the thick, damp, eerie smog was the close-by coughing of lost souls as I felt my way home, a mile up Watling Street, by walking with one foot off the curb and by counting the crossroads.

What the dark, poisonous, creeping smog heralded was the enforced end to Britain's centuries-old laissez faire attitude to air pollution. What it also heralded that first night was the end of Britain's long Industrial Revolution, you might say. London's administrators were forced almost overnight to leap into radical action, and drastically change all the laws governing industry and domestic use of coal.

The newspapers were reporting, after the first night, the deaths of 250 people killed by that choking smog. It had enveloped not only our pub but much of southern England. The next night 500 people died from being unable to breathe while in the poisonous black blanket, 800 the next, and altogether 4,000 'deaths-by-suffocation' attributed to the smothering smog which had come down on 5 December and didn't rise until 9 December.

Altogether *12,000 people*, mainly the old and those already suffering from respiration problems, were killed by that 'pea-souper' over the Thames River.

Google history reports: "In some places, visibility had literally gone down to one foot, meaning that you couldn't see your own feet when looking down nor your own hands if held out in front of you." (I have already vouched for that.)

"London was at a standstill and at least one theatre had to close because smog filtered in and rendered the stage invisible to the audience."

I should add that in Dartford – one of the worst-hit places during those fearful five days and nights – we always managed to get to Wat ye Tyler and see our friends under indoor lights, and even feel our way home again through the blackness. I think we lost one old patron in the suffocating blanket of coal dust and fog ... But it is possible he passed away, not from fogginess, but because he was snaffled by one Dog's Nose too many.

Who knows?

Not only was history made by the Great Smog of 1952, it also altered Britain's face. When I returned only eight years later, Charles Dickens and Jack the Ripper's smoggy London was no more. Instead the city had turned a strange sandy colour that almost caused you to reach for your sunglasses. The familiar old dark face of Parliament was suddenly turned almost golden. So were Piccadilly, Trafalgar Square, Westminster Abbey and Buckingham Palace. And they still smile wanly, 50 years on.

But Dartford remained dark-visaged for decades afterwards, preferring to cling to its relatively recent historical past. The conservative community claims that its founders, one of whom was excavated at the turn of the 20th century, were there 250,000 years ago*, and that the second lot of famous Dartfordians were a visiting band of Saxon robbers, who came pillaging up the Thames and decided to stay. Their progeny are still there, running the shops.

Westminster Parliament looking golden on a fine summer's day. But when I first visited it in the 1950s, the entire edifice – and all of London – looked like those black towers you see lurking in the background of this picture.

That knowledge will be making the old codgers in Dartford call for another Dog's Nose. They would be even more astonished at another scientific finding: The ancient 'English' hunter-gatherers of 9,000 years ago – like the much later ancient Brits who painted their bodies with woad and ran around semi-naked 7,000 years later, had a capacity for intelligence as great (or as little) as that of mankind today. (Much shaking of disbelieving heads in the Dartford Conservative Club lounge. Including Maggie Thatcher, the Dartford grocer's daughter who would never at any time put up with tattoos, woad-painting and similar sorts of idiotic nonsense.)

At least Dartfordians could remain sure of one thing. Kent's famous cherry orchards are unique, and the very first in Britain. They were planted on tribal Cantii land by the Romans, who built a road lasting a thousand years, and for Chaucer's rollicking pilgrims to travel on in their journeys to Canterbury. Almost all travellers on that road would stop for sustenance at a Dartford tavern.

In Henry VIII's time, one of his women, Anne of Cleves, lived across the road from the Wat ye Tyler pub.

But what the boys in Wat ye Tyler remembered best was old Wat and his hell-raising friends – Jack Straw and John Ball. These three great freedom fighters of the 1300s considered themselves as miraculous survivors of the Black Plague and deserving of a better life afterwards.

Instead they were oppressed with the ancient feudal system's equivalent of Pass Laws – and hit with Poll Tax, just like furious black freedom fighters were in Sharpeville and Soweto during apartheid in South Africa, 600 years later. So Wat and Jack and John marched on London at the head of 60,000 protesters, toyi-toying and chanting freedom-and-equality songs such as:

"When Adam delved and Eve span
Who was then the Gentleman?"

The mob also threw a few stones, took over Fleet Street, raided the prison and released the inmates. They marched on the Tower of London where King Richard II was hiding with his mother. The 14-year-old king immediately agreed to abolish serfdom and allow the peasants to go where they wished and to rent land.

Unfortunately, however, the protesters had also burnt down a few buildings, including the Savoy ... which happened to be, at that

Tyler and his friends Jack Straw and John Ball became icons of British protest for the next 400 years. And may yet make a comeback as a symbol in some campaign demanding rights.

time, not a hotel but a palace and the home of John of Gaunt. He called up his vigilantes, who killed Jack and John and Wat. This allowed King Richard to withdraw his promised land reforms.

"That's the way things are starting to go in South Africa these days," I told my new friends in those early days of apartheid at home. The lads in Wat Ye Tyler simply buried their muzzles in their Dog's Noses in that place of fine historical learning. I hope I didn't add: "Funny how history repeats itself."

Drama in a West End Theatre

Dartford had a Metropolitan Court in the 1950s which dealt with court cases of national interest – murder on the high seas, bigamy and fraud in big business, rape in the dell – reports of which, as Fleet Street freelancers, we dictated over frenetic phone lines to numbers of national newspapers.

We were garnering, at good rates of payment, more national headlines than many of Fleet Street's fulltime staff did. The secret was that our courts were a domain that was, in practice, exclusive to just three reporters in Kent. Thus we could time our stories to hit the slow periods between daily Fleet Street deadlines.

We cherished our Fleet Street headlines as much as the fee each produced.

For instance, the report dispatched at 7am, headed: "Court sentences Thames-side woman for advertising her child for sale", was bound to be published in more than one of the three afternoon national papers.

Elsewhere in Kent and most counties, justice was dispensed in the lower courts by voluntary, often very amateurish justices of the peace (JPs). Their style is captured (but not done justice) by the story told everywhere of the constable giving evidence against a prostitute.

The constable stated: "She made a scandalous proposition to me, Your Worships, which I cannot repeat in public." After much urging the lady who headed the Bench said irritably: "Then write it down!"

The proposition made to the blushing policeman was passed as a note which four of the five JPs read. The lady chair of the Bench then nudged awake the retired colonel dozing up there beside her and handed him the note. His eyes opened – then widened in amazement as he read the unsigned, but lurid solicitation.

"*What! D'you want to do it right now?*" he asked her.

Unlike the JPs, the metropolitan magistrates in Dartford were wide-awake, professionally trained legal experts who dealt with all major crime. The *Dartford Chronicle* took its local metro court so seriously that it published in every weekly issue a brief summary of every case on the week's long court roll. This allowed me to be assigned there every single day, not only to gather a formal digest of every court record for our local weekly, but to stimulate local interest by scribbling stories in shorthand, and feeding Fleet Street with early-deadline Kentish cherries. It left lots of spare time for many other activities, because one could rely heavily on meticulous court records for the gems that might be missed while pursuing out-of-court interests.

One of our 'perks' as reporters in outer-London was a steady

Noel Coward, man-about-town par excellence.

supply of free tickets to London's West End theatres, for which we spent loving care on our published reviews. But on one memorable occasion the *Kentish Times* was sent, not a reviewer's ticket, but a formal invitation and two complimentary seats upfront for the launch of Noel Coward's latest comedy, *Relative Values*. (It transpired that the *Kentish Times* was featured in Coward's script – though not included in a later film of his play.)

The *Dartford Chronicle* branch editor handed the invitations to the paper's two Commonwealth representatives, a New Zealander and me.

We were not going to hire, at our own cost, 'white tie and tails' or even black-tie, so we buttoned up our overcoats under our chins, and caught a commuter train to Charing Cross station. After an elegant scotch at the Savoy we adjourned to the theatre in The Strand where we were ushered into the centre of the third row – almost the best seats in the house.

We surreptitiously removed our coats and settled in, knowing it would not be possible, dressed as we were, to visit the bar with the other smartly attired folk at the interval.

Interval was a near disaster. Instead of leaving the auditorium, most of the audience stood up in their seats and peered at us. Some even pointed fingers.

"Don't look round," said Geoff, and we slunk down in our seats, the cynosure of all eyes. Or were we being studied as two sinister aliens in a world of post-Edwardian fashion? I had to determine which, so I turned around. And there, in the seat immediately behind us, was Noel Coward.

Death of the King

The quiet and steadfast king, George VI, died not long after enduring all those 1939-1945 war years. His funeral in 1951 was a spectacle that might almost compare with the descriptions of ceremonials held in

Queen Victoria's time at the apex of British power 50 years earlier when an entire world empire was on parade, from Swazi warriors to Chinese Sepoys, from grandiose Maharajahs to the royalty of Europe amid clinking harness and sparkling spurs.

King George's funeral was in that mould, a grand if sombre occasion indeed. Belatedly, I joined the silent spectators who had been standing four-deep in the cold streets from before dawn to witness the solemn parade. The procession lasted most of the afternoon.

Sixteen months later this public mourning would be followed by celebration of the young Queen Elizabeth II's Coronation. It would be a dazzling and stupendous affair. I didn't think I would want to witness Elizabeth's coronation though. As a reporter I might find a good vantage point, but the drawback of being on a provincial weekly newspaper was that, in the long months leading up to the great spectacle, every meeting on the subject, from debates on the proposed local bonfires and bunting, to who would get invitations to local banquets and speeches – and who should organise what in the local High Street – all these tedious details would have to be reported in the *Dartford Chronicle,* with similar local reports proliferating in sister editions of the *Kentish Times*. When the great day dawned, the local events would need to be chronicled by some unfortunate beings all over again. The prospect was too much to bear.

Admittedly, England and its mature and slowly and steadily changing society were returning in some ways to its role as a cultural champion in a comfortable garden of cherries. But it was too small. Too comfortable. It was time to move on; time to get back to the hard realities of South Africa. It was time to try and witness at first-hand the antics of the ruling white community and to watch the emerging battles over racial political differences – between white South Africans and white Nationalists, of course; but also the increasing racial confrontations between the white racial minority rulers and the black and brown majority who were showing early signs of standing up to their oppressors.

On the hard veld, cherries would be difficult to find ... though not as hard as finding them in much of bombed continental Europe in those bleak, fire-blackened years.

I was not aware that South Africa was descending into madness ... yet I was soon to discover that most people at home didn't realise it either. Soon the apartheid nation entered Africa's greatest war – hoping to keep it secret from its own voters! It was a heavily censored war, yet one journalist managed to cover it widely and accurately, and several South African editors were able to venture – fleetingly – behind the lines during a whole decade of bush-fighting. ☐

* Palaeontological details from Peter Ackroyd's *The History of England* Volume One (Macmillan 2011).

14. Africa's greatest war.

Freedom cannot be censored into existence.

President Dwight D Eisenhower 1890-1969

"The Biggest War in black Africa's history"* was a military conflict as strange as anything in fiction. It involved a series of major battles involving tanks, jet fighters, helicopters, missiles, poisonous gas, and newly evolved weapons of modern warfare tested for the first time. The war was at its most intense over the 14 years between 1975 and 1988.

It was a war that was never declared, never finished, with no recognised heroes or acknowledged defeats, with no winners and no recognised losers. This intense and sophisticated African war was never adequately recorded.

For a while its very existence was denied.

It was almost impossible to report accurately on such a war – though, once we had broken through the military censorship, several of

Symbols of a war in the bush. An Angolan soldier standing beside new weapons from the industrialised world which were being tested almost unseen by Cold War combatants.

us managed to meet the supposed leaders of the Angolan sides, President Neto's cabinet and Jonas Savimbi and his generals, and paid several brief but indelibly absorbing visits to the war zones and headquarters of both armies.

The picture of the government offices of wartime Luanda remains vivid:

> *The Minister of Finance, a western-educated economist, is explaining his problems of running a socialist economy in such bad times. The signs of Luanda's topsy-turvy nature are obvious when you learn that a taxi driver can make a 600km return flight up the Atlantic coast each day in order to sit in a taxi rank in the capital (jet fuel in this war is much cheaper and more available than gasoline). A policeman directs the thin traffic of the centre city by standing on a case of beer imported from Germany. The beer represents either his salary or his bribes. No one drinks cans of Heineken in Luanda ... Heineken Lager, in this taut time, is the African port's main currency.*

It was a fruitless war in which about half-a-million people died, and another four-million were forced to flee their homes, while their nation, free of Portuguese control after 1975, was reduced to bankruptcy.

The Unita leader was shot dead in an ambush in February 2002.

After all these years I can still see his bearded visage – and a smile as broad as the distance between soccer goal posts. Almost literally.

His face – with a deliberately posed snarl replacing his customary broad smile – appears on a huge canvas that holds back the surrounding forest. The canvas walls hide a parade ground on which Savimbi's well-equipped soldiers are marching.

When it appears that the war may soon be over, Savimbi is offered a lowly post in a government of reunification. (I remember writing that he should accept the post – Minister of Fisheries – because, with his force, energy and charisma he should be able to lead a national government even from that lowly ministry.)

The giant portrait-on-canvas is of General Jonas Savimbi, university-educated leader fluent in French, English and several other languages. His aggressive pose dominates the parade ground where troops are drilling at his military HQ, situated in a deep forest region known as 'the End of the World'.

However, reunification and peace never come. Nor does anything occur that is sensible, logical or mundane. Outside forces are at work – not least of them the oil sources of Cabinda, and the fixed attention of Moscow, Havana, Pretoria and Washington.

Here's what happened in Africa's first modern war and its media coverage:

Secret invasion

Late in 1975 we got wind of the fact that South African troops had secretly invaded Angola. That hostile move was in itself a secret that could not be sustained, for the troops included large numbers of 'Our Boys' – an appellation taken over from WWII when it was used with more pride and with justifiable patriotism by South African volunteers of all races fighting against Hitler.

In 1975 – unlike previous wars – the 'whites-only' sons on the Citizen Force were compulsorily serving first one, then two years in the military with large numbers of them going against their will as well as their moral principles and political inclinations. It was from these conscripts and their worried parents that newspapers got wind of the invasion within 24 hours of its launch; though neither Parliament nor any formal sector of society was officially aware that the nation was already illegally at war.

Our information was officially denied in Pretoria and dismissed as 'rumours'. We were warned that a mere reference to troop movements or any military matter whatever was totally forbidden under the Defence Act, not to mention laws covering treason and espionage.

Utterly frustrated, I suggested in my *Undercurrent Affairs* column in the Johannesburg *Star* – decades before the days of digital blogs – that things were happening on our borders which the public should know about; but as we could not tell them what they were, they should listen to the BBC News. (Life was uncomplicated for government authorities before the invention of the internet.)

Regrettably, the BBC and every other news source we knew of, were neither excited by nor much interested in "a bush war" in which every authority on both sides denied being involved.

Blindness to Bush Wars, even today, blights the reputation of the world media. These crimes happen on a huge scale in South America, Africa and Asia. Often they involve slavery, genocide, rape, massacre and

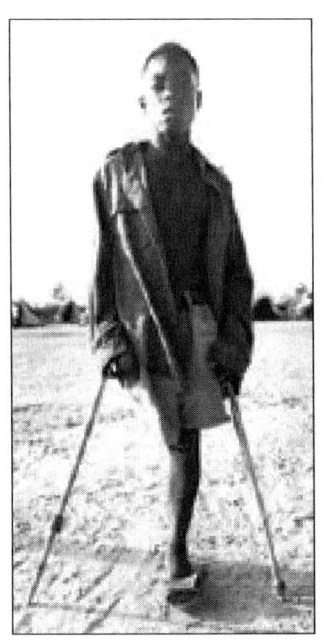

This crippled youth is the symbol-of-war that lasted longest. In Angola when peace finally came, a contest was held to choose Miss Landmine. All the contestants were young females with wounds and crutches. All had to pose on one leg, as this young casualty of war does.

torture on an intolerable scale. Usually they gain attention too late, and bring justice after delays that make justice irrelevant.

In Angola, although all was denied and nothing was supposed to be published, we were allowed to 'discover' very soon that South Africa was not alone in the underhand Angolan War. The USA, through the clandestine efforts of the CIA, was involved. So were Cuba and Russia on the MPLA side. And China, like South Africa, was offering support to Savimbi's Unita forces.

"A convoluted Communist-Capitalist hot war? A bush war with the 'non-support' of a non-defence force in South Africa?" These were hard to credit.

Very soon, PW Botha, as Minister of Defence, conceded that there were South Africans entering Angola under arms, as the outside world was beginning to confirm … but they were 'mercenaries', he lied.

Mercenaries? Then they did not fall under the reporting limitations of the Defence Act. So, without deferring to any defence or civil authority, *The Star* immediately began reporting on the war as best we could. But it was not possible even to say precisely where and how war was being waged. Whatever might be happening would be happening somewhere in the unmarked bush in a faraway country; somewhere in a region described long ago, then officially named in Portuguese, as "The End of the World". It was a place with no real roads, no maps, no telegraph lines and no permanent infrastructure.

As the forces on both sides mobilised, setting up formal bases and assembling armies, the undeclared war became a very hard reality – to the point where casualties and bodycounts increased and a total blackout was placed on the names and numbers of dead as well as wounded. We were not to know until years into the war that, in fact; we had "exposed" the deaths of most South African casualties, for they were very small. This was because of the peculiar way in which politics and the need for secrecy dictated how military attacks were planned.

(Instructions to army units, it was disclosed many years later, were: "You will not risk capture of any of our armaments – especially the new state-of-the-art G5 ultra long-range guns. You will use only small detachments of personnel, and ensure every casualty – and all equipment – are removed from any field of engagement.")

Even so, censorship could not last. We were rapidly learning methods of overcoming it so that the Angolan War became a regular news story, and thus an accepted phenomenon of Africa and, yes, of the Cold War. The conflict transformed the African continent in 12 months. It did so just as surely as colonialism had changed it over decades in previous centuries. However, bush battles, like brush fires, are hard to extinguish. They went on at different levels of intensity for another decade until the Cold War collapsed. And they are still going on – in very different guises and on a somewhat smaller scale – a quarter of a century later, in several areas of West, Central and East Africa.

Future wars tested in Africa
The book *The War for Africa**, written contemporaneously, still provides one of the best real insights and overviews of the Angolan War. Its publishers pointed out highlights of its content thus:
- A war springing out of deep disagreements between the Cuban and Soviet allies of Marxist Angola.
- An advanced Soviet MiG fighter battles an older French Mirage warplane 30,000 feet above the forests of Africa.
- The Angolan economy is crippled, the budgets of Cuba, South Africa and the Soviet Union subjected to terrible strain.
- The Angolan war spelled the end of the last great neo-colonial attempts at African conquest.
- It offered opportunity for democracy to 100-million people in five countries.

The book's author, Fred Bridgland, is to my mind among the best overseas journalists who covered Africa in this era. He had already won reporters' awards in Scotland where he subsequently joined the national daily, *The Scotsman*. He served Reuters from New Delhi. His African war dispatches appeared in the *Washington Post, New York Times, The*

Times, London, *The Economist* and *The Spectator*. Some ideologists accused Bridgland of being the mouthpiece of the capitalists, but this was not so. He was not, of course, sympathetic to the foreign communist cause, but he reported fearlessly; quoting opinions and reporting on the facts he could find – only on what he could see or check.

He was a regular foreign correspondent of *The Star*, Johannesburg, supplementing our own Africa News Service which was highly professional, but increasingly hobbled by international sanctions and South African passport problems. The chief of the American CIA's Angolan task force said that Bridgland destroyed the intelligence agency's operation "in one stroke". This was not merely an unintended compliment. It was probably on the record to give a false impression of the CIA's involvement as wholly indirect or 'peripheral'.

In any event, the South African Defence Force (SADF) involvement was palpable. Encouraged by the CIA, it had moved into southern Angola to protect Savimbi's rebel faction from the Cuban forces – though on an infinitely smaller scale than the invited Cubans who claimed to have sent in 50,000 troops (in fact, probably about 30,000). The SADF grew increasingly anxious as the CIA-led support evaporated. Instead of trying to suppress information, the SA government began to acknowledge its role, and attempt to justify it to local voters and to the world.

The opposition press corps was offered on-the-record military briefings, and told how "our boys" were fighting an honourable, limited war – without using terrorist tactics or poisonous gas, as the latter had once been used unsuccessfully by the 'enemy' in an early encounter.

Because single-sourced information of this kind made little news, newspaper editors were invited to "go and see for yourselves".
The first two things we discovered were:
- There was evidence of the efficacy of poisonous gas being used by Cuban forces in the far reaches of the jungle battle.
- There were rumours – established as fact later – that South Africa had supplied Savimbi with "weaponable" teargas.

However, our direct experience of the war merely increased our impressions of its surreal qualities.

Let me give you samples of it.

Before dawn one morning, a handful of us were briefed for a flight to a South African base on the Angolan border. Our pilot was Polish, offering a dashing demeanour, a raffish (i.e. Royal Air Force-type) moustache, and an almost impenetrable accent. We would be travelling in a civilian, propeller-driven plane, he said, but because of the newly created threat of Sam missiles, we would fly the last 250km over the Okavango Delta at a height of no more than 60 feet.

"Any questions?"

In the silence that followed I asked jocularly: "Yes. Are there any trees higher than 60 feet?"

It turned out not to be a joke. Anyway, our hair rose higher than that. But that wasn't the end of it. As we approached one airstrip nearest the Angolan border, the old aircraft suddenly climbed so steeply it felt as if it were going to stall – then dropped like an elderly, would-be Stuka dive-bomber to the runway below us.

"What the hell were you doing?" we asked our 'driver', a patently frustrated fighter pilot, we thought.

"Missiles," he explained. "That's the standard way to avoid them here."

Later one of the editors said he had heard our pilot saying to his ground crew: "If anyone had told me I'd be flying a bunch of ignorant civilians at 60 feet in missile territory, I would have said they must be mad."

I prefer to think that is apocryphal. Yet, what was undoubtedly true was that the Russians finally entered the war directly by supplying, not only the best, state-of-the-art fighter planes, but also missiles and the best-trained fighter pilots to fly their own planes. For a while this provided unchallenged air power and tipped the war markedly, though temporarily, in favour of Luanda's Cuban and Russian backers. (China, I remind you, favoured Savimbi's Unita.)

Probably before the intervention of state-of-the-art MiG fighters in the Angolan skies, Tertius Myburgh, editor of the South African *Sunday Times,* persuaded his contacts to allow several of us anti-war editors to make another trip, "unofficially and at our own risk", this time. We flew deep into Angola, then travelled through the bush on a six-hour truck ride to interview Savimbi.

Visions of the heat and the wild beasts did not deter us. In reality what threatened us with seeming near-death was hyperthermia. That and an overwhelming sense of emptiness.

The emptiness first revealed itself in the metal shell of an ancient Dakota we boarded at the Angolan border. The plane had no safety belts, no seats or any furniture, in fact, no windows and – worst of all – empty spaces in place of doors. We felt cold and apprehensive flying low over empty 'enemy' territory. But it was nothing compared to the return journey. Thinking we had found relative sanctuary when we finally got back into our dear old plane, we lay on the cold metal floor, trying to avoid the strong draught while we were wet, semi-naked, and blue with shivering.

The plane rides, however, were merely sidelights to the journey. Landing on a hastily cleared strip in the thick bush to the welcome of singing crowds and clapping of tribal hands, we transferred to the back of a fully loaded truck. We lay there, bumping and rolling with the vehicle as it brushed a winding path through trees for most of the day and much of the night. In all that time we never saw trace of another soul or single dwelling. We never saw a fence or a gate or a real road. Or a tame animal or a wild one. Or even a bird!

The topography was flat, seemingly waterless, featureless, yet choked with forest trees. It was well named 'The End of the World'.

When we recounted all this to Jonas Savimbi, he laughed often and smiled constantly. His African generals remained politely quiet and concerned, but looked small and unimpressive beside him. When they conducted an analytical, socio-political and military briefing for us in one of the tents in this camouflaged canvas camp, however, they showed how highly trained and highly skilled they were in the technology and strategy of war. We were almost sorry to leave this 'empty land', for Africa is filled, even there, with surprises.

We were supposed to depart as the moon set in mid-evening. But no moon could be seen. The rain fell steadily. Cold rain in a hot climate. The back of the truck soon collected several pools of rainwater, which sloshed over us as we tried to sleep. That was when hyperthermia raised her awful head ... and stayed with us all the way, through empty land and cold and then empty skies (fortunately) as we took to the air without encountering a fighter plane or missile.

The weird and the bad

A final sample of a weird war occurred one evening while we were with Savimbi's enemy, the MPLA. The war seemed to be almost over – peaceful enough to allow a visit to the future 'victors' in Luanda. We had witnessed the effects of war in that lovely, palm-fringed bay with thousands of shacks crowded with war refugees, a broken economy and crumbling buildings.

Three or four editors, on yet another mission, now found themselves in Luanda's tallest hotel. We had gathered in one bedroom to consume just a little of Luanda's war-time currency – canned German beer. We needed them in order to recover from the shock of climbing, fully-loaded, up to the 15th or maybe 20th floor. The lifts were inclined to lock their doors and get stuck in inaccessible places when the electricity went off. Which was often. We did not wish to experience jammed lifts more than once.

We were recovering from our climb up the stairs and enjoying the elevated view of the sweep of the harbour when we heard rapid explosions in the docks below us.

"It sounds like gunfire," said someone as we retreated to where the case of beer stood.

Then followed more shots, and the soft thud – of bullets – right outside our brightly lit window. "Turn off the lights," said someone, getting up to do it himself.

"Who'll walk down and find out from the hotel what's going on?" someone asked his fellow beer drinkers.

There was no answer to that, but when we had finished the beer and set off to find dinner, we asked the question. We received the usual answer.

"Something's happening," we were told.

"What? The shooting?"

"Yes"

"Why?"

Shoulders shrug. "A battle? A false alarm? Drunken soldiers? It just happens."

It happens that the war reached its inconclusive climax in 1988 at the final battle of Cuito Cuanavale, where the full might of Cuban land, air, and ground-to-air missile forces had rallied with Angolan government troops and a relatively small group of unnumbered South African freedom fighters to clash directly with Unita's guerilla forces; which were backed by South African guns, aircraft and an unknown, but strictly limited number of specially trained infantry.

For the first time, a series of really heavy battles ensued. Both sides claimed victories. The SA Defence Force withdrew from its Western

Front and from Angola the following year, before the fall of the Berlin Wall.

When it was all over official statistics from both sides offered the following claims concerning the final battle at Cuito Cuanavale:

On the one side: 20 Cuban army brigades of 50,000 men supported by 475 tanks, 50 amphibious craft and 3,000 military and technical personnel from Russia and East Germany, 100 helicopters and 80 MiG fighter aircraft and numbers of South African freedom-fighting volunteers.

On the other side: 3,000 South African and 8,000 Unita troops backed by sophisticated artillery, 'special force' units operating behind the lines and outdated Mirage fighter aircraft accompanied by subsonic Impala jets used to create havoc among communist troop-carrying helicopters.

Precise figures of battle casualties are unknown, except within the easily identified and accounted for SA Defence Force personnel where independently confirmed and strictly accounted for deaths numbered only 34.

So who won the war?

"We did," said the propagandists of both sides.

However, after the final battle, the SA military were treated back at base as heroes. The renowned commander of Cuban forces, Comrade Ochoa Sànchez was put on trial in Cuba and sentenced to death and executed.

Nobody won.

And the very, very ugly

Meanwhile, another undeclared, unreported war was waged on Africa's east coast, stretching inland towards Malawi. Whole districts were crushed and the people living there were captured, tortured and dispersed by rebels challenging the Frelimo government for power in Mozambique.

The rebel forces burnt down villages, killed most of the occupants and abducted the rest – using the young women for sex on the march, and the young men as slave bearers and gun fodder.

About 600,000 Mozambicans – a large proportion of the north-western region's population – fled into Malawi for protection, where they were housed and fed by US and UN agencies. Their homes across the border lay deserted, ravaged, and empty.

It was only in civilised, peaceful Malawi that we had any way of collecting information about the trackless bush war next door. My friend George Trail, the American ambassador, led me to the Malawi/Mozambique border and invited me to see for myself the refugee camps where his staff had been supporting the refugees and seeking information on the war for months. It was all distinctly hush-hush. "See for yourself. Don't quote me as a source", said the ambassador, who unofficially wanted the world to know what Washington already knew.

Back in Johannesburg, over a single week, I devoted three full-length double columns over five days to the horrifying details concerning the victims of the Mozambique war. The coverage brought no reaction from any authority or readers at home or abroad. No one cared, it seemed, except the protagonists. And they could not communicate. If they could, the first reaction no doubt would have been denials of the acts of genocide, rape, arson, torture and slavery. Both sides kept mum.

Bush wars are like that.

What did you do in the Wars, grandpa?

If my grandchildren were ever to pause to ask: "Grandpa what did you do in the wars?" I'd have to say: "I travelled, and I ducked, and I fought for my drinks. And I learned something."

"And what would that be dear grandfather?"

War is inglorious, dishonest and ugly. War just happens. No one is told – perhaps ultimately no one quite knows – why it happens. It causes pain, emotional suffering, death, destruction, tragedy. It happens. But it seldom happens that people are able to negotiate agreements to solve conflicting interests. Instead, nations – or people – take up the weapons that have been supplied and stored up, and send other people, in a cloud of words and a mist of glory, to go off and kill other people. Especially their own people, or their nearest neighbours.

"That's what I thought, grandpa. But sometimes it seems like there's no other choice."

Anyway, the Berlin Wall fell. The Soviet economy collapsed. And all the 20th-century wars in Africa, South America and Asia ended, momentarily and almost simultaneously. And, of course, as a direct result, the apartheid regime collapsed and its ideological demagogues ran for cover. The effects of the Cold War, like the miserable effects of factional Islamic armies, have been consistently underestimated.

The Cold War itself continued across the world for several more years. It caused more brutal unsolved murders and stories of spies that were so convoluted that they seemed incredible ... until they happened on your doorstep. It happened to the Johannesburg *Star*'s crime staff in the 1980s; with international complications worth examining next. ☐

* The War for Africa – twelve months that transformed a continent by Fred Bridgland (Ashanti Publishing Ltd).

15.
Master spy and global murders.

Assassination is the extreme form of censorship.

George Bernard Shaw, writing in the 1930s

A small weekly newspaper in the United States bravely broke US law by publishing on February 24, 1980, leaked details of brutal assassinations of 11 innocent people on four continents.

The names of the victims; the names of the murderers; the methods of ensuring death, and silence, were all published for the first time on that date, at the height of the Cold War – but published only in the State of Delaware, where the newspaper was encouraged to defy disguised censorship in "The Land of the Free".

The great newspapers of the free press of America, Britain, the British Commonwealth and Europe did not publish a word of that globally significant and sensational information.

In Africa, those investigative journalists facing strong total denials of such evidence, suddenly knew why they had been so easily rebuffed by their nation's State Security. It was because the *Sunday News Journal* of Delaware was quoting evidence given *in secret* to a Grand Jury in Washington, the capital city in which three of the assassins' victims had been killed by a bomb set off in their motor car.

The FBI must have been hugely upset by this crime on its doorstep. Unable to deliver results, the Bureau must have pushed for a closed Grand Jury hearing, in the absence of normal prosecution. The 'leak' thereafter of this evidence to a small, willing newspaper, seemed obvious, even to us on the other side of the Atlantic. Our New York Bureau picked up the report and cabled it to us within hours.

It confirmed all our wildest suspicions. It demonstrated how easily South Africa's State Security had been able to deny every report *The Star* had published relating to the sensational murder near Johannesburg of a top politician and his wife. It answered the question *The Star* had been asking for two years and two months since the night of those disturbingly melodramatic murders on its doorstep.

Every possible lead in *The Star*'s investigation was officially denied as soon as it was published. It is significant, too, that when the *Sunday News Journal* in Delaware finally published those leaks of Grand Jury evidence (possibly, as stated earlier, a secret tip-off from angry FBI agents) even these could never, in the name of the CIA or 'National Security', be officially confirmed.

For the same reason, none of the major US newspapers seemed able to imitate the Delaware *Sunday News Journal* or print a single paragraph about 11 assassinations carried out on four continents – including the double murder in the US, for which an ex-Cuban in the US, Virgilio Paz, finally went to jail.

Who killed Robert and Jean-Cora Smit?

Jean-Cora Smit, an innocent housewife, was waiting for her husband to come home when a large, swarthy man with a Mexican-style drooping moustache knocked on the door, entered and pulled out a Beretta Brigadier handgun. He fired at her, silently at close range. He and his accompanying assassin were expert hired killers.

She died without knowing why. Or was she first brutally stabbed again and again, 14 times, with a long butcher's knife? And then shot?

Hope, and logic, suggest the former. The probability is that her body was not mutilated until her husband came home – where he was immediately assassinated with another gun. Bullets crashed at close range into his shoulder, chest and head; until he was dead.

Perhaps only then was he stabbed – and Jean-Cora's body mutilated until blood ran on the floor. Blood was smeared on furnishings and the letters *Rau Tem* were scrawled in blood on the wall. Thus were created false leads and a deliberate atmosphere of horror before the assassins pocketed their weapons and gloves, and coolly walked out into the suburban night.

The precise details must differ, but it is part of the murder scene that tens of thousands of South Africans must have absorbed and carried with them after

The smoking gun ... A Beretta Brigadier 9mm handgun was alleged to have been carried across three continents for use in murders ordered by different spy agencies.

reading the *The Star*'s big-headlined story on 23rd November 1977. The image of the skilled, yet purposefully brutal murders of Dr Robert Smit and his wife, remain especially vivid because of the worldwide consequences and what they represented: the truth about blatant, cold-blooded, political assassination, committed on a global scale.

The *solution* to these sensational murders' mysteries – and nine others – also appeared in evidence leaked to the Delaware *Sunday News Journal*.

It reported:
"*In President Nixon's time in the early 1970s the CIA set out to eliminate certain foreign leaders and activists. When this was discovered by the US Congress – and forbidden – the CIA turned to like-minded and furtive Secret Services in unstable countries to commit murder in return for political favours.*
"*The main protagonists were fanatical Cubans, ousted from Havana and operating from a base in the US as members of 'Omega 7' or 'ZERO'.*
"*However, these were mere 'hit men'. The senior partners in crime with the CIA included:*
Pinochet's Secret Service in Chile known as DINA
A fascist organisation in Italy, and South Africa's Bureau of State Security (BOSS)."

One of the links of this spy murder syndicate to the Smit murders was the evidence of a protected witness, Ricardo Canete. He had been employed by the CIA to infiltrate the Cuban Nationalist Movement and was allowed a plea bargain by the FBI, requiring him to give, under oath, checkable evidence – much to the embarrassment of the secretive CIA.

Canete told the Grand Jury that two Cuban Nationalists – the men sought for carrying out bomb-blast murders in the US capital, Washington – had escaped from the US by using CIA counterfeit money and South African Kruger Rands, supplied by despot-ruled Chile. Canete said he showed the FBI some Kruger Rands that were part of the currency used by the wanted killers while they were hiding in Manhattan.

"I was told at the time that the boys (moustachioed Virgilio Paz and bespectacled Jose Suarez) were bragging that the gold coins had been given to them by the South African Bureau of State Security (BOSS) … that Paz had been given a Beretta Brigadier handgun by a Chilean secret police official in Miami two years previously. This was the smoking gun used in the assassination of Robert and Jean-Cora Smit in South Africa. (When we sought evidence from all possible South African police sources of the calibre of the handgun, the official information supplied to us appeared to mix up the calibres of two such guns.)

The bullets of Paz's Beretta nevertheless left a bloody trail from the United States to Italy to the city of Springs in the Transvaal. And the trail of the Cuban killers employed by the CIA and Chile's DINA, and by South Africa's BOSS, seemed to stretch from South America to North America, then from southern Europe to South Africa.

The number of trained members of the international hit team was not known, but the 'working unit', including back-ups, was thought to be no more than half a dozen. One of them appeared to be an agent named Townley, uncovered during one of the Johannesburg *Star*'s investigations.

BOSS, it was alleged, was granted not only use of these foreign assassins, but was also allowed to operate freely (though somewhat secretly) in the US in return for providing information on communist activities in Africa.

Unchallenged evidence under oath

The Grand Jury was given the names of some of the cabal's murdered victims who were:

Former Chilean General Carlos Prats, an Opposition Senator, and his wife Cora, killed in an October 1974 bombing in Buenos Aires.
Chilean Minister of Defence, Osca Bonito, blown up with five other people in a helicopter in Chile in March 1975.
Chilean exile Bernado Leighton and his wife Ana, seriously wounded in a botched assassination in Rome in October 1975.
South African economist Robert Smit and his wife Jean-Cora, murdered in Springs, South Africa in November 1977.
Ronni Moffit and Orlando Letelier, who died in September 1976 in a Washington car bombing. This crime on home-ground in the US capital led to FBI investigations; Grand Jury secret hearings and a public trial and sentencing of three plotters of the hit team during 1977-1980.

You had to be a journalist in South Africa in the 1970s to understand the unlimited power of BOSS and its subordinate secret agencies. They not only destroyed evidence, they planted false evidence and threatened possible witnesses with death. (BOSS agents once stole a car from a *Star* staffer in Johannesburg and used it in an attempted assassination in far-away Cape Town; then abandoned it afterwards back in a street in Johannesburg, to the bewilderment of the journalist owner.)

Despite this published list and all the other relevant evidence available, the apartheid government stuck to its denials.

The Johannesburg *Star* published the evidence on Page One, and – deliberately placed the apartheid state's denials on an inside page. For once, no Cabinet Minister complained about being provided with lesser and unequal publicity. Two decades later the Truth and Reconciliation Commission's findings were restricted to "it should be noted that the attorney-general's investigation confirms a politically-motivated killing involving security forces."

And so the "mystery" is allowed to continue in SA, even now when the murderers and their clients were damned in court and publicly denounced in *The Star*. Even 35 years after the murders, the *Cape Times* in South Africa carried a denial by one of the murderers, released from jail ... but he would deny it, wouldn't he? He had already confessed once, to shorten his imprisonment. There was no benefit for him to volunteer more information.

The SA Nationalist Party's government also continued to deny the findings, which were also shunned by most newspapers and much of the electorate.

The denials found space partly because of the ruthless power taken by the man who held even the nation's apartheid leaders to ransom.

The Spy Master

Tall, brooding 'Lang Hendrik' cast a long and menacing shadow.

It stretched darkly across all of South Africa and far into the murky world of international violence – and international intelligence networks.

As chief spymaster of the apartheid state when it was at its height in the 1960s and 1970s, Hendrik van den Bergh purposely inspired fear. It fitted his task and his vanity; but while he needed to be the *eminence grise*, his behaviour showed that he also wanted recognition. He appeared to be fascinated by total power, conspiracies and vengeance. He seemed responsible only to his own ambitions. He was accountable to nobody, not even it seems to his friend the PM.

Yet his ambitions were carefully self-controlled. Clearly he had no talent and no wish to be a president, prime minister or mere party politician. He intended, instead, to guard the Nationalist State – and help control the nation from behind the scenes. His danger lay in his fanaticism. His ultimate power lay partly in his awareness that he had carefully become involved in an underground international network of contacts, informers and professional killers. He plugged this unleashed power of his into the career of his early political friend and comrade-in-arms, BJ "Jolly-John" Vorster.

Secret spymaster Van den Bergh must have considered himself all-powerful; the last man with whom you would wish to cross swords. His nature was strange and unpredictable. And his reach was so long it seemed impossible to avoid.

He telephoned my colleague, Rex Gibson, after the newspaper he edited, the *Sunday Express,* revealed that *The Citizen,* ostensibly an independent pro-government newspaper, was being secretly and illegally financed by the Nationalist government using taxpayers' money to the tune of millions.

The phone call was made to Gibson's home, then an unlisted number in a relatively new suburb. Van den Bergh framed the implicit threat cautiously, but his tone and language were vaguely sinister.

"Mr Gibson, we don't care what you publish," he said, "But we will find out who your source is and then we will act."

What action he contemplated was unstated.

For the next three nights, a mysterious car positioned itself on the quiet street outside Gibson's home as darkness set in. There were no street lights and the car's occupants – shadowy figures – parked so

Lang Hendrik', police General Hendrik van den Berg, second from right, smiling down on a colleague in subterfuge, Dr Eschel Rhoodie, far left, whom he despised. Standing with Rabin and Peres in 1975 in Jerusalem.

that the car faced the sliding glass doors in the editor's lounge. Then the engine was switched off and the headlights turned to full bright. They shone directly into the lounge.

The message was obvious, yet General van den Bergh also put it in words: "I have men who will kill for me."

But that came later ...

Powerful friends

Right from the beginning, young Van den Bergh, without knowing it, had been singularly fortunate in his firmly chosen career. At the age of 20 he was already a policeman. Later, he jeopardised his career by refusing to go to North Africa with a police contingent seconded to fight in the early African desert war against Hitler.

Instead, he secretly, but actively, supported South Africa's declared enemy by joining the right-wing *Ossewa Brandwag* (Ox wagon sentinel or night-watch), a para-military movement founded by a young attorney, Balthazar Johannes Vorster, whose members adopted Nazi-style uniforms and the Hitler salute.

Ironically, they used 'terrorist tactics' against Union Defence Force targets, and loudly opposed the white voters' majority support of Churchill's War against the Nazis.

For this, Vorster and Van den Bergh, born in the same year and still under 30 years of age, were interned under wartime security laws. Ironically, again, the two were imprisoned without trial. I remember Vorster telling me about this three times, when the political tables were turned and he was Minister of Justice, defending his notorious 90-days detention-without-trial bill.

"No one complained when I was locked up," growled the trained lawyer. "And I didn't whine about it."

"But that was in war, not peace time," I countered as a political correspondent probing for his motives in the early 1960s.

"I am fighting a war against communism," said Vorster. "Do you think the communists worry about secretly locking people up? They even torture them – in your so-called 'peace time'," he later told a group of us.

Twice more, while I was a parliamentary and political correspondent and checking his version and motive for jail without trial, he repeated to me (but "not for publication,") his justification for suspending rule of law.

BACK IN 1940 Vorster and Van den Bergh had been sent to Koffiefontein, a prisoner-of-war camp in an old mining compound on the hot, dry veld where they would have met Nico Diederichs, organiser of *Die Reddingsdaadbond*, a trust set up to promote racially-exclusive trade unions for Afrikaans labour and for exclusively Afrikaans business, somewhat in the pattern of several racially exclusive 'black' organisations that arose later. (Diederichs was also associated by some investigators with the gruesome murder decades later of Robert Smit and his wife.)

In the 1950s, after the war and the National Party's victory over General Smuts, Van den Bergh rose quickly through the police ranks and was soon able to devote the rest of his life to his secret service and spying networks.

Vorster, relatively new to Parliament, introduced Van den Bergh to Prime Minister Verwoerd. Soon after, the policeman was promoted to Major. Within 36 months he was Lieutenant-Colonel, then full Colonel in charge of the Police Security Branch. Following the Rivonia Treason Trial and 'his triumph' of capturing the ANC leaders, Van den Bergh became the youngest police Brigadier in SA Police history. And, soon after, he claimed to be the youngest police general.

The BOSS – 'as cold as ice'
In May 1969, through his close and long-term relationship with B J Vorster, now prime minister following the assassination in Parliament of Dr Verwoerd, Van den Bergh was allowed to create, virtually single-handedly, the Bureau of State Security (BOSS). It brought together all the basic security services of the police, the military, the navy and the government; causing unease throughout the country and anger within the government's own party ranks; because Military Intelligence and similar agencies were automatically and heavily downgraded by this takeover.

The portentous change required only two simple bills which Van den Bergh's friend, Prime Minister Vorster, rammed through Parliament, despite sometimes vociferous protests from several cabinet ministers, and many Nationalist Party members and bureaucrats. They feared, perhaps, the threat to their own ambitions rather than the real dangers to the nation of an organisation with such centralised and unbridled powers.

When the English-language newspapers highlighted the initial letters BOSS, journalists believed the acronym would be a constant reminder of the blatant authoritarianism of Van den Bergh's powerful new Bureau of State Security. Instead, Van den Bergh no doubt would merely have smiled at the naiveté of the journalists for doing his PR for him. 'Lang Hendrik', standing "six feet seven" in his police boots, *wanted* the title BOSS (though some bureaucrat decided to change the organisation's title to Bureau *for* State Security as a normal, though self-defeating, PR reaction).

It probably didn't bother Security Police chief 'Lang Hendrik' van den Bergh that he was easily – though hesitantly – associated with the bloody and horrifying assassinations of Nationalist Party candidate Robert Smit, South Africa's former representative on the International Monetary Fund, and his gentle wife.

The boss was confident of his own safety. He even sent two of his senior agents, instead of the usual discreet single observer, to monitor the evidence, the exhibits and the detective work being done at the site of the politically-fraught Smit murders which he had probably arranged.

His support of the police in this matter was innocently appreciated by the police detectives investigating the case, for 'Lang Hendrik' had also been head of the Police Security Special Branch and they knew his greater, all-powerful secret service would do a thorough job. Most police could not know, however, that Van den Bergh's aim was to cover up – not uncover – the crimes.

The police were palpably embarrassed when they failed to solve the high-profile, cold-bloodedly dramatic assassinations. More significantly, they refused repeatedly to tell the press of their theories concerning the mystery.

Yes, 'Lang Hendrik' was safe – as were the actual imported assassins, as well as the secret service agencies in half a dozen countries which had aided or abetted him – and he them – in the past.

Most of the press did not have a clue, literally.

The Star had exposed BOSS, but the result puzzled us. The noise we had anticipated at the revelations of the US Grand Jury concerning the Smits' assassinations was no louder than that in a fenced-off, shrouded tomb. Governments, including South Africa's naturally, were tight-lipped, and it didn't pass the notice of Johannesburg's newspapers that the world's free press was equally silent on the inner details of 11 other similar assassinations brought to the attention of an *off-the-record* US grand jury hearing.

The Cold War, it seems, as the hostile heat increased, secretly subjugated rule of law in some of the main democracies of the West. The silent CIA had no intention of offering excuses.

Even great newspapers such as *The New York Time*s and *The Washington Post*, operating at the geographic source of the espionage assassinations and their exposure in Washington, felt obliged to stay silent about the grand jury's *sub rosa* findings. They did not react to the Delaware *News Journal*'s coverage of judicial leaks, or respond to the Johannesburg *Star*'s own requests for more details of the evidence heard by the secret grand jury. The phrases *CIA ... secrecy laws ... Communist threat ... Agitprop ... patriot duty ...* must surely have been whispered in the appropriate ears? Nor did we have any playback from the BBC or British and European press on the leaked official evidence of the nine other relevant assassinations affecting several countries.

This was the Cold War, in which petty dictators flourished. And, around the world, spy networks were holding things down to their own satisfaction it seems. Hendrik van den Bergh's reputation stayed shadowy at home and strong among secret circles abroad, where it mattered. This despite the fact that circumstances suggested (though without much tangible proof) that 'Lang Hendrik' was occupied with other illegal issues besides assassination.

Who shopped Mandela?
Van den Bergh had a direct hand in almost every major issue involving security of the Nationalist government for quarter of a century.

In 1961, when Nelson Mandela returned from his secretive tour abroad and was slipping through police nets at home, it was Van den Bergh's security contacts in one of the countries Mandela had visited, they believe, who must have supplied information leading to the capture of the 'Black Pimpernel'.

Someone in the international spy network must have tipped off the SA security branch to the existence of the ANC hide-out at Lilliesleaf farm in Rivonia.

Some credence for this was provided by Van den Bergh himself, when asked, two decades later in his retirement, "Who shopped Nelson Mandela?"

"I am the only man alive who knows," said Van den Bergh.

It is absolutely clear, however, that Van den Bergh kept a 24-hour watch on all white and black political opposition movements and on incipient political uprisings (except for the Sharpeville "accident" which he confessed he did not foresee). He certainly was ultimately responsible for the tapping of thousands of telephone lines, including the homes of many journalists, and for placing contacts and would-be informers within the editorial staff of newspapers.

One of Van den Bergh's few weaknesses as a security cop was that he liked to boast and to have some sort of recognition for the immense 24-hour job he was doing. But he was careful never to go on record, as his deputy Alec van Wyk once mistakenly did in enthusiastically defending the role of BOSS.

Van Wyk told a press conference that BOSS had highly trained undercover agents working in the UK, the US and elsewhere … just as the CIA and MI6 also had worldwide agents, even in South Africa.

"The secret agencies even met to discuss 'issues of mutual interest'", he said.

There is inconclusive evidence in Prime Minister Harold Wilson's memoirs that it was Van den Bergh's agents who tipped off the Labour leader that Jeremy Thorpe was having a homosexual relationship with Norman Scott; a person thought to be a 'security risk'.

There is conjecture, too, that General van den Bergh was approached and took advice from Sir Percy Sillitoe of MI6 in earlier days, when the famous British spy was in Rhodesia with the British South African Police. There was talk of BOSS abetting in the murder of one of the criminals (Waldeck) who was ignorantly upsetting the smooth supply of arms to South Africa. There were also other rumours which could never be confirmed.

Making enemies

What is beyond conjecture and known to many of us, is that 'Lang Hendrik', acting on behalf of his ally, Prime Minister Vorster, was deeply involved in the local and international ramifications of Connie Mulder and Eschel Rhoodie's Information Scandal (Infogate). The chief of BOSS was involved in helping Nationalist colleague, Eschel Rhoodie, set up a temporarily influential news magazine, *To the Point*, using public funds in the same way as *The Citizen* newspaper was launched.

Slush funds of taxpayers' money were secretly used to gain influence among selected right-wing media proprietors, businessmen and politicians across America, Europe and other parts of the world.

This slush fund, however, became fairly well-known, as were many of its recipients abroad, and was generally approved by the party. Its prominent recipients, such as the politically connected American newspaper publisher, John McGoff, had strong right-wing support across America, and afforded BOSS and the South African Department of Information's operators immunity, if not respectability, for a while.

The Cold War communist threat proved to be BOSS's strongest sword – and shield.

As the 1970s progressed, BOSS became increasingly powerful, much to the dismay of Defence Minister PW Botha who perceived that it and the Department of Information were wielding more influence than the Ministries of Defence and Foreign Affairs together.

Van den Bergh knew that his success had created for Vorster and himself at least two powerful enemies in the Nationalist Party, but he did not fear them. He should have, because P W Botha was able to use the *Rand Daily Mail*'s 'deep throat' and the *Sunday Express*'s exposure of Minister of Information Mulder, and of Information departmental head, Eschel Rhoodie, to bring down – not only Van den Bergh, but to destroy Prime Minister Vorster as well.

It was the kind of classical political party rift revolving around the governing party that decades later split the ANC. The irony in Botha's success was that the "Erasmus Commission" he appointed convicted Prime Minister Vorster on evidence that applied equally to PW Botha himself. It was clear that the secret state-funding of *The Citizen* newspaper – as well as much bigger slush-funding at home and abroad – came from PW Botha's National Defence Budget, the only national budget items whose details were kept from Parliament and the press.

The Erasmus Commission, as a kind of prompted after-thought, placed all the blame instead on Vorster and Van den Berg.

Leaving loudly

Van den Bergh, however, would never go quietly, as his friend and mentor Vorster did. At the height of his power 'the BOSS man' telephoned, for the second and last time, his nemesis, *Sunday Express* editor Rex Gibson. The call came after Judge Erasmus, a legal officer more noted for his malapropisms than his judicial wisdom, issued his final report on the Info Scandal. The *Sunday Express* learnt that a key sentence from witness Van den Bergh's evidence had been omitted from the official transcript and proceeded to publish what it believed the missing sentence to be. It was damning.

The *Sunday Express* bravely pointed out that the sentence missing was the quote by the head of BOSS telling Judge Erasmus: "My men will do anything for me. *They will even kill for me.*"

Within days, the fallen head of National Security decided how to counter his accusers. He prepared a petition and manned a table in Church Square, Pretoria, urging passers-by to sign it. It was addressed to the government and it said:

"Charge Van den Bergh."

There was no need to add an additional three words: "If you dare." Government didn't dare. The head of BOSS was never charged. And thus did Van den Bergh demonstrate for the last time his power and his menace.

Even after his retirement, Van den Bergh, who was famously unretiring by nature, found it hard not to interfere. He predicted, correctly, that the infamous Civil Cooperation Bureau (CCB) conceived by his rivals, Military Intelligence, to ensure political control of key towns and cities, with its 'death squad' set up on the remote, heavily guarded Vlakplaas, was far too loose and undisciplined. Their slapdash units would kill 'the wrong people' and would cause more harm than they were worth, he declared.

'Lang Hendrik', who had been married twice, retired to the countryside where he farmed chickens for nearly two decades. He started to write a book and then abandoned it; averring instead that he would never reveal his secrets. He died in Bronkhorstspruit, at the age of 82 in 1997, outliving by nearly a decade and a half, his slightly younger patron, ex-President Vorster. They had risen to power together; reached the very peak together. They had also suddenly been found out, outwitted, and chopped down together.

Recently, a former neighbour of General van den Bergh's from long ago recorded on the internet: "While I was in my garden, I saw him pass, one metre away. When he happened to meet my eyes, he never greeted, he just stared you down, and honestly had eyes like a snake. As cold as ice."

On such social tweets are reputations built or destroyed. □

16.
'The bravest editor in the cemetery'.

Give me the freedom to know, to utter, and to argue according to conscience, above all liberties.

John Milton, in the 1600s

In 1988, at the very moment when the free press seemed near death in South Africa after 159 years of struggle against colonialism, nationalism and apartheid, another free press was beginning to come to life for the first time in the changing, former totalitarian, communist Soviet Union.

In the rest of the world, journalists lived in hope or despair.

A survey in the mid-1980s showed that, of 150 nations reviewed, 130 of them stifled their press or attempted serious censorship of the independent media in some way.

It grew worse and 1988 became an unusually hazardous year.

In that year, the editor of a Mexican newspaper rose solemnly to his feet to address more than a hundred delegates at an emergency Conference on Censorship called in London by the World Press Freedom Committee.

"The greatest challenge for a Mexican is to address a world assembly like this," he said, " ... after lunch." (That took care of the sombrero stereotype) ... "I was awakened from my siesta," he went on, "to hear the chairman introducing me as one of the most courageous editors in Mexico. If he repeats that outside this venue, I may become the bravest editor in Mexico City's cemetery."

I asked him, in the same spirit later: "Are you advocating censorship of this anti-censorship conference?"

"Certainly not. I'm pleading for accuracy – I'm not brave. And I'm pleading for personal privacy on the grounds of personal safety," he added, falling naturally into a playful issues-and-ethics quiz, in which editors sometimes solemnly or satirically engage.

In Istanbul that same year, at the annual meeting of the International Press Institute – in which my friends Raymond Louw of the *Rand Daily Mail* in South Africa and Cushrow Irani of *The Times of India* were ceaseless fighters for press freedom wherever it was in jeopardy – I met a number of insouciant but nervous Turkish newspaper people. They included the editor-in-chief of a large and popular Turkish newspaper who was accompanied by his Responsible Editor.

"What is a Responsible Editor?" I asked him.

He beamed at her.

"She's the one who goes to jail," he explained. (Press freedom was already erratic in Turkey in 1988.)

"Don't you feel a little uncomfortable about that arrangement?"

"Can you think of a better arrangement?"

Indeed I could not. Though I thought the intensely emotional Responsible Editor seemed a little too passionate about her desire for martyrdom in prison.

Yet my own temporary 'arrangement' was not nearly as good. In a way, it had been forced upon me. I had visited President Mugabe to reason with him, or protest his action, in jailing a Scotsman with the Irish name, O'Dowd. He had been arrested and locked up – in his capacity as the temporarily acting editor of the Harare *Herald,* Zimbabwe's biggest daily (and at the time, still independent) newspaper. He had been imprisoned without being informed why, or for how long he might be held incommunicado and in solitary confinement.

Robert Mugabe at the height of his reign.

"Are you imitating South Africa's apartheid-style methods?" I asked President Mugabe, who was pretending ignorance, although I could see what appeared to be a relevant file before him on his desk – the same desk at which I had hitherto interviewed an equally anti-press PM, Ian Smith.

The new Zimbabwe president bristled nicely, and we finally reached Mugabe's concept of a solution. His 'arrangement' was that he would release the acting editor, if I would guarantee that the prisoner-without-trial left the country immediately, never to return. It could not be my decision, of course, but it was 'arranged' and the newly freed, dour Scottish newspaperman became a top-paid supernumerary among the Johannesburg *Star*'s line of assistant editors. The irony of a Scotsman finding press freedom in internationally banned South Africa may have been lost on Mugabe.

O'Dowd, the released prisoner, enthusiastically described to me his experience of solitary confinement in a Zimbabwean jail filled with political prisoners who conspired to communicate with each other's cells in all kinds of innovative ways. The food wasn't good though, he admitted.

"But you actually enjoyed your stay in prison?"

He nodded. And I immediately appointed him Jail Editor.

We both laughed, but he didn't stay long enough to test the 'arrangement'.

In 1988, there were worse things than jail without trial to think about.

Chillier in Chile

In Chile, the ultimate form of censorship – assassination of journalists and editors who questioned the Pinochet government – was still happening. We discovered that the killers might have once included South Africans, for the Chilean and South African governments had a cosy 'arrangement' of their own, as described in the previous chapter. The deal entailed swapping, across continents, trained assassins to ensure anonymity for those who committed murder to ensure 'state security'. Extreme censorship by assassination was not new to us. It had been happening in countries like Ecuador and Argentina for a decade. And it looked as if it was starting to happen – or at least for the authorities to make death threats with impunity – to journalists in South Africa.

During that busy year, at a conference of the French-based FIEJ (World Association of Newspapers), we were briefed by Emilio Filippi, director of *La Epoca* (*The Times* of Chile) on President Augusto Pinochet's decision, after 13

Pinochet was helped to power by the CIA, and when finally deposed, charged with 300 crimes. He was accused by his opponents of being responsible for countless murders and much torture.

years, finally to allow one daily opposition newspaper to operate in his country ... provided it didn't criticise his government. This arrangement by *La Epoca* was denounced by the non-democratic left wing as well as by the dictatorship's militant right wing – and was deprecated by many of us in between. Yet the paper announced in its first issue:

"We are committed to democracy ... in order to ensure stable and just co-existence. We are against dictatorships of any colour, now and in the future."

The first edition also carried a cartoon in which one citizen asked another: "Do you think it is too much 'terrorism' to ask for free elections?"

The 140,000 copies of the first edition, its highest circulation ever, were sold out by mid-morning, its owner told us.

Earlier, during a brief sabbatical granted after a decade of editorship under somewhat sweaty circumstances, I had been able to collect the views and experiences of relevant editors around the world for a proposed book to be titled *Ten Tight-ropes*. But *La Epoca*'s chilling balancing act of being tolerated by Chile's dictatorship, though negotiated with great bravery, seemed too tricky to be relevant to any tight-roping towards freedom. The existence of a newspaper in the position he described, was one which world press leaders had already rejected, in general terms and on principle, at our emergency debate in South Africa ("Conflict and the Press") the year before.

It is a fundamental *'to be or not to be'* issue, this idea of 'publish by permission of the government'.

No independent newspapers could possibly consider it, especially in an authoritarian state. It is a line not to be crossed, though many do, even in free countries, at the behest of their power-seeking proprietors.

The FIEJ conference debate on the subject in Rome that year revealed an even stranger 'walking-the-tight-rope' challenge for the world's media. It concerned an act of huge and historical significance.

When in Rome, think Russian

"*Perestroika ilitol 'koperedishka? Pozhivem, uvidimi.*"
(Roughly translated: "Real change or just a breathing space? We shall see.")

"Could you, Dr Laptev, help us to understand what Perestroika entails: how does it relate to Glasnost and the 6,000 Russian newspapers under your government's control?"

My role in asking this question as chairman of a debate at the FIEJ Rome conference is relevant only because it created, on the platform, an unexpected and extraordinary coincidence ... an ironic juxtaposition of similar positions and opposite views. It was also a reminder to all of us that every story has at least two interesting and usually conflicting sides.

I was introducing, to a professional international audience, the World Free Press Organisation's main conference speaker, Dr Ivan Laptev. He was chief manager *and* editor-in-chief of *Izvestia*, the studied and stilted propaganda organ of the Communist Party which he was transforming in 1988 into a lively, investigative newspaper.

Its circulation across 11 time zones had suddenly jumped by 1.7 million copies to nearly 10 million and rising. I congratulated him on his paper's new style and reminded him, and the international assembly he was about to address, that his newspaper (The News) had been perceived in the past to have no news. Its co-state newspaper, *Pravda* (Truth) seemed to have carried none of that elusive quality.

He responded with polite honesty and candour.

He was reluctantly experiencing great difficulty with the changes in his motherland, he said. Nothing he had encountered had ever been as hard to deal with as reformist President Gorbachev's new policy of *glasnost*, except possibly the controversial concept of *perestroika*.

"It is saddening. It is not easy after eight decades to disclose, publicly, bitter truths about the recent and distant past, hitherto concealed," he confessed.

While a lack of consensus among Russia's newspapers was by 1988 as inevitable as it was necessary, it was also, for the confused Soviet press, a major problem. But then I suddenly heard Ivan Laptev saying, "*Dealing with freedom is like working in a minefield.*"

I could not believe my ears.

Those sentiments had been publicly uttered in similar words 25 years previously by a predecessor of mine who was editor of *The Star* in Johannesburg when the South African press was forced to deal – not with freedom – but with threats against it.

Editing an independent newspaper in South Africa, said Horace Flather of *The Star* in 1963, was like "*walking through a minefield blindfolded!*"

His statement, coming not long after news of the Sharpeville massacre, shocked the free world. However, by comparison with 1988, we felt that Flather's editorial walk on behalf of our newspaper in the 1960s had been a stroll through a rose garden, avoiding small thorns.

And now Dr Laptev was contemplating a walk through the minefield – backwards. He was still on the other side. It allowed me to encourage an interesting discussion among the international press delegates to the conference.

Everything is relative it seems, including walks in opposite directions across no-man's-land to reach for freedom.

YET, IF GORBACHEV'S *glasnost* was obscure to the editor-in-chief of *Izvestia* in 1988, the 'democracy' of Russia's next leader, Boris Yeltsin, was a total mystery to him. Indeed the seldom sober 'liberalist' who marched on the Duma and grandly 'set Russia free' made *everyone* in the USSR nervous. Yeltsin's melodramatic, unpredictable style antagonised even his close supporters. His early fall, and the swift take over by Putin, was greeted with relief.

One of the West's finest Russian-speaking 'Moscow-watchers', David Remnick of *The Washington Post* in 1988 and of *The New Yorker* into the 21st century, wrote recently that Putin was seen by Moscow's intellectuals as having the vision of an army sergeant. Yet he was nevertheless preferable to the wild liberator before him who had created chaos.

"Putin spent most of his adult life as a KGB officer, but his résumé gives off a different, more varied, resonance in Russia than it does abroad," Remnick reported.

The problem in Russia was that its Constitution was promptly ignored by a judiciary intent on protecting the state. Even 12 years after the fall of communism the head of USSR television told Remnick with evident satisfaction that:

"Freedom of speech is a relative notion. It does not exist anywhere in its ideal form. It is an ideal that does not exist in nature, only in theory. In reality freedom of speech depends (in Russia) on the government, on the editors and producers ... "

Everyone had a different sense of what freedom of speech meant, added the Russian editor-in-chief. This sophistry may have been partly to blame, during the years of Putin-style democracy, when *Izvestia*'s circulation fell from 10 million daily, to about quarter of a million.

BACK IN THAT crowded year of communist change I also attended the first of the international free-press rallies in which Alexander Pumpyanksy of Moscow's *Novoe Vremia* restored the equilibrium of my era by announcing humorously to the Free World:

"For me, *glasnost* is reality. If the emperor has no clothes we must say so. If he wears a Soviet-made suit, the Soviet press must admit that he is badly dressed."

We also learned of a very different situation being experienced at that moment in Cuba. Communism's much vaunted offspring in the Americas was poverty-stricken, and President Castro was cutting and patching and inventing 'news' with extreme dedication. Cubans were not even allowed to hear about Russia's reformist *perestroika*! General Castro forbade its citizens to hear or see anything but his own government's propaganda. Cuba's only non-government publication was *News from Moscow,* printed in Russia in Spanish. But now it was being distributed by the Cuban government with all mention of *glasnost* and *perestroika* censored from it.

President Putin, plotter par excellence, but accused by Russian intellectuals of having the vision of an army sergeant.

Bookshops in Cuba sold books about Brezhnev, but nothing about his democratically-minded successor, Gorbachev, let alone Yeltsin. And Cuban soldiers sent abroad 'to save Angola', were forbidden to talk in detail about Angola. Letters, books and articles about the outside world were censored or banned. Only official communiqués were published, FIEJ was told by a Cuban newspaperman who had recently left home.

Today, journalists find it strange that the last era of Castro's Cuba is still revered by some ideologues across the world – and by a majority of members and Cabinet Ministers in the ANC 'democratic' government.

Democracy, and the Press's role, in a nutshell

My most privileged moment at the Rome Press Congress in 1988 was to introduce Adv. Soli Sorabjee, former Attorney-General of India and chairman and founder of the formidable anti-corruption organisation,

Transparency International. He discussed the essentials of press freedom in the best speech on the subject I have ever heard. Its essence might be summed up and cherished as:

A free press depends on three things:

An aware society *that subscribes to the belief that the 'right to know' is a fundamental individual right. (The press and other media are there to provide this awareness.)*

A parliament accountable to the people. *(The free press's role in this is to provide the means for that accountability.)*

An independent judiciary *to protect individual rights. (A free and independent media's role in this is to help protect the independence of the judiciary ... and vice versa.)*

His summation evokes an elegant, rounded, balanced whole. It offers a succinct definition of a securely balanced tripod on which true democracy rests, with a free press acting as the binding that holds together these three great democratic pillars.

It is another metaphor of the press being 'the Fourth Estate'. Adv. Sorabjee's summation offers today a salutary and useful guideline for all who become confused by political leaders seeking to 'discipline' the press for being too critical, too negative and too whatever-else-they-can-think-of.

Adv. Soli Sorabjee, international defender of freedom of speech. Formally Attorney-General of India.

In South Africa in 1988 the heavily censored free press was still alive. No one was crying "Murder!", but only because our country was then still in the second act of a horrifying plot. Yet the script was so familiar – one could trace it across dozens of nations – we would have been naïve not to recognise its likely denouement ... a Declaration of Emergency proposing death to South Africa's 150-year-old free press.

However, the world faced a worse crisis at that time than our grave but limited one at the far end of Africa.

A major move was afoot in the

United Nations to create a World Information Order regulating global communication. It was as chilling a threat as you could imagine. Yet it merely bored most of the world's population ... The passivity of inward-looking democrats aggravated the magnitude of the threat.

Fortunately, the bureaucratic, communist-style decree supported by Russia, China, even India and the rulers in much of the Third World was so alien to every concept of freedom of information that it could be dealt with virtually behind closed doors and soon dismissed. But it remains a reminder of how dangerous public apathy can be to basic rights and 'boring' ethical principles.

A powerful group of undemocratic nations already seeks repeatedly for the UN to endorse censorship of the internet.

In trying to reflect the grand principles of press freedom and its role in democracy, I fear that boredom might be bearing down as I write. So I shall quickly conclude the above snapshots of the world's press dilemmas in 1988 with some words from Alan Paton, famous author of *Cry the Beloved Country*. He told the University of the Witwatersrand, early in those bad old days:

"You fight for liberty because it has to be done, whether you are going to succeed or not. And if you do not fight for it, you will lose it forever. If it has to be restored to you, you will not know what it is."

Britain's press, of course, haven't had to fight for the *principle* of freedom of expression for centuries. But it has had to fight many dubious threats and difficulties. Let's look at a strange example: *The Times* being forced to describe, in sensational detail, rape and murder and the bawdy classes at its front door. ☐

17.
The Times vs. 'Jack the Ripper'.

To class the 'Jack the Ripper' story with one of these modern murders is confusing Indian curry with ice-cream. And disrespectful to the professionals too.

Sir William Connor, famous 'Cassandra' columnist

It began in 1785 under the name *The Daily Universal Register* and became *The Times* on 1st January 1788; a time when its front page carried only advertisements. Its significance and long-term influence are based on the fact that during its first 120 years it was owned by its editors who were interested in journalism, not power. The family of John Walters was the founder, and he was followed as editor by his son, then his grandson. These were the best of times for the famous paper.

The Times is unique. And it was a major source of the world's independent free press.

It used 'time' in its name two-and-a-quarter centuries ago, a title that has since been copied across the world. Thus it is usually known as THE Times (Also known recently as "The Times, London" and, mistakenly, as "The London Times".)

The paper employed talented and highly professional reporters and correspondents whose only aim it was to report independently on national, social and world events of interest to the literate ... which, in that era, consisted of the ruling British class, differing in its concepts of overseeing the extension of a global Empire.

The Times wielded its influence within this wealthy, well-educated class because Britain's ruling parties (with sophisticated, highly aware members) were so sharply divided in their politics. The newspaper's non-party stance and wide reporting sometimes carried greater weight than that of the government itself. In those circumstances *The Times* earned the ironic sobriquet, The Thunderer.

During its first two centuries *The Times* recorded, not only world history but several versions of its own official history, all easily accessible. So let me add merely two personal passing insights into the culture of *The Times* a decade before its current owner degraded it.

But firstly, we should look at the story a century ago that reported on 'Jack the Ripper'.

How on earth could old-fashioned, fact-fanatical, world-surveying, *The Times* deal with this frenzy on its doorstep?

The headline to this chapter might have been suitable in *The Times*' hundredth year, 1888, when most of the newspaper-reading world was engrossed in what today might be termed "the unsolved mystery of the brutal, bloody, serial sexual murders of a killer who called himself Jack the Ripper".

The newspaper was operating not far from where major work was underway in building Tower Bridge across the Thames. It was just a short walk into another world which was the East End, where prostitutes paraded the fog-shrouded lanes in its slum area.

Vice, crime and poverty filled its foul air. And now reporters of small scandal sheets had joined the newly-rising popular press that flocked like vultures onto the gory sites. There were fake notes and prank letters littering the scene.

The Times simply published what it saw and what its readers said each day. And it castigated the police for losing their own bloodhounds as well as losing the bloody trail.

Why is it that 'Jack the Ripper' *still* remains the subject or inspiration of books; films; plays; sociological history; a flourishing tourist trade in the 21st century and a string of websites?

On 13 October 1888, The Illustrated London News offered this image of what were known as the "Whitechapel Murders" ... The police would be wondering: "Is this yet another victim of the self-described 'Jack the Ripper'?"

There are several reasons – and a place to study them might be the website www.jack-the-ripper.org, which is a fine example of how a website can out-perform almost any newspaper in analysis, if not fact-accountable news.

But the main clue to the fascination of this famous unsolved case of the 19th century is the serial killer's escape from justice, despite public challenges issued in advance of his gruesome murders in the name of 'Jack the Ripper'.

Some officials and politicians claimed at the time that the name was the invention of a well-known journalist, who also wrote the Ripper's gory, sensational notes to the authorities! But the critics of the critical press *would* say that, wouldn't they? Fake notes and prank letters to the authorities were being produced in various styles by uneducated residents and upper-class visitors – and probably journalists and others, all of whom ought to have known better.

So how did a purist newspaper like *The Times* of London deal with this uniquely challenging situation?

The Times simply continued to do what it did best: It reported the facts precisely as it found them.

On Easter Monday in the early Spring of 1888 the expertly dismembered body of Emma Smith was discovered in Whitechapel, London. Within a month, the police came upon the severed and mutilated corpses of three other 'ladies of easy virtue'. At this point, Scotland Yard received a dramatic, taunting message:

> This is the fourth. I will murder 16 more and then give myself up
> – Jack the Ripper

The challenge issued by an apparent self-confessed serial killer – and his mounting, indescribably gory evidence – galvanised *The Times*, though the already long-established, soberly responsible newspaper never was and never would be best equipped to report on crime and horror. Despite this, *The Times* also galvanised its readers into action through its detailed, constant, measured and impartial reporting.

The significance of its influence on activist citizens can be discerned even in the brevity of the following extracts taken from months of the newspaper's reports.

Some of these extracts suggest that if Sherlock Holmes had been a real person at that time, he might, from his point of view, have dubbed

the most horrible street-crime in British history as:
"THE MYSTERY OF THE MISSING BLOODHOUNDS".
Three months into the appalling saga *The Times* reported:

October 1 – *In the early hours of yesterday morning two more horrible murders were committed in the East End of London, the victims of both cases belonging to the same unfortunate class. No doubt seems to be entertained that these terrible crimes were the work of the same fiendish hands ...*

The (second) deceased's throat was (also) terribly cut; gashes on the face and part of the right ear cut off. There were other indescribable mutilations. It is stated that some anatomical skill seems to have been displayed in the way in which the lower part of the body was mutilated.

At three o'clock yesterday afternoon a meeting of nearly a thousand persons took place in Victoria Park. After several speeches upon the conduct of Sir Charles Warren (the Commissioner of Police), a resolution was unanimously passed that it was high time both officers should resign and make way for some officers who would leave no stone unturned for the purpose of bringing the murderers to justice, instead of allowing them to run riot in a civilized city like London.

October 1 – *Letters to the Editor of The Times:*
Sir, I beg to suggest the organisation of a small force of plain-clothes constables mounted on bicycles for the rapid and noiseless patrolling of streets and roads by night ...
-Your obedient servant, Fred Wellesley.

October 2 – *Two communications of an extraordinary nature, both signed "Jack the Ripper", have been received. The first stated that the writer would in his next job "clip the lady's ears off" and send them to the police. The second communication was a postcard to Scotland Yard: " ... I gave you the tip ... Double event this time. Number One squealed a bit; couldn't finish it straight off. Had not time to get ears for police."*

October 2 – *Letters to Editor:*
Sir, I cannot help thinking that these Whitechapel murders point to one (insane) individual. I was myself all but the victim of an assassin who believed he had a mission to destroy me ... Edgar Sheppard MD.

Sir, As a magistrate of more than 30 years' experience of criminals ... I have no hesitation in saying that the best way ... is to offer a substantial reward ... Harry White

October 3 – Great satisfaction was expressed throughout the city at the promptness with which the Lord Mayor has offered a reward ...

October 4 – Letters to Editor

Sir, As regards to the suggestion that bloodhounds might assist in tracking the East End murderer, as a breeder of bloodhounds and knowing their power I have no doubt that, had a hound been put upon the scene of the murder, while fresh, it might have done what the police have failed in doing ... Percy Lindley

October 9 – Police are instructed not to remove a body of a murdered victim, but to send notice immediately to a veterinary surgeon ... who holds several trained bloodhounds in readiness to be at once put on the scent.

October 10 – Sir Charles Warren witnessed a private trial of bloodhounds in one of the London parks at an early hour yesterday morning.

October 15 – Mr George Lusk of the Whitechapel Vigilance Committee has received a letter (stating): " ... I think you are all asleep in Scotland Yard with your bloodhounds. I will show you tomorrow night. I'm going to do a double event ... JACK THE RIPPER".

October 19 – Mr George Lusk has received several letters purporting to be from the perpetrator of the Whitechapel murders ... one letter was accompanied by a cardboard box containing what appeared to be a portion of kidney. The letter said: "From hell, Mr Lusk. Sir, I send you half the kidne (sic) I took from one woman ... 'T'other piece I fried and ate. I may send you the bloody knif (sic) that took it out ... " CATCH ME IF YOU CAN."

The pathological curator of the London Hospital Museum examined the contents of the cardboard box and pronounced it to be a human kidney.

October 19 – Sir Charles Warren's bloodhounds were out for practice at Tooting yesterday morning and were lost. Telegrams have been dispatched to all metropolitan stations stating that, *if seen anywhere they should be sent immediately to Scotland Yard.*

October 25 – *A petition to the Queen reads: "To Our Most Gracious Sovereign, Lady Queen Victoria. We the women of East London feel horror at the dreadful sins that have been lately in our midst and grief because of the shame which has befallen the neighbourhood ... We call on your servants in authority to close bad houses within whose walls such wickedness is done, and men and women ruined in body and soul".*

November 10 – *(Another murder, and at this point The Times held back none of the gory details of a young woman's dismembered body.) ... Ears and nose cut clean off. Severed breasts placed on a table beside her bed. Stomach and abdomen ripped open. Kidneys and heart placed on table beside breasts. Liver and lower portion of body and uterus missing. A more horrible or sickening sight could not be imagined.*

November 13 – *Arrests made, but all suspects set at liberty. As will be seen from our Parliamentary report, Sir Charles Warren (Police Commissioner) tendered his resignation on Thursday last.*

'JACK THE RIPPER' was never identified and never caught.

However, *The Times*' direct, sober reporting, and the consequent active intervention of members of the public and of parliament, helped usher in a number of reforms in housing conditions, policing and government.

The Times goes on a small manhunt

Seven decades after Jack the Ripper's crimes, I happened to be temporarily on *The Times* (in its 173rd year, I think it was) when all of Fleet Street was focused on a 'sensation' of similar scale which the entire press quickly dubbed 'The A6 Murder'.

Like the Jack the Ripper case, the rape and murder on the national highway grew into a mystery that is still alive in Britain more than half a century later.

Once again *The Times* in 1960 was reluctantly, but cautiously and calmly involved. It was merely following up the media's common headline of the day announcing:

"UK POLICE'S BIGGEST MAN-HUNT EVER."

A senior reporter and I set off in his car for an address near the village of Maulden, just off the A6 highway in Bedfordshire, where the headquarters of the police manhunt had been set up about 48 hours previously. They were hunting for a killer who had rapped his gun against the window of a Morris Minor parked in a lay-by on the A6 – at a place named Deadman's Hill.

He had forced its occupants, a 36-year-old research scientist and his 23-year-old laboratory assistant and lover, to drive him for several hours around northern London and back into the countryside. Then he shot the physicist at close range in the small car, and raped the girl on her dead lover's body. He ordered her out of the car and, as she pleaded for her life, he fired five bullets into her, leaving her for dead.

She lived to tell the tale and tried to identify the killer.

My colleague and I expected to be held up at police checkpoints throughout our journey to the murder scene where we expected to witness, or be turned back from, "the biggest manhunt ever".

Nothing happened. Not on the A6. Not at any junction on our route from London.

My colleague was philosophical about this, which I – though a foreigner – expected this Englishman to be, for he was a Toynbee, one of the few names I have never forgotten. His is the family name of four generations of favourite philosophers, economists, historians, writers and journalists.

We did not discuss these relationships. We were concentrating on a media-hyped manhunt.

Finally we reached the very headquarters of the police search. It was a stately home in the countryside with a broad gravel driveway behind open gates and a baronial front door beyond. There was not a single vehicle in sight of this graceful, peaceful mansion.

A matronly receptionist quickly answered our knock and welcomed us in.

"Yes, this is the right place. The Bedfordshire police are in charge, and we have been granted the manor house as office space," she said.

But where was the 'action'?

Where were the police motorcycles and two-way radios and roadblocks?

Where were the police dogs? Helicopters?

"Where is the communications room?" we asked.

She led us into a large room at the far end of which sat an elderly man in plainclothes behind an expansive desk. Communications? He gestured to the two phones, one on each side of his chair. Where were the police mobile units? Where were the foot patrols? Why was there no activity at this HQ?

"Well, all possible units are out on the job," he pointed out.

"Where?"

"Wherever they're needed," he explained patiently.

"Is this really the biggest police manhunt ever?"

"Yes, I believe it may be. London HQ says so. The media, except you, say so. Throughout the shires, the counties and the country we're all doing everything that needs to be done ... Can't have a dangerous, armed suspect running free, y'know."

On our way back to London we discussed the story to be written.

Was there one? Yes. The existence of a supposed mad, runaway killer could not be taken lightly. But our story wasn't the big, black headlined version of the popular media.

Toynbee would write ours just the way we saw it and the way we heard it directly on-site.

That was the coldly factual eyewitness story that appeared in *The Times* next morning in the manner I have just described; though not in the precise quotations I use above, for my memory of it after more than 50 years is imprecise, and my notes and relevant cuttings from *The Times* are long lost. But *The Times'* report was a sedately accurate 'backgrounder' on the scene I've just outlined, written and published as a full broadsheet-page column below a moderate headline.

The sequels, deeply significant, are still making history today, *half a century* later.

Police used all their inter-departmental and criminal files to pinpoint suspects. After fast investigations of the most likely leads, they quickly arrested two men. Both had only minor non-violent criminal records. The first was Peter Alphon, a man of no fixed address who was placed in an identity parade a month after the murder, but whom the second victim and miraculous survivor, Valerie Storie, did not point out. Instead, she picked out an innocent volunteer in the line-up.

The next man arrested and placed in an identity parade was a petty criminal, James Hanratty, hesitantly selected by the surviving victim. He was later tried and sentenced to death.

His hanging on the gallows at Bedford Prison in 1962 occurred during widespread public protests by anti-capital punishment movements and by family support groups who believed James Hanratty's conviction was a frightening miscarriage of justice.

There were many reasons to suggest that the first suspect arrested, Peter Alphon, was the murderer. He had both publicly confessed and then denied it.

Over the years *three* commissions of inquiry, so far, have investigated the 50-year-old murder case, before and after Hanratty's execution.

His body was exhumed when scientific DNA testing became available and proved to match certain items of clothing in the case. But this forensic evidence is still being challenged. The first suspect, Alphon, made headlines again when he died in 2009.

The London *Daily Mail*, headlining a few years ago the 50th anniversary of Hanratty's hanging, reported that:

"An appeal eight years ago, the second, was dismissed because of the new DNA tests, but it is now claimed that this finding has been proved to be unreliable. The latest challenge centres on doubts about DNA tests used by Appeal Court judges ... "

On the eve of his execution Hanratty told his family: "I'm dying tomorrow, but I'm innocent. Clear my name."

They have been campaigning on his behalf ever since. And so have many other campaigners against capital punishment and possible injustice.

It should remind us that, when it comes to democracy and justice, the role of the popular press is at least as vital as the role of quality newspapers seeking to defend accuracy and quality.

Protecting the black sheep

The rare opportunity given me to explore the quality and culture of *The Times* at first hand, and at all its levels in a very short period, has proved in a long lifetime to be even more extraordinary than it was inexplicable.

I was allowed opportunities which no *Times*' journalist could ever hope for.

To this day I do not know (and care not) why and by whom I was nominated and accepted as South Africa's second Commonwealth Press Union Fellow – and definitely the last, because Verwoerd removed our country from the Commonwealth at a time that happened to fall between my acceptance of the assignment and my arrival in Britain.

So there I was in Fleet Street again, ensconced in the top-level offices of *The Times* during Britain's 'never-had-it-so-good' decade of the 1960s, and during The Thunderer's 'never-been-more-benign' era.

One can appreciate the excellent balance of *The Times* in that period merely by glancing at a brief timeline of *The Times'* history:

From 1788-1905, the paper was run by its remarkable family of independent owners. In 1906 it was bought by one of Britain's first 'press barons', Lord Northcliffe who, fortunately, after only 16 years sold it to John Jacob Astor. For 45 years the Astors ran *The Times* through a trust fund. Its independent editor modernised the paper and brought news to the front page for the first time only in 1966.

Even this did not help raise revenue, so Astor sold it the following year to Roy Thomson, Canadian owner of a media chain whose flagship had been *The Scotsman* in Edinburgh. Lord Thomson ('call me Roy'), faced with intractable demands and often vicious dealings with the trade unions, felt impelled to sell the newspaper, or close it down.

Unfortunately Rupert Murdoch was allowed to buy it. He immediately bypassed legislation and reneged on his promise not to interfere with its editorial policies.

Yet he saved *The Times* from certain closure.

Murdoch, who was prepared to fight the overweening trade unions literally in the streets, took over *The Times* in 1981 and the separately run, highly profitable *Sunday Times*. He promoted Harold Evans (the editor who had vitalised the *Sunday Times* weekly and led the world in investigative journalism) to edit the daily.

However, Murdoch promptly, and some claim illegally, intervened in editorial matters. This led to the walkout of Murdoch's newly appointed, famous editor ... a matter we shall deal with when we inspect Murdoch's role in the free world's media.

MY BRIEF SPAN on *The Times* was at the height of the Astor era, when the newspaper was in its traditional home beside the Thames at Grays Inn Road, and when Gavin Astor was chairman of *The Times'* trust and David Astor, lifetime friend of George Orwell, set up a similar independent, non-profit trust for his own newspaper, *The Observer*.

I had hardly been long enough with *The Times* to get used to its own pub when I was called upon to report to the foreign editor. He proved to be the deputy foreign editor's deputy who decided I should deputise for him while he joined his superiors in at least one week of absence from the newspaper. It was mid-August, when almost all of Britain seemed to be away on holiday.

It's hard to panic during such a languid time, but I nearly did. At that stage I had attended only the news editor's conferences, and had met very few of the paper's many editorial executives.

"All you have to do is take the calls from our foreign bureaux, and report what they tell you to the daily conference," he said.

"Don't bother to question them ... they won't take that from an unknown newcomer like you".

In fact, I discovered later, I would simply be following the foreign editor's normal routine. *The Times* accepted that its foreign correspondents knew exactly what was required of them, and would file accordingly. If something were out of the ordinary, they would alert us, or be alerted by the foreign editor.

Correspondents were expected to judge whether news elsewhere might be extra hot and reduce their own daily contribution accordingly. It was a trusting, delicate, back-to-front, carriage-and-horse, yet a clear communication procedure.

"Berlin, two columns. The situation is reaching crisis point," I heard myself as the acting third deputy foreign editor saying to the assembled, though thinned-out might of the Editorial Conference:

"Beirut, half a column."

"Bucharest, three-quarters."

"Pretoria, three paragraphs ... at last, not much happening there ... "

The chief sub seemed irritated at the unnecessary comments. No one asked about content. Either they guessed, or a sub-editor would communicate directly with the correspondent involved through the unstable transcontinental telephone – or more likely undersea cable – systems of 50 years ago.

ONE DAY I RECEIVED an invitation from the owner of *The Times*, soon-

Christine Keeler, whose sexual encounters with a Minister of the Realm and a Russian agent created havoc for a 'never-had-it-so-good' government.

to-be Baron Lord Astor, to attend a lunch at his estate in the country. My only reservation about such a privileged invitation was that it involved him – Lord Astor of Hever – not the *Observer's* Lord Astor, nor the eldest Lord Astor, Viscount Waldorf Astor, whose great home on the bank of the Thames was famous for its wild parties and its glamorous and powerful guests.

Soon the smashingly and exuberantly attractive Christine Keeler would be cavorting there in the arms of the Minister of Defence; until it became clear she was also cavorting with a Cold War member of the Russian Embassy.

Christine Keeler's face and figure would be on the front page of every daily and Sunday paper in the land (except *The Times* which had to publish the story on an inside page as it still had advertisements which filled its front page).

It was hard to find a male in Britain or in Parliament who would blame Cabinet member, John Profumo, for being seduced by the exquisite young Keeler ... until he told a little lie about his romantic meetings. For this he was quite properly fired ... You couldn't tolerate a politician who lied, could you?

What next?

Profumo turned out to be, in the decades to come, one of the more upright, contrite, caring and genuine characters ever to enter politics.

'Caring, upright, genuine' were attributes one might apply to Lord Astor – not the Thames parties' one, nor the one who later owned *The Observer* – but the dutiful yet kind one who invited an unknown entity to a private lunch, because it seemed to him the decent thing to do.

It was an informal occasion with only one other guest, Sir William Haley, outside of numerous friends and family.

Sir William had already been editor of *The Times* for nearly a decade and should have been an 'insider' in the Astor circle. But he did not act like one when I met him. Indeed, except among Nationalist politicians back home, I have seldom experienced such frost.

Sir William was really august.

No other word for it. And, he seemed to me to be irritated beyond measure by my presence as an upstart temporarily on his staff whom he had never seen before, because I arrived when he was still on his summer vacation away from editorial conferences. I was acutely aware of his reputation. He had once been editor of *The Guardian*. He had served as post-war, director-general of the BBC for eight years, and created its august Third Programme. He had been a director of Reuters and of Britain's Press Association.

He had every right to ignore me most of the time at this informal luncheon. Which he did. But at last, I noticed he also refrained from saying anything more than absolutely essential to anyone else.

I never bothered to find out more about his august personage until I fished out this memory of the occasion. And now I see that he was born outside of Britain on the island of Jersey, the son of a Yorkshire clerk and a French grocer's daughter. And French was his only language as a child. He left school at 16 to become a radio operator on a tramp steamer and his vast education came out of an encyclopaedia! Fittingly, he ended his career as head of Encyclopaedia Britannica in Chicago where he resigned over a difference of opinion with his American employers.

August indeed. But also an immense figure whose worth I failed to discern, even as a passing signal in the dark. I did not know that Sir William, unlike a wartime predecessor on *The Times,* had a reputation as

Britain claims to breed more varieties of sheep than any other nation. This Welsh black sheep is one of several strains. It has the qualities required of a journalist: 'hardiness and self-reliance', also known as 'bloody stubbornness'.

an outstanding and fair-minded newspaperman who had fought against appeasement in Munich as hard as any editor in Britain.

He also fought to publish war news, "however unpalatable", as long as it did not harm the war effort. Yet ... and here I belatedly found a partly shared and very rare trait of his in journalism: "Haley was found to be too shy to work as a reporter, so much so that he transferred to sub-editing in his younger days".

It makes me belatedly wish I could have met him again – a man who, five years later in 1966, moved *The Times* into the modern world and news onto the front page after saying that the newspaper had lived in "magnificent isolation" long enough.

"Every newspaper has to live in its day and age," he said, then banished birth and death notices and other advertising 'smalls' from page one.

INSTEAD OF SITTING in the cold silence among Lord Astor's diners that day, I accepted with alacrity my host's kind invitation to wander around the estate with him.

As the two of us paused on the hillside to look across at another meadow, I experienced one of the warmest social gestures I can recall. Astor said, "I get so tired of all the academic stuff and the office politics, I prefer working down here on the farm. I want to show you one of my major projects. Look at that breeding stock in that meadow over there."

I tried to make out the browsing dark shapes.

"I'm building up an entire flock of Astor black sheep," said the deprecating chairman of *The Times'* trust. "In this family it's quite a challenge."

I thought much later of the elder Astor, Lord of Cleves, known to run the best parties in the land – but yet to be publicly associated with the two most famous prostitutes in Britain.

But talking of reputations, do remember *The Times'* 200 years of exemplary and ethical behaviour – and its sensible approach to the Jack the Ripper tragedies. ☐

3

Past and future of the press.

18.
Pulitzer and the birth of 'popular' newspapers.

*"What are the news?" he would ask ...
until one of his foreign correspondents
in Europe cabled back:
"Cannot find a single new!"*

Joseph Pulitzer was the famous and eccentric editor-publisher of *The World* in New York. "It is said" that he insisted on the plural form of the verb for news.

I have deliberately used the phrase "It is said" as a reminder that it signals a dubious source. In fact, it was probably the fierce publisher of the *Chicago Tribune* who once insisted on saying, "the news are".

"It is said" is a signal relating to gossip, not news.

However, it was in this era of a new 'Yellow Press' that gossip was often used in place of news ... a pollution that Pulitzer never set out to produce.

The American route to the modern, 'popular' mainstream press can be traced back to Joseph Pulitzer.

Pulitzer was an immigrant to the USA in the late-1800s when New York City's population was three-quarters immigrant. He studied English, bought the struggling *The World* newspaper and turned it into 'the biggest in the world' by aiming it at the new NY citizens of many languages. He demanded from reporters short, sharp sentences about relevant city dramas. He insisted, it is said, that the news "were" best told in big, sensational headlines.

One of his biographers gives us real news from the pages of the old *The World* newspaper. He quotes a report on *The World*'s front page, which appeared soon after Pulitzer took over. It concerns neither politics nor economics, but the fate of a destitute widow named Margaret Graham:

She had been seen by dockworkers as she walked on the edge of a pier in the East River with an infant in her arms and a two-year-old girl clutching her skirt.

All at once the famished mother clasped the feeble little girl round her waist and, tottering to the brink of the wharf, hurled both her starving young into the river as it whirled by. She stood for a moment on the edge of the stream. The children were too weak and spent to struggle or to cry. Their little helpless heads dotted the brown tide for an instant, and then they sank out of sight.

The men who looked on stood spellbound. Graham followed her children into the river but was saved by the onlookers and was taken to jail to face murder charges.

Now *that* 'are' the news. Indeed, that 'were' trying to be Pulitzer prize news. Most newspapers might simply have reported: "Margaret Graham, address unknown, was arrested yesterday on a charge of murder for throwing her two children into the East River, New York." Then – quite correctly and in the interests of justice – diarised the date of the court hearing for a full report on the case.

Another story?
'It is said' of Mr Pulitzer that he illuminated his eccentricity in his later years by his determination to buy up vast tracts of empty land in America to emblazon them with a message to readers who might be out there in Space and out of reach of *The World*. He was dissuaded only when he was asked: "What message? And what language will you use?"

It is a fact that Pulitzer bought New York's *The World* in 1883, and by the time of his death in 1927 he had taken its circulation from 15,000 to 600,000 to become bigger than the *New York Times*, bigger than his new 'down-market' rivals the *New York Sun* and *New York Journal*.

The World became the biggest circulation newspaper in America, in fact.

He did many good things for journalism in the years bridging the 19th and 20th century. He helped establish the prestigious Columbia Graduate School of Journalism in New York. He hired the best journalists he could find.

Pulitzer did many things to create his 'new journalism', but none has coloured his fame as much as his feat in publishing the world's first comic strip in full colour.

He hired a cartoonist to draw 'The Yellow Kid', a strange little character who carried topical comments aimed at adults more than it appealed to children. The Yellow Kid became the most popular feature of New York's *The World*.

But then came Pulitzer's war with two other newspapers which, in the early 1920s, fought for domination of New York. The one was the *New York Sun*, which stooped to anti-Semitism to attack him in person, and the other was the *New York Journal,* which whizz-kid William Randolph Hearst bought, and took as far 'downmarket' as it could go in publishing sensationalist journalism.

The Yellow Kid, an unlikely icon of an unwelcome tendency in 'popular' journalism.

Hearst moved to New York and grabbed The Yellow Kid feature by the simple device of offering *The World's* cartoonist a fee he could not refuse. Only then did Pulitzer realise he had been too trusting in signing contracts.

The result was a bitter circulation war that took all three newspapers down to the gutter.

But Pulitzer's heart was not in it. Hearst kept The Yellow Kid and, fortunately for Pulitzer, it was Hearst who also held onto and inflated his mantle as King of the Yellow Press.

Joseph Pulitzer, a great and inventive newsman, died at the height of that battle. His *The World* ended four years later.

Hearst's 'yellow press' and his own unreported scandal

William Randolph Hearst, lived a life as sensational as the "yellow press" he virtually invented in the 1920s. He turned his papers into America's first broad mass readership chain of downmarket newspapers during the 1930s. Hearst was born in Beverley Hills, the only child of a self-made

William Randolph Hearst and his famous film star mistress Marion Davies. A cause for murder?

multi-millionaire miner and rancher. At 23, while a student at Harvard University, Hearst junior became 'Proprietor' of the *San Francisco Examiner* ... which his father had won as payment of a gambling debt!

Resigning as business editor of the university's *Lampoon,* William Randolph soon built one of the world's richest and most powerful newspaper empires. At his peak, Hearst owned 28 metro newspapers and 18 magazines; along with several radio stations and movie companies. Fortunately, it was a very temporary empire, for it became synonymous with 'lurid journalism'.

This description was the only understatement associated with Hearst's sensational network of papers, which were ruthlessly downmarket and became instantly successful in the wild era of Prohibition.

Californian Hearst was no doubt inspired by his early New York rival, Joseph Pulitzer – but that newspaper proprietor sought working-class readers using fine skills that deserve emulation everywhere.

Hearst, in his early days while starting his newspapering career on the West Coast, emulated Pulitzer in employing the best journalists available. These included great names such as Ambrose Bierce, Stephen Crane, Mark Twain, Richard Harding Davis and Jack London – forming a bouquet of writing talent out-rivalling at first even the sophisticated magazine, *The New Yorker,* launched in that same era on 21st February 1925. (However, while Hearst's newspapers quickly lost their recognised writing talent, *The New Yorker* went on to publish short stories by some of the best-known American writers of the 20th century, including Dorothy Parker, Roald Dahl, Vladimir Nabokov, John O'Hara, Philip Roth, JD Salinger, Irwin Shaw, James Thurber, John Updike and EB White.)

"(The) Depression weakened Hearst's financial position and by 1940 he had lost personal control of his vast communications empire," according to one biographer, Jeff Wierichs. "Hearst upset the left wing in America by being a pro-Nazi in the 1930s."

Hearst was in fact a strangely mixed personality. He ordered his newspapers to champion 'the little guy', which they did for a while, with some excellent investigative journalism. However, this promising path was soon lost through Hearst's insatiable thirst for money and power. He was a snob, possibly a megalomaniac and an extreme racist. His own life

Hearst Castle, new but bigger than most in Europe. Above is merely the swimming pool. Hearst also owned a castle in Wales and made huge property investments across America. Also several Hollywood studios and many newspapers.

was filled with sensation and gossip. Hollywood was ripe with rumours of the mysterious death of a movie producer who had joined Hearst and his mistress on a pleasure cruise.

Did he try to murder Charlie Chaplin for flirting on the yacht with the press baron's famous mistress, 'world heart-throb' Marion Davies? Did Hearst shoot the movie producer (Thomas Ince) by mistake in a jealous confrontation on deck with the other two whom he suspected and then found in a compromising position?

The details of this shipboard death were blatantly suppressed. The lack of any inquiry and of any official records remains a mystery even today.

Hearst was seen as the inspiration of the wicked characterisation of an all-powerful media owner in Orson Welles' momentous film *Citizen Kane*. In this particular case, all Hearst's power in Hollywood failed to suppress the film and its accusations.

However, his highly publicised aura of power led celebrities, politicians and film stars to continue to scramble for invitations to Hearst's 130-roomed castle, on an enchanting hill above Hollywood – a lifetime project intended to rival the most famous castles of ancient Europe.

The bravest and most celebrated wit of the times, journalist Dorothy Parker, was once mistakenly added to the guest list for a nationwide celebration in this Gothic setting. She was appalled at the arrogance, hypocrisy and snubs she believed she experienced there.

Hearst, though co-habiting in his castle with his movie-star mistress Marion Davies, informed his guests that one of the rules of the house was: "no lovemaking between unmarried couples". Dorothy Parker broke the rule and was asked to leave. As she departed she wrote these lines in her inimitable style in the powerful tycoon's visitors' book:

Upon my honour
I saw a Madonna
Standing in a niche,
Above the door
Of the famous whore
Of a prominent son of a bitch.

Freedom of speech in America is a brave, beautiful and often ironical thing. Especially in the light of one of William Randolph Hearst's most quoted remarks: "News is something somebody doesn't want printed; all else is advertising."

THE EXCESSES of Hearst's press and of other mass readership newspapers that burst on the scene in the 1930s have taught us a great deal about freedom; its hazards; its threats and its supreme value. It has taught us that freedom of information flourishes best in a dedicatedly democratic country and with an educated population which has bred, from primary school, champions of an open society that boasts freedom of choice. In the 1930s, the USA led the world in this. And, after William Randolph Hearst had extravagantly over-reached himself, the public's reaction was strong. The patterns in the US press quickly changed.

While Hearst represented the first form of 'mass media' through his chain of newspapers, most of them, including one of the biggest p.m. papers in the world, his *Los Angeles Examiner,* died, and the 'yellow press' retired to the poorest suburbs, attracting readers who were entertained by manufactured scandal and inventive stories of monsters and rapist aliens.

The *Los Angeles Examiner* left a legacy of scandal greater than its proprietor's own. It had led the field in covering the sensational 'Black Dahlia' murder – with so many 'inside exclusive' reports that some journalists accused the paper of making up its stories about the mysterious murdered woman. But the boot was on the other foot and the paper tracked down and captured a rival newspaper's agent who was stealing the *Examiner*'s exclusive investigations even before they were printed. Such frantic effort.

However, the rest of the American press followed a new course by immediately reforming and ending the

slide into 'tabloid' journalism. They were led in quality by some major newspapers recognised as 'the ten best' and included *The New York Times* and *The Washington Post* at the top, which were followed by a changing list that included *The Boston Globe, The Philadelphia Inquirer,* the *Chicago Tribune, Miami Herald* and *The Detroit News* (once the biggest circulation English-language afternoon newspaper in the world).

Each had a distinctly different personality. The best of them remains, I believe, *The New York Times,* which was bought by Adolf Ochs in 1876 for a sum of $75,000. Ochs ran it for 39 years. His son-in-law, Arthur Hays Sulzberger, ran it for the next 26 years, just before mass education and mass immigration were reaching their heights, and competition among newspapers for new readers in New York became frenetic. *The New York Times* rose above it all, disdaining the Pulitzer-imitating, exuberant reporting of many news sheets. *The New York Times* soon dominated even the sophisticated and cultured *Herald*, which eventually died in its battle against the uncompromising and huge breadth of straight news reporting of its main rival.

America's biggest newspapers avoided the extraordinary battles and even more extraordinary personalities who fought for dominance in Britain's modern press. As the following chapters show, the stories of the British 'press barons' outpace fiction. □

19.
The Press Barons who wanted to be Emperors.

Britain's press barons provide a gallery of portraits of truly extraordinary men – all 'self-made'. Regrettably, most of them single-handedly grasped for political power. Few of them escaped from overweening ambition and over-confidence. One of them dominated the 1920s and 1930s and set the world stage for today's mass media.

The handful of self-made press barons influenced much of the English-speaking world for almost a century.

Yet, as mentioned earlier in this book, some of the 20th-century press barons were not English ... and not the least helpful in aiding newspaper readers, let alone English culture or justice or recognition of fairness – or truth.

Untitled Robert Maxwell is a prime example, described at the beginning of this book. So is Australian/American Rupert Murdoch and Canadian Conrad Black who was ennobled as 'Lord Black of Crossharbour', but committed a felony in the USA.

Yet there were other 'non-Britons', such as American Lord Astor and Canadians Lord Thompson and Lord Beaverbrook who benefited Britain and its newspapers in peace and war. Then there were the enigmatic Lord Camrose and phlegmatic Lord Kemsley, also known as ...

William Berry, journalist and later self-made press mogul who became Viscount (Baron) Lord Camrose. © National Portrait Gallery, London.

The humble Berry Brothers

They were two self-made Englishmen – well, Welshmen, actually – who came from humble beginnings and ended up owning much of Britain's "quality press".

The Berry brothers, William and Gomer, created a small empire of English papers led by their flagships *The Financial Times*, *The Sunday Times* and *The Daily Telegraph*. They did so while still recognised as 'the Berry boys', and not yet known as Lord Camrose and Lord Kemsley.

The Berry boys lived in the small Welsh town of Merthyr Tydfil, where their father was an estate agent. William, the second of three sons, began his career as a journalist working for a local weekly paper.

Then Billy-boy Berry set off for London – at the age of 21 with 100 pounds in his pocket – to establish a commercially orientated publication, *Advertising World*. He invited 19-year-old Gomer Berry to assist him with the second issue, thus starting a brotherly partnership which lasted 35 years.

But it was their elder brother Seymour who actually paved their way. He made a quick fortune as an industrialist, then helped them buy up some small newspapers. They saw that a new 'popular' press in Britain had, since their childhood in the 1880s, mushroomed as newspaper versions of the magazines 'penny-'orribles'.

William, who took education seriously, aimed higher. He aimed his small newspapers in the 1920s and 1930s at the newly-educated middle class, with the purpose of informing them and helping them become post-Edwardian businessmen and professionals – male readers with ambitions and grave demeanours, if not serious minds.

In 1919 the two brothers bought *The Financial Times*. Two decades later they bought *The Daily Telegraph* and its direct competitor, *The Morning Post* which they merged within their main asset. William led the way to its triumph. Instead of trying to attract readers with gifts, as other would-be popular newspapers did, he decided to change the format of *The Daily Telegraph;* to maintain the quality of its news coverage, and to halve the price from two pence to a 'penny'.

From the start, brother Gomer Berry (soon to be Lord Kemsley) concentrated his energies on the Sunday Times. Once he was in sole command he became editor-in-chief and the circulation trebled. Like brother William, the younger Berry was soon a baron of the realm. © National Portrait Gallery, London.

Under his guidance as editor-in-chief, the circulation doubled immediately to 200,000 and grew to well over a million copies by 1949. As Lord Camrose, William followed by his sons, ran *The Daily Telegraph* as their own journalistic enterprise for more than half a century.

When William and Gomer decided to split up in the early 1930s, the younger brother kept the provincial daily papers and *The Sunday Times*. As Lord Kemsley, Gomer devoted his life to this newspaper, while continuing to build on his own publishing empire, which included, briefly, *The Times*.

It is important to remember that the brothers' success depended on both of them becoming hands-on editors-in-chief, exercising their journalistic judgements on a daily basis, as well as personally ensuring good management and high standards. Editorial independence indubitably existed.

From the start, brother Gomer Berry concentrated his energies on *The Sunday Times*. Once he was in sole command he became editor-in-chief and the circulation trebled. Like brother William, the younger Berry was soon a baron of the realm.

By 1937 Lord Kemsley had considerable power to use, but wisely refrained from exercising it, abjuring politics and focusing instead on his expanding chain of newspapers.(I still have today a copy of his instructive book on journalism which he signed and gave me when I was taken on, albeit for only a brief spell, as a recruit to his news organisation in 1950. He wrote only the preface of his book, for he designed it as a professional in-house product of Kemsley Newspapers so that it became a continually updating and relevant journalistic guide of great benefit to newspapering for many decades.)

Meanwhile, eldest brother Seymour Berry, the first industrialist in the family, became richer than, and almost as powerful as, his younger brothers. He was created a Viscount in his own right, while journalist William's son succeeded his father in the newspaper business and became yet another Viscount.

Their path to fame and fortune in newspapers had been rendered easier by the chaos in which the previous so-called 'Napoleon of the Press', had left his own newspaper empire at his early, demented death.

IF YOU THINK three Berry barons, in one generation of one family, might be somewhat excessive for the House of Lords, you should look at the awards of the *previous* generation, the best-known family of press barons – "a wild bunch of Irishmen"*, to quote one of their biographers.

That Irish family's titles eventually included:
Alfred Charles William Harmsworth, 1st Viscount Northcliffe
Harold Harmsworth, 1st Viscount Rothermere
Cecil Harmsworth, 1st Baron Harmsworth,
Sir Leicester Harmsworth, 1st Baronet,
and Sir Hildebrand Harmsworth, 1st Baronet.

Lords of the Kingdom

Two ambitious English boys – originally from Dublin and sons of a poor country widow – ended up owning the major half of the British metropolitan press.

Elder brother Alfred Harmsworth has been hailed (and criticised) for being "the father of popular journalism". He is also recognised (and also criticised) for being an early pioneer in 'tabloid journalism'.

But he was much more than both those claims, and hailed by some with the dubious title of 'Napoleon of the Press', for he shaped the worlds of advertising and news into the formula which created the modern mass media.

Alfred came to England as a child shortly after the British Education Act was passed in 1870 and enabled him in his school days to read *Tit-Bits* ('a weekly storehouse of information'). He was among the first to appreciate the explosion in potential newspaper readership

Alfred Harmsworth was an extraordinary individual with huge talents and an overbearing manner that allowed him to do whatever he wished. His mistress lived openly with him in a normally rigid society with the three children she bore him. His wife took a lover, in desperation, and his variety of high society and lowly-born sexual consorts were manifold. Yet no one in the moralist society that ruled in the early 1900s seems to have challenged his behaviour - let alone in the press which he dominated. It was assumed by many that his increasingly erratic behaviour and early death were the cause of the dreaded disease of his era: syphilis.

which the law of compulsory education produced, so he started his career as a self-taught journalist by writing and publishing a periodical called *Answers*, aimed at his questioning, newly educated generation.

His mother sent Alfred's younger brother, 19-year-old Harold, a lowly shipping clerk, to straighten out Alfred's financing when he launched the half-penny *Daily Mail* – a paper very different from the products of early American popular journalism.

His *Daily Mail*, which he edited, focused on men who might have the ambitious aim of earning R1,000 a year.

In the manner of the informative *Tit-Bits* magazine of his youth, Harmsworth designed his paper to help men like himself with news and features that would, "explain, simplify, clarify."

The Daily Mail, promoted as 'The Busy Man's Journal' was deprecated at first by an envious rival as "a paper by office boys for office boys". Harmsworth always knew, however, that he knew better than anyone. *The Daily Mail* sold almost 400,000 copies in London on its first day and within 24 months was making profits not equalled by *The Times* in its greatest days.

Harmsworth had touched a new, relatively exclusive would-be businessman's market. His *Daily Mail* not only maintained its circulation above *The Times,* but also attracted effective advertising in forms never known in the press before.

Alfred had created a business bent on profit – the first newspaper to become a public company. That achievement took it three-quarters of the way towards the lofty ideal of editorial independence in a corporate market. Alfred's newspapers remained, perhaps forever, supporters of the conservative view; dominated by his 'hands-on' style, yes, but also because those two papers were deliberately designed for conservative readers. He instinctively knew his market.

But he quickly over-reached himself.

In his search for another set of new readers he launched a second newspaper, *The Daily Mirror*. It was aimed specifically at women, few of whom, in that era, could read or leave home and secure an independent job. *The Daily Mirror* attracted 265,000 readers at first – but within three months was left with only 25,000 buyers and huge costs.

Men and women of the 'lower classes' at this time were also rarely considered worthy of the attention of newspapers. Yet he encouraged the newly appointed editor of *The Daily Mirror* to turn it around and face the broadest (downmarket) end of newspaper readership. The experiment was an almost instant success.

His *Daily Mail,* aimed at the middle class, thrived even more. It offered its mass readership new benefits such as exclusive world news services and, for the first time ever, financial news pages, 'background' news, a daily magazine and Women's Page! (How ironic it all seems today when the 'Women's Page', regarded as a nasty male chauvinistic device, was dropped in the late 20th century to ensure political correctness. This despite the loss of many woman readers who had preferred the special attention in their favourite papers.)

Biding his time for *The Times*

Alfred, as Lord Northcliffe, spent 10 years trying to buy *The Times* from the third and fourth generation of its founding/editing family, the Walters.

Northcliffe achieved his ambition; finally, by pretending he was not the least interested – then buying a controlling share of *The Times* secretively; almost by proxy, in order to get the required approval of a judge and acceptance from society, for the change in ownership of Britain's oldest and best-known paper.

Northcliffe promised himself as well as everyone else that he would not interfere in the editorial processes and opinions of *The Times.* "I cannot," he said, on the grounds that if he did, its aura of editorial independence would fade and so would the newspaper.

Fortunately he chose strong editors, because his promises were quickly overtaken by his demand for power, wherever that was supposed to be.

He *did* interfere. He interfered personally and blatantly for years – until a new editor he appointed, Geoffrey Dawson (formerly editor of Johannesburg's *Star*) impugned him and resigned.

The next famous *Times* editor, Wickham Steed, was fortunate in having Lord Northcliffe as a proprietor in the period in which the owner's health markedly declined and his interests became less focused on his newspapers. Yet Northcliffe's overbearing nature and his threats aimed at Lloyd George and other politicians, led to the perception of many that he was now becoming *dangerously* powerful.

It was thought that he might influence the upper classes through *The Times;* the middle classes through *The Daily Mail;* the working classes through *The Daily Mirror*, and the counties through his provincial press. He might hold Parliament or the government to ransom.

Power in the press, however, seldom works so simply. Newspapers provide information, but their opinions seldom change readers' minds. And in Northcliffe's case his greedy sense of power and ill-disciplined antics may have helped drive him towards insanity and behaviour that went almost beyond his social scandals (which, like Hearst's scandals in America, never appeared in any newspaper).

One of the most prevalent and extreme of Northcliffe's scandals was that his widespread love-life had led him into deteriorating health and loss of full sanity through the dreaded disease of its day: syphilis.

HAROLD HARMSWORTH was overwhelmed by his brother's bullying and Napoleonic ambitions. The younger brother was more interested in money for its own sake, rather than the power it might provide. He was a narrowly dedicated capitalist, keeping his feet on the ground and avoiding all pretensions to editorial or political talent. His newspapers flourished, resulting finally in him receiving the title of Lord Rothermere.

However, while Lord Northcliffe was accused of being a warmonger who was against Germany, Rothermere publicly courted Hitler and called for appeasement. Harold's stance was quickly rejected by all of Britain as WWII broke out.

Nevertheless, the two Harmsworths, without being fully conscious of it, were creating a family newspaper dynasty in the form of their unstable nephew, Cecil Harmsworth King.

Lord Rothermere. He assumed a subservient role and listened to others - but not to his brother, 'warmongering' Lord Northcliffe. Instead he listened to Goebbels and Hitler. © National Portrait Gallery, London.

Megalomania becomes King, and vice versa

The rise to fame and entitlement was meteoric for Cecil Harmsworth King, nephew of both those Lords who owned much of Britain's press. Cecil King was educated in the very best schools ... it was said of him that he really believed he was born to rule.

The young man's instant progress to the board of *The Daily Mirror* was never enough for him, of course, and he was soon conniving for greater recognition. He did it in a most devious way.

As soon as he was able to, he organised a putsch in his newspaper's boardroom in order to get rid of his chairman. He did so by manipulating a required unanimous vote at a secret meeting – without the chairman being informed of its purpose or having notice of the meeting to which he would have recorded a blocking vote.

The 'back-stabbed' chairman was Guy Bartholomew, who was also editor of *The Daily Mirror*, and had built up its reputation and readership almost single-handedly. When Bartholomew first found that the newspaper was a failure as a publication designed for women readers only, he about-turned policy and boldly sacked its genteel all-women staff ("It was like drowning kittens," he averred).

Then he had gone on painstakingly and creditably to build up *The Daily Mirror*'s image and fashion it as "the voice of the 'lower orders'".

Bartholomew had championed the women who had filled the factories in WWI; thrown open the columns to letters of three sentences – and presented 'Jane' to the world on a daily basis.

Jane (with her ever-present dachshund) in a comic created by The Daily Mirror, became a figure far better known than the Mirror itself. For at least a decade her desperate daily efforts to keep her clothes on were syndicated and watched by readers of both sexes on four continents. The comic strip above concerns one of the rare occasions when she stripped naked voluntarily, not accidentally, but as demurely as ever.

Scantily dressed 'Jane', in a world-renowned comic strip, shed her clothes so compulsively, but maintained her morality so convincingly, that she was loved by the entire British nation, and was required reading in a special edition for the American armed forces. All this happened under Bartholomew, whose ignominious firing was made possible by duping him, and emphasising his drinking and increasingly gross behaviour.

Having ruthlessly engineered Bartholomew's departure, Cecil Harmsworth King chose up-and-coming Hugh Cudlipp to edit and lead *The Daily Mirror*. At the age of 23, Cudlipp became the youngest chief editor in Fleet Street. He and King turned the *Mirror* into the world's largest selling daily newspaper.

King was chairman of the International Publishing Corporation (IPC) by 1963 when it was claimed to be the biggest publishing empire in the world. His assets included some 200 papers and feature magazines and 20 other trade and technical magazines on three continents, plus music, radio outlets and a chain of news agency businesses.

Later, King also became infected with the peculiar press baron curse of megalomania. He was convinced that Prime Minister Harold Wilson's return to political power was due to his newspapers' efforts, and when this was not officially recognised by the government "he charged into battle like a blind-folded bison with a grudge turned loose in a liquor store in the dark", to quote Francis Williams who witnessed the ensuing events.

In May 1968, King composed an attack on Harold Wilson, demanding that

the prime minister should be driven from office without delay. The newspaper proprietor issued instructions that his proclamation should be published prominently under the title "ENOUGH IS ENOUGH" on the front pages of both *The Daily Mirror* and *The Sun* over his signature as chairman of the International Press Corporation. He did not trouble to inform the board.

It resulted in his own personally created board (with his protégé Cudlipp as a member, I assume) meeting secretly to fire him in his absence ... as he had fired Bartholomew.

Francis Williams, who once worked for Prime Minister Atlee, for the Labour's *Daily Herald* and for *The Observer*, wrote in his book *Dangerous Estate*: "Cecil King was brought down on the same principle that had arisen when Lord Beaverbrook and King's uncle, the first Lord Rothermere, had demanded of Baldwin the right to be consulted on Cabinet appointments in return for their support."

King must have forgotten that his predecessors had been demolished by Prime Minister Baldwin with the contemptuous phrase, given him by his cousin, Rudyard Kipling, that they wanted "power without responsibility, the prerogative of the harlot throughout the ages".

Francis Williams also wrote of Lord Alfred (Harmsworth) Northcliffe: "Not since Napoleon has any man enriched the nobility with so many of his relations."** (Alfred ensured that his poor Irish mother's two sons became viscounts, a third became a baron, and her two grandsons become baronets of the British Realm, which was hated in Dublin. His mother outlived him – and never forgave him for not bequeathing *The Times* to her.)

THE EXTRAORDINARY dominance in the English press of the above two families (Welsh and Irish), marked a low period for *editorial independence* in British newspapers and the negative example which Alfred Harmsworth set in the wider world caused his successors to try and avoid similar pitfalls.

The many counter-influences included:
- Canadian Lord ('call me Roy') Thompson, who ensured in the 1960s editorial independence for all his publications around the world, including the Edinburgh *Scotsman* and *The Times*
- American Lord Astor who guarded the trusts set up to protect the editorial independence of *The Times* and *The Observer*

- Canadian Lord Beaverbrook (William Maxwell Aiken), who appointed a ground-breaking editor to *The Daily Express* and turned his own attention to politics and guaranteeing munitions to fight off Hitler's attempts at invasion of Britain.

The arrogant role of *some* of the once poor, migrant press barons was extremely worrying. Fortunately, however, the key to maintaining and advancing standards of journalism in the United Kingdom belonged – as it had done for 200 years – to strongly independent-minded newspaper editors.

The Berry brothers, Lord Camrose and Lord Kelmsley, were themselves lifelong editors-in-chief, caring emphatically for the reputations of their papers such as *The Sunday Times* and *The Daily Telegraph,* which William Berry and his son edited for almost 50 years up until 1986.

One of the 'villains', Lord Northcliffe, fortunately valued strong editors for *The Times*, including Wickham Steed and "Dawson of *The Times*" mentioned earlier. The latter was sufficiently independent-minded to fight with his proprietor and then quit; not returning to *The Times* until Northcliffe died.

William Haley and Harold Evans, referred to elsewhere, were both the epitome of editorial independence and honoured that principle. So did Arthur Christiansen of the brilliantly edited and designed *Daily Express;* and Hugh Cudlipp who, despite Cecil King, made *The Daily Mirror* sparkle while challenging norms and bringing reforms in British society.

One of the most famous of all was CP Scott, editor of *The Manchester Guardian* which he served for 60 (!) years. In his later years he was also its owner, and *The Guardian* has grown into an international newspaper under another wilful editor with decades of experience.

Across Britain, and despite the feverish chase after peerage titles, editors held their ground against such ambitions and power-seekers. They also upheld the 200-year-old principle of *editorial* independence.

This ideal of a free press forms the cardinal thrust of this book, which will continue to be posed in its later chapters. □

* *The House of Northcliffe* by Paul Ferris (World Publishing, USA 1972)
** *Dangerous Estate, the Anatomy of newspapers* by Francis Williams, (Longmans 1957).

20. US champions of press freedom.

It was the best of times.

Charles Dickens

Newspapers may have been a mixed blessing, but what is not in question is that the often-maligned USA has more honest, freedom-loving newspapers today than any other combination of states and nations on Earth. They set the world standards of balance, truth, accuracy and popular appeal as well as demonstrating the media's faults. They come, of course, in all sizes and shapes. A glance at typical varieties can tell us a great deal.

Let's start at the top. The two leading newspapers, *The New York Times* and *The Washington Post*, have been so much in the forefront in news publishing that I need merely offer small personal insights as reminders of the characters of those papers as I knew them in the last century.

The Washington Post

The most colourful yet ambiguous, so far as my observations went, was *The Washington Post* under Katherine Graham, at the time of the drama and triumph of the newspaper over Nixon's 'Waterloo' at Watergate.

Political activity was frantic and campaign buttons were the craze when I went to meet for the first time, the suddenly internationally famous editor, Ben Bradlee. I wore in my lapel a large button which I had come across somewhere in New York and which seemed fittingly ironic in Washington. It read: 'I am a victim of the Press'.

"What the bloody hell are you wearing that goddamn thing for?" he asked, and added: "I've also got one of those fucking buttons around here somewhere." He produced it and said with a straight face: "The goddamn newsroom gave it to me. God knows why." (Or something stronger to that effect.) His button read: 'Thou shalt not swear'.

The Washington Post's news-gathering and news-editing systems were just like those of most of the best-known newspapers of the free world, and it was among the pioneers in adapting those universal systems in the 1980s to computerisation. A reporter from *The Calcutta Times* or *The Toronto Star* could walk into that newsroom today, I imagine, and feel at home at her desk and familiar with the system in minutes. But there was one surprising aberration at *The Washington Post* which astounded me and which I never liked. The Leader and Op-Ed pages were divorced from the system!

Ben Bradlee was Executive or Managing Editor, and undoubtedly king of the news departments at the heart of the paper; but he was entirely divorced from the newspaper's 'brain' and its voice, except through his direct contact with the head, Katherine Graham. Yes, it certainly ensured full separation of news from comment, but it felt to me to be too artificial; too remote-controlled. It was, in my opinion, simply wrong.

The Executive Editor shrugged his shoulders. "It's Katie's paper. What Katie wants, Katie gets," he told me; an observation I could never forget.

Naively, I couldn't understand it, and I knew I could never accept editorship of a newspaper in that form ... until I belatedly got to know properly and understand Katherine Graham.

After her husband's untimely death, she had become the humble, shy and reluctant boss of one of the world's greatest newspapers in the free world's hottest political seat. And in that heated kitchen, the grieving would-be housewife gradually became supreme; partly through her incorruptible spirit, but mainly through her heavily tested courage.

The chemistry was undoubtedly at work in her (separated) leader conference room. Years later, at a moment's notice and without hesitation she came to South Africa, despite international sanctions and boycotts, to help us defend press freedom at its darkest hour. I admired and adored her ... but I continued to question the lobotomy, or rather 'pre-frontal leucotomy' of *The Washington Post*'s editorial brain – isolating it from its body.

The New York Times

Later I learned that the journalist whom the English-speaking world admired most in my era, columnist James 'Scotty' Reston of *The New York Times (NYT)*, had held the same opinion about who should be responsible for comment in the paper. The *NYT* is also a publisher's paper more than an editor's, despite its great leaders such as Executive Editor Reston.

The New York Times

LATE CITY EDITION

—NEW YORK, TUESDAY, MARCH 25, 1980—

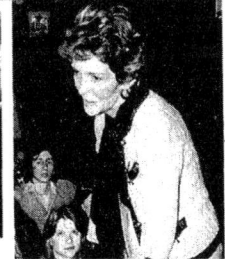

Salvador Archbishop Assassinated By Sniper While Officiating at Mass

Churchman Was Known as Outspoken Advocate of Justice and Rights

THE SHAH ARRIVES IN CAIRO AND ENTERS A MILITARY HOSPITAL

STAY PERMANENT, SADAT SAYS

Former Ruler Will Not Comment on His Plans — Some Egyptian Groups Voice Opposition

'Scotty' Reston's publisher was friendly, unassuming Arthur Ochs Sulzberger, known as 'Punch'. He invented the title 'Executive Editor' for its first incumbent of his era, Turner Catledge, who was given second-in-command of everything ... except the editorial (opinion) page.

'Punch' Sulzberger felt more of an owner and proprietor than his father Arthur Hays Sulzberg and his uncle Orvil Dryfoos had done in the past. They had married the daughters of Ochs who had owned the newspaper, and they felt diffident about exercising owner's privileges. On the other hand, 'Punch' was certain of his family and their proprietorial rights. He was determined enough about his 'difficult duty' and in the way he should use those rights. (He had begun on the bottom rung as a junior in departments throughout the paper.)

As chief executive, his division of command of the newspaper and its opinion pages effectively divorced the *NYT*'s dedication to 'pure news' from comment. But it also eliminated interpretation and sometimes contextualisation of the news. It unintentionally introduced a minor element of a major flaw demonstrated by news agencies whose range of coverage is, through lack of contextualisation or interpretation, sometimes of a bland conformity.

Reston was shocked at the way his newspaper had divorced its twin roles. He thought of joining his friend, Katherine Graham, on *The Washington Post* – she even offered him a share of stock. But he felt compulsive loyalty to *The New York Times*, though possibly this loyalty was rendered moot by the irony that Katherine Graham was going to hold onto the 'Punch' leader-writing system which Reston had objected to and which deprived the Executive Editor of full control.

In the event, both publishers proved more courageous than

any employed editor could be, and the system has worked with near-perfection – so far as editorial ethics and honest judgement and public service are involved – in these two exceptional and world-famous former family-run newspapers.

But the system is still deprecated by many of us. Our reason is that when editors of the Free World fail in their sole duty, which is to journalism and the public interest, they are easily fired. This cannot not happen in the case of an owner.

For clarity's sake, we need always to remember that an owner-editor is seen to represent, automatically, editorial independence. 'You know what you are getting'.

You should also know what you are getting from the *appointed* editor of the newspaper you read. The editor has the duty, according to free press ethics, to ensure he or she is able to act independently of the employer, and has the right to act freely and fairly. The editor should resign if or when this principle fails.

The Pentagon Papers

When I used to visit it, *The New York Times (NYT)* in Times Square, NY, was the best newspaper in the world. It is still the world's best, as far as I know, though like all newspapers and life itself, the *NYT* has changed.

Before stating my reasons for providing it with an unqualified superlative accolade let me declare my personal bias. In my youth I was informed that the most reliable newspaper on Earth was *The Times*, London. (We shall re-visit that view.)

But during my time as a reporter we used to read, daily, the superb analytical reports and opinion columns of Scotty Reston, who was simultaneously at that stage a deputy editor, political correspondent and (British-bred and trained) head of the *NYT's* Bureau in Washington. Our Argus Group in Africa had lifting rights on nearly all the *NYT's* material and we published regularly his articles covering world affairs, as well as Washington's issues.

Scotty Reston – despite his carping critics and his mistake in his declining years of believing nearly everything Henry Kissinger told him – was indeed the best, in the view of most journalists everywhere. He was fair. He was honest. He was trusted by his contacts, by his readers and by his newspaper colleagues ... until Kissinger successfully misled him over government policy on Vietnam.

His nearest rival as best journalist of his era (in my perspective) might have been Alistair Cooke of *The Manchester Guardian*, later the BBC in London, but his reports from America were more leisurely, infinitely less known or influential and, of necessity, more detached and unchallenged. Then there was my friend Harold Evans, courageous campaigning editor of the London *Sunday Times*, and later of *The Times*, before he clashed with new owner Rupert Murdoch ... but Evans was of a later generation (mine), and was cut down in his prime by Murdoch.

Reston was 'tops' as a specialist reporter as well as a commentator, despite being open to instant attack from the powerful men he criticised. He was thought by his rivals to be 'too close' to his contacts and too respectful of confidentiality – but it was he who persuaded *The New York Times* to publish a leaked copy of the US Military's Pentagon Papers – documents classified as 'military secrets'. It was a military report about the Vietnam war which threatened severe punitive (and political) retribution if revealed. The newspapers' exposés of these are to the eternal credit of 'Punch' Sulzberger and, later, Katherine Graham. In the cause of the public's interests, neither newspaper-owner flinched from backing their editors under intermittent and intense political pressure.

THE *NYT* HAS PUBLISHED daily, in disputatious eras from as far back as the American Civil War. It still bears scars from major editorial campaigns and from winning its unsurpassed 100-plus Pulitzer Prize Awards.

In 1851 the newspaper's founders had stated in their first issue: " ... we do not believe that everything in Society is either exactly right or exactly wrong; what is good we desire to preserve and improve; what is evil, to exterminate, or reform." Clearly, in recent times, they were out to reform or discourage the latest US president, Donald Trump.

Back in 1896 one of the United States' newspaper dynasties, the Ochs-Sulzberger family, took over the upmarket paper and was obviously happy with the founders' statement of policy. Today the newspaper, according to opinion surveys, is seen by 40% of the public to have a liberal slant and 11% believe it has a conservative slant. The owners will be happy with that too.

What particularly pleased me as a newsman was that some have claimed that the paper is pro-Palestinian and others have claimed that it is pro-Israel. A few earnest books have accused the Jewish-owned *New York Times* of being anti-Semitic!

That is the newspaper culture our Argus Group of newspapers used to aspire to ... newspapers that attract criticism from diametrically opposed sides. *The Star* in Johannesburg enjoyed such a position, in a grim sort of way, while operating in a hostile state in which apartheid MPs, under the safety of parliamentary privilege, called us communists (a heavily punishable crime in SA at the time) and the communists and other anonymous leftists called us apartheid racists. And in Cape Town *The Argus* and *The Cape Times* at that time were constantly criticised for being pro-Zionists – or pro-Islamists.

The Star enjoyed the direct relationship it had with *The New York Times,* so much so that we had our own office in their building off Times Square. For various reasons, I grew to know the *NYT's* inner workings and editorial systems fairly well, which led to my discovery of the best example of a great newspaper's unique culture. The *NYT's* Editorial Board met one day in 1980 for a precisely formal lunch in their dining room high in the building and I was, for some reason, their only guest as far as I could make out, as I was next to the host and there were no name cards ... which is the point of this reminiscence.

Instead there was a discreet card in front of each table placing, bearing a message of 30 or 40 words. The diners seemed familiar with it. During a momentary hush around the spacious table, I was able to read those words quickly. I wish I could tell you what they were, but I wouldn't anyway, even if I could remember them. It seemed to me the conjunction of those words belonged exclusively to *The New York Times*.

They were about belief, and service, and appreciation and other things that might make up a prayer. The words had all the elements of an 'old-fashioned', elegant, pre-meal grace; a rite long gone from daily business life. But the printed card at one's seating place carried no reference, or implied reference, concerning any god or any religion. All could enjoy the reminder of life's spiritual gifts and responsibilities; none need take offence.

There lay the culture of *The New York Times*: Offend the corrupt and the evil-doers, yes. But respect the beliefs – and non-beliefs – of every human being. Consider the widest view. Offer no needless offence. (It was one of the greatest qualities of Sulzberger and Reston and the changing editorial board, but in the view of many outside and envious journalists, it was their greatest weakness.)

That's how I interpreted the dining table message. Nobody present had any thought of discussing it ... or re-reading their newspaper's silent 'grace'. But the culture of honesty, fairness and excellence was represented around that table by the journalists present, whom others around the world might still recognise a whole generation later, because of the lustre of their bylines and reputations.

They were: Arthur Ochs Sulzberger, chairman and publisher. Charlotte Curtis, associate editor. Robert Curvin, member of the editorial board. Max Frankel, editor, Editorial Page. Mitchell Levitas, editor, *NYT* Week in Review. Karl Meyer, member of the editorial board. AM Rosenthal, executive editor. Seymour Topping, managing editor.

There was no way, however, that I was able, or wished, to emulate their subdued style during our editorial guest lunches at the Johannesburg *Star*. Ours were often argumentative occasions in the rooftop restaurant overlooking the city. Lunch-talk of contentious debate and wit was encouraged. Once, only once, it nearly got out of hand. A famous American black orator was our visiting guest, as were several local newspaper editors. Our over-worked chief guest (one of several black visitors technically illegally drinking a glass of wine on our premises in that apartheid era) was overcome with jetlag and ennui ... while a South African guest was holding forth at great length and criticising the USA, our American visitor quietly went to sleep, his head resting awkwardly on my shoulder. In this position it was not easy to end the luncheon debate, swiftly and as silently as possible. The *NYT* would not have approved. Nor did we on this unique and rowdy occasion.

Newspapering 'for the fun of it'

Now to assess the rest of the American press, beginning, at random, with the leader in newspaper-chain-building, Howard W Scripps, who took pride in the quality of newspapers he bought and helped upgrade.

He was the 13th child of a poor family who, at 24, started his own newspaper, the *Penny Press*, in Cleveland, Ohio. Soon he proved to be a genius in the newspaper industry, one who grasped the nature of its basic functions and who bought newspapers – then newspaper companies – 'for the fun of it'.

What he enjoyed most was to buy small newspapers that were losing money, and uplift them into his stable of successful community papers. In the end he had 23 newspapers – some of them big and influential – as well as his own news agency (which became *United Press International)* and his own features syndicate.

Scripps chose young men as editors and offered them 10% of stock in their own paper, with a loan from him if needed to buy that investment, and a blanket instruction to build profitable newspapers by honestly servicing their communities.

It was an early franchise system, with built-in standards. Editors were told "to make it harder for the rich to grow richer, and easier for the poor to keep from growing poorer".

For example, he told the young editor of his Houston, Texas, newspaper:

" ... Serve that class of people, and only that class of people from whom you cannot even hope to derive any other income than the one cent a day they pay for your newspaper." (In other words, advertising was a secondary objective that would follow success in the first.)

The first objective was: "Be honest and fearless ... Most men fear to speak the truth, the bold, bold truth. You must have no fear and embrace the truth," he told them. "Be diplomatic, but don't be too diplomatic ... It is rare indeed when ... a conscientious man can lose anything by fearless, frank speech and writing."

And rare indeed to find such an editorial-minded, multi-newspaper owner.

By 1960 the number of newspaper chains in the USA had reached 59, between them controlling 325 daily newspapers, accounting for about a third of the total newspaper circulation of the nation. However, while they benefited from franchise interchange and syndicated Washington columnists, chain proprietors were mainly interested in business, and advertising revenue, allowing it to reach 80% of income. Business managers started being promoted over editors. The papers became monotonous through the timid conformity of many of their editors.

On the other hand, the independent-minded ones who followed their own instincts and bucked the system, were rewarded – if they succeeded – and their efforts resulted in greater profit as well as quality.

SAMUEL NEWHOUSE built himself a newspaper chain that grew to be the most powerful in America, with a combined circulation of three-million and a monopoly in six major cities. He was in the business, not for fun, but for money. It was said that he was uninterested, and hopefully disinterested, in the editorial content of his newspapers for he never read them.

Instead, he read all their balance sheets, constantly. He travelled across most states of America to check personally his newspapers' accounts.

"He just treats newspapers like so many hardware stores," said a contemporary in the 1970s. "When he buys a good paper, it usually stays good. When he buys a bad one, it stays bad. He's interested only in the cash."

This allowed for a certain amount of local independence, but it meant that a powerful segregationist newspaper in the 'Deep South' could preach racism if this was popular with its readers at that time. If a northern paper supported integration, well, so be it. He left them all with one irreplaceable quality: independence.

In one of the few speeches he ever made, Sam Newhouse, or his full-time PR unit, said of his newspapers: "Their accents are from the far Northwest, the East and the South – accents from all regions of our land. But despite the differences in accents they are united in one common aim: the newspapers' dedication to the truth."

The truth about newspapers has, as usual, two sides. 'On the one hand' there is a lot to be said in favour of newspaper chains and their dispersed control of editorial opinion. 'On the other hand' there is much to criticise when the motive for selling news is primarily and exclusively to make money.

And there is *everything* to condemn in a paper when a publisher is interested mainly in personal power.

When 'Mr Integrity' talks ...

While the USA is undoubtedly the champion of freedom of the press, it is also fortunate that it has – as champion of print in the transitional period to a digitised communications world – one of the richest, most famous and most independent publishers on Earth. This might also apply to the new owner of *The Washington Post,* Jeff Bizos, but I am referring to Warren Buffet as the paragon of virtue.

Back in 2012, when independent newspapers around the world were beginning to panic at the prospect of digital websites grabbing their decreasing circulations, Warren Buffet started buying more newspapers.

He wrote the same letter to each of them. It read:

END OF THE DEADLINE

Warren Buffett of Berkshire Hathaway Inc. by Fortune.

"May 23, 2012. To the Publishers and Editors of Berkshire Hathaway's Daily Newspapers. "Until recently, Berkshire has owned only one daily newspaper, The Buffalo News, purchased in 1977."

[It was a pioneering newspaper almost 40 years ago. We at Johannesburg's *Star* visited his small newspaper in the 1980s to learn about their pioneering progress in the earliest days of conversion of editorial rooms from typewriters to computers.]

Buffet added: "Now Berkshire owns 26 dailies. I've loved newspapers all of my life – and always will. My dad, when attending the University of Nebraska, was editor of the Daily Nebraskan. I have copies of the papers he edited in 1924. He met my mother when she applied for a job as a reporter at the paper. Her father owned a small paper in West Point Nebraska and my mother worked at various jobs at the paper in her teens, even mastering the operation of a linotype machine. From as early as I can remember, my two sisters and I devoured the contents of the World-Herald that my father brought home every night.
"In Washington, DC, I delivered about 500,000 papers over a four-year period for the Post, Times-Herald and Evening Star. While in college at Lincoln, I worked fifteen hours a week in country circulation for the Lincoln Journal (earning all of 75 cents an hour). Today, I read five newspapers daily. Call me an addict.
"Berkshire buys for keeps. Our only exception to permanent ownership is when a business faces unending losses, a remote prospect for virtually all of our dailies. So let me express a few thoughts about what lies ahead as we join forces ... I believe newspapers that intensively cover their communities will have a good future ... You should treat public policy issues just as you have in the past. I have some strong political views, but Berkshire owns the paper – I don't. And Berkshire will always be non-political.

" ... I am sure my successors will follow the ideas I am laying out in this letter. (Indeed, letting them know of this hands-off principle is a secondary reason for my writing this letter.)

"You will determine your paper's destiny; outsiders will never dictate it.

"We must rethink the industry's initial response to the Internet. The original instinct of newspapers then was to offer free in digital form what they were charging for in print. This is an unsustainable model and certain of our papers are already making progress in moving to something that makes more sense.

"We want your best thinking as we work out the blend of digital and print that will attract both the audience and the revenue we need ...

"Times are certainly far tougher today than they used to be for newspapers. Circulation nationally will continue to slip and in some cases plunge.

But American papers have only failed when one or more of the following factors was present:

(1) The town or city had two or more competing dailies
(2) the paper lost its position as the primary source of information important to its readers or
(3) the town or city did not have a pervasive self-identity.

"We don't face those problems.

Indeed, the papers we own and are buying have been successful on both the journalistic and business fronts. They have earned the time, money and respect that subscribers allot them. I'm confident your paper will continue to do so.

I look forward to our future together."

Warren E Buffet

His letter spread hope to the free press around the world. Yet owners are aware that he was referring to special circumstances. Greater challenges face the printed press today.

Before we look at the future, let us look first at the price of true and constant independence, and at how *editorial* independence has been badly damaged in recent times by new owners of the press in many countries. ☐

21.
The man who saved South Africa's 'black' press.

> *If you sometimes get mad at me, because the sentiments I express keep you awake at night, then I am glad. I do not see why I should bear the brunt of insomnia worrying about what will happen tomorrow. If many of us can keep awake at night, then maybe we will do the sensible thing – talk together about our joint future.*
>
> Percy Qoboza

Percy Qoboza went to jail twice for no crime of any kind – unless trying to form a civic committee to save children and parents of Soweto after the 1976 riots was a crime.

Soon he owed much to the man who saved him ... the man who went on to save the black press from extinction in South Africa's apartheid era.

The Minister of Justice paused in his clamp-down on *The World*, but only when it was brought home to him the probable international outcry he would cause in the real world by arresting Percy, the editor, and his deputy on the newspaper.

The Minister of Justice backed off, and said the state merely wanted to question the editor about his role in the extraordinarily vital and administratively efficient 'Committee of Ten', a voluntary civic group which was trying to extricate its bruised and angry community from its chaos.

Percy's brief detention without trial – without any charge ever mentioned – raised the South African temperature a few more dangerous degrees. It was an anger not merely prompted by the fear that if he could be summarily locked up and interrogated, so could we all. It meant a great deal more than that.

Layton Slater, the quiet, behind-the-scenes chairman of Argus newspapers, fired off a hand-delivered protest to the Minister of Justice "registering the strongest possible protest at the treatment

213

meted out to the editor of *The World*". He told the Minister that "Mr Qoboza is a courageous editor who nevertheless seeks peaceful solutions to this country's problems." Slater prophesied dire international retribution should the editor not be released.

Percy, and our colleague, Aggrey Klaaste, were released within 18 hours. Percy remained as urbane and philosophic as ever.

It was in this philosophic period of his life that he and I became close friends. At that time South African law forbade inter-race mixing, to a degree that a white and black man having a beer together was technically illegal. (There were also crazy laws disallowing professionals – white and black doctors, or lawyers and newsmen for instance – socialising with each other. But these decrees seldom worked in practice.)

Nonetheless we felt more free when we visited Ian Smith's "Rhodesia"; free enough for Percy and I to face what we both thought was certain death in a motor car when we set out to examine the Operational Area of the bush war raging at that time. Our white colleague who was driving suddenly collapsed and momentarily lost consciousness, causing our vehicle to go out of control. We were about to crash at full speed into the back of a stationary army truck, when Percy had the presence of mind to lie down on the front passenger seat and simultaneously jerk the steering wheel around. The vehicle swerved sharply again, causing only half of the top of the car to be sheared off as it smashed into the back of the truck. We crawled out of the wreck, covered in shattered glass and shards of metal, but hardly scratched. The unconscious driver and his side of the vehicle were untouched.

"It took the brains of a black man to save our lives," said Percy after a very long silence.

"You've gone grey," I pointed out. "In fact you were nearly turning white when it happened."

"Just disguise," said Percy, "I thought you white boys were out to kill a kaffir."

We always talked like that, though in formal terms I was a decade older than he, with a great deal of professional seniority. He loved to shock white men with startlingly racial comments. And I enjoyed watching his baiting, then privately pulling his leg after he strutted his blackness before astounded visitors in those dark days of apartheid.

I mention all this to show why I am able to assert that Percy was an independent-minded journalist who, as editor, would act independently of anyone, including Slater, the silent, caring boss of Argus Newspapers.

One grows tired of reading new 'history' referring to people like Qoboza and Aggrey Klaaste being 'curtailed' by white management when, in fact, their papers were supported in most cases by efficient management, just as whitey editors were. One tires, too, of reading that these journalists avoided politics in order to please their masters. It simply was not so.

In fact, back in those days, we were not only supported by management, but Layton Slater, always the unknown name behind the scenes, also assumed major personal risks in providing black journalists with salaries even when, for political reasons, they found themselves out of work. It happened, for instance in the case of one reporter who was banned, but not before he joined a strike against his own paper, and saw the newspaper being closed down by the government as the result of the prolonged strike.

A manager asked: "How long will we go on paying a man a salary after four years and nine months – three times as long as the employee actually worked for us and libelled us? Where does it stop?"

"Yes, but where does compassion stop?" someone quipped.

When the counter question was put, the manager pointed out defensively: "If the true facts were known, it will be found that the company's compassion and generosity is without parallel in labour relations, not only in South Africa, but abroad as well. We have more than discharged our legal obligations and we have also met totally our moral obligations in this case."

Perhaps ... but they would go on paying, because Layton Slater's policy, laid down the principle that 'every member of our staff is innocent until proved guilty'.

THE WORLD'S ROOTS went right back to 1903 with the launch of *Ilanga lase Natal* (The Natal Sun) by one of the future founders of the ANC, John Langalibalele Dube. Thirty years later the Argus Company bought it from a new white owner and in 1950 named it *The World*.

"Why?" I asked at the time as a reporter working in Durban, Natal Province.

"Because we are losing readers to English-language competitors – and because we have legal problems we don't even understand in Zulu editions".

In 1974, as *The World* was reaching its 25th anniversary, Percy Qoboza became editor of the paper which was now publishing in English in Johannesburg and competing directly with *Drum* and *Golden City Post*. Two years later he was arrested and spent his first day and night in jail. Two years after that he saw *The World* closed down by edict again during a national panic by the government in mid-October 1978, when numbers of political and other organisations were also banned.

"*Sign of* [Government] *Failure*" I headlined the first of the occasional front-page 'leader' columns which *The Star* went on to publish in times of crisis or cases of appalling injustice.

Despite prolonged protesting by newsmen and newspapers for the second time after mass closures, Percy was locked up for six months ... and came out as seemingly unruffled as ever. But *The World* was banned; 'forever'.

AND SO WE CAME to the moment when Layton Slater stepped to the fore. All staff of *The World* – not only the journalists who were a small minority in *The World*'s publishing building –but the entire complement of the newspaper's staff would be paid full salaries until a solution was found, he said.

This time *The World* was gone for good, but Slater's pledge to pay salaries held firm. It took two years of financial loss – affecting also *The Star's* fortunes – before a way around the autocratic government's policy could be found. Rescue came through an obscure newspaper title, unused but still registered, named *The Post*.

The World re-appeared as the same paper under that unfamiliar, different name. (It was a manoeuvre, strangely reminiscent of *The Star* in its early days a hundred years earlier – when it was blotted out by Kruger's government in the 1800s, only to return in days, blazing as the *Comet* until the real paper reappeared soon afterwards.)

But a relentless apartheid government was not to be defied in the 20th century. Soweto's *Post* of 1978 was closed down again forever by official decree in 1980 ... and all its staff were suddenly out of work on full pay again.

The game was nearly up, in the face of a limitless crisis of non-production ... until someone in a small office on the top floor of *The Star*, arrived with a file about an inoperative little weekly paper named *The Sowetan*.

The Bantu World founded in 1932, a forerunner of the paper Percy Qoboza transformed that was banned in 1978.

Dr Aggrey Klaaste. Photo courtesy of the Sowetan.

"It isn't much of a title, and in name only it seems restricted to one giant suburb instead of being a national emblem ... but we're alive again as a national newspaper," the newspaper's staff was told when all its employees had been rounded up.

Percy began the battle of rebuilding the paper, but soon left. Joe Latakgomo, a senior journalist with about 15 years on the thrice-named modern newspaper, took his place, but moved to *The Star* after receiving death threats. Then Aggrey Klaaste took hold of *The Sowetan* and adopted a proclaimed policy of caring for the people of Soweto – and all their kin for hundreds of kilometres beyond.

The paper went bounding upwards. Aggrey told me that he had remembered several of *The Star*'s many efforts at community-building and followed suit, quietly and firmly, with his campaign called Nation Building. It held more significance than any we had attempted, and on a greater scale. Soon *The Sowetan* leapt over local and tribal prejudice and even racial prejudice as the nation shifted sporadically into democracy. Both Percy and Aggrey died young, but both knew they had done enough to win their personal battles.

They must have relished the memory that Dr Nthato Motlana, widely-known physician and anti-apartheid activist, and chairman of the historic Soweto 'Committee of Ten', (put together in the editorial offices of *The World- Post- Sowetan*) remained their active supporter.

All this is well-remembered. What is forgotten is that the hero of *The World's* struggle was the late Layton Slater, general manager of the Argus Group. It was he who almost single-handedly, behind the scenes, and in spite of constantly tense financial threats, won the war ... the state's open and physical war against *The World* and its phoenix-like journalism. Layton Slater had the faith and the courage to continue to pay for *all* newspaper staff in all departments as well as the expenses of sustaining the paper and its property while it was legally inoperable.

It was a memorable time when you were paid your full salary not to come to work until you might be needed at some unknown time in the future.

Today *The Sowetan* is one of the largest national newspapers in South Africa and has already adopted its fifth shape since its birth in KwaZulu-Natal – that of a 21st-century online newspaper often criticising the corruption of the nation's recent leader, President Zuma. □

22. The price of true and constant independence.

Most people sell their souls, and live with a good conscience on the proceedings.

Logan Pearsall Smith, 1940s

Editorial independence in a big, established newspaper is an unwavering ideal. In practice it is a mission sought by most journalists – but for obvious reasons rejected by many proprietors.

Given the driving compulsions of money and power, the concept of editorial independence sounds unconvincingly idealistic. Yet editorial independence can and does exist in some of the most respected papers across five continents.

It exists where some proprietors respect truth and published press values ... and where newspaper women and men – and readers – demand nothing less. Even then, it can exist only where newspapers operate at a practical profit – without allowing profit (or any proprietor's interest in potential power) ever to be the prime publishing motive.

Editorial independence was surprisingly strong in the USA and Canada when I personally witnessed it in the 1980s, in dozens of newspapers from Miami to Toronto and from Vancouver to Buffalo and Boston. And there existed many declared policies of press groups that guaranteed it, as I noted in the previous chapter.

It also exists in a number of long-established, usually family-owned, newspapers in Britain, away from London where *The Manchester Guardian* long ago set a standard that continues today in its international editions.

Editorial independence, as demonstrated in the previous chapter, is very difficult to define, but it seems to have survived the hiccup at *The Times* – London's great paper founded by editors, not entrepreneurs – and protected by family and trusts for much of its first 200 years. Its editorial independence was still intact in 1961, when I was able to ascertain within *The Times* the existence of this ephemeral quality. It was temporarily lost, of course, when Murdoch gripped *The Times* too tightly.

The Times experience showed that independent editors of

newspapers could survive only where real trust or a clearly written, bilateral declaration between management and an editor exists – together with a strong will on both sides to enforce it. A legal financial trust may not be good enough.

Editorial independence seems to last only where a newspaper is owned by its editors, of course, but more significantly, where it has ethically dedicated proprietors, such as Katherine Graham of *The Washington Post,* who was prepared to take legal responsibility for every move her editors made whenever freedom of information was at stake in America. She supported the judgements of her editors – even when these threatened the very existence of her family's newspaper.

The New York Times has had, so far as I am aware, an impeccable record of editor/proprietor accountability and independence through almost all of its history. So too, with its policy of even-handed reportage ... except in wartime and on issues where it is campaigning for truth. The most recent example of this was its coverage of the Donald Trump presidential campaign, where truth, in the eyes of much of the world, was an interestingly entertaining mobile feast.

Yet, even editorially independent newspapers who build their reputations almost *solely* on campaigning in favour of their definitions of truth must inevitably be seen as one-eyed by readers who can see both sides of a disputed issue. Only in extreme times, or in the face of populists such as President Trump, should a one-sided press be seen as a saving grace.

Another element required for stable, long-term editorial independence seems to be that the newspaper must be a serious one, carrying sufficient *gravitas* to fend off political and other predators. By 'serious', I mean one which readers can take seriously, i.e. a major daily or weekly that boasts deep roots in its society and regards itself accountable only to its readers and its reputation for fairness and established journalistic ethics. *The New York Times* is a prime example.

The ideal of editorial (not proprietorial) independence should never be confused with newspaper claims of being 'independent of all political parties', a status which often turns out to be a convenience rather than a conviction.

Reaching for the stars

The most effective way I can describe this finely balanced complex of sensitive conditions is to resort, once again, to my own experience of a once truly editorially independent daily which I had the good fortune to serve during my last 20 years as a full-time journalist.

Its first 125 years of history affirm the fact that editorial independence is a culture that was deeply distilled; despite constant threat from within, as well as from outside racist autocrats. It required century-long devotion to independent speech and freedom of information that had to be actively maintained, with conviction, against all odds every day.

Johannesburg's *Star* – possibly because of the conviction born at its birth and carried in its DNA – was a newspaper which was forced to survive probably more threats to its existence and more crises over its first 100 years than any other in the world.

That is an astonishing claim when you think of the editors of *La Prensa* murdered by an Argentinean regime; the switch-back political roles of the newspapers of Bogotá bent on survival at all costs; the lives sacrificed by so many journalists in the world persevering in their independent reporting across the globe, and the forced closure of newspapers in Hitler's Germany as well as in Italy, Greece, Spain, Russia and Cuba – wherever they challenged tyranny.

Yet the unchallenged, unqualified facts about the Johannesburg *Star*'s perilous history speak for themselves. So do its actions. Except for a sad period of lapses between the two World Wars, almost every major challenge the newspaper faced arose from the paper's unquestioning belief that editorial independence was the foundation stone of proper journalism. Here is the story:

(Heart) Breaking News

In its first 20 years in the Transvaal, *The Star* was burnt down twice; closed down; attacked by armed mobs and later occupied by 'enemy' troops and shut down during 20 months of the Anglo-Boer War.

In the 50 years of apartheid some of its staff were imprisoned, and some were assaulted. Two cameramen over the years were shot and killed. Many of its staff were arrested and some held in jail without trial. A few were seriously threatened with death. For three years the newspaper endured, together with all the South African press, successive decrees of Emergency Regulations; most aimed – unsuccessfully – at total censorship.

The story of this historic newspaper began with its humble founders, Tom and George Sheffield.

George borrowed money and bought a printing press and Tom devoted his life to being editor, sub-editor, reporter and text-reader. They launched the *Eastern Star* on the first day of 1871 in the face of much press competition among the 1820 Settlers of Grahamstown in the eastern part of the Cape colony before South Africa was born.

They lived on the smell of printers' ink for 15 years until, in desperation during yet another economic depression; they hauled their press by train to Kimberley and by ox-wagon, fording the great Vaal River and trekking 300 miles through the veld of the Transvaal *Republiek* to where the world's biggest gold-rush was in progress. They were interested in newspapers, not gold, but they had arrived in a mining camp with many foreigners, no official name, no post office and no recognised streets.

Yet the two men survived; re-launching their paper in 1887 when the first buildings were given numbers ... and possibly was the first metro newspaper in the world to exist before its nascent city streets did.

Tom Sheffield told his potential readers that the paper would be "loyal" to the laws of the land, but "not subservient" to President Kruger's State, for which the paper would "advocate reforms in the interest of all".

Soon the *Eastern Star* was fending off no less than six rival papers on the goldfields. The paper was saved by a man riding a horse (possibly white) who persuaded the Sheffield brothers to join in creating a newspaper *company* with large numbers of shareholders in Cape Town and London as well as in the Transvaal *Republiek*.

The visitor, a Cape newspaper owner, had ridden north to set up a goldfields paper of his own, but instantly changed his plans; joined up with the Sheffields' paper (the biggest in the mining camp) and registered the *Argus* Company in Cape Town, where his paper – and company law – were defined and stable. Then the 'man on the white horse', who had ridden a thousand and more miles over barren veld, took over control and editorship of the newspaper in 1890, dropping the word *Eastern* from *The Star*'s name and, ensuring the paper's editorial independence he recruited only fiercely independent editors from the world-class newspapers of the day.

Who was this paragon?

As a young school teacher from Leicester in England, Francis

Joseph Dormer, had sailed to Cape Town to take up a senior educational post – but instead became a freelance war correspondent whose frank despatches on Lord Chelmsford's sensational *defeat* by the powerful Zulus (pitting spears against guns at Isandlwana in 1879) had so impressed the *Cape Argus* that they enlisted him as a copy-editor. He was soon editor of *The Argus,* and – with finance from an acquaintance, Cecil Rhodes, whom he had met at sea on his way to the Cape – he bought the newspaper, and announced *The Argus*'s policy as: "... in every respect independent and, we trust, impartial ... public interests will alone be kept in view. It will be the mouthpiece of no party ... (nor) any individual playing his part on the political stage".

The latter statement was aimed at Rhodes, his press sponsor, with whom he soon fell out – fortunately once more for independent journalism. Dormer fought even his own Argus Board to prevent Rhodes placing one of his "lackeys", as Dormer described him, in a senior editorial post.

Instead Dormer tolerated an Irish editor who not only caused *The Star*'s temporary closure by the State, but also a riot by a mob intent on burning the place down.

During Dormer's own editorship, *The Star* modelled itself on *The Times* in London and soon *The Star* was able to provide *The Times* with an editor from its own Johannesburg staff and later an editor-in-chief (who, as I mentioned earlier, became known in London before WWII as "Dawson of *The Times*", and its first editor to find it necessary to resign from that still august newspaper on the principle of editorial independence).

In the modern era, *The Star's* shareholding was held mainly within the financial houses of the biggest mining groups whose nominated representatives on the Argus Board were there on the understanding that they might intervene in any of the newspaper's affairs *only* if it failed constantly to pay its own way.

Financial independence is, in any case, obligatory for any publication claiming independence of its editorial content. There are no exceptions.

EACH CHALLENGE for *The Star* in its war in defence of the delicate, ever vulnerable balance of independence is a long story, but I shall try to sketch the historic challenges in a few lines:

1890 *The Star* burnt down, attracting thousands of people to the blaze. Its new editor-owner Francis Dormer miraculously found alternative presses over the weekend, published reports of his own paper's destruction, and an editorial which said: *"With the intelligence which never fails to animate a crowd at a fire – zealous volunteers began to throw the mirrors and crockery into the street from the first floor window to prevent them from burning."*

1892 The newspaper was attacked and damaged by a raging mob because its acting editor, an Irishman named RJ Pakeman, was seen to be belittling in his editorial one of Queen Victoria's sons who happened to die within days of this criticism made in faraway South Africa. Suspecting that gold diggers and prospectors from around the world, even when liquor-inflamed, would never display such emotion over a distant sovereign's sensibilities, Dormer wrote a biting editorial to inquire whether the mob attack was not "instigated by vulgar trade jealousy" of half a dozen rival newspapers?

But he did not fire acting editor Pakeman.

1897 A cartoon in *The Star* that raised the ire of the Transvaal's President Paul Kruger led to the paper being forcibly shut down by his police. The paper immediately re-opened as *The Comet,* but a week later the paper was able to win a court judgement ruling the president's act unconstitutional. Pakeman was the one who had approved the cartoon for publishing – and was probably praised, in hindsight, by the absent editor-in-chief.

1913 Thousands of rioting white miners marched on Johannesburg, burnt down the railway station, killed a cameraman and a black bystander, and tried to set fire to *The Star*. Armed staff fended them off. The strikers were protesting at the job promotion of black mineworkers; a cause which the newspaper supported.

1922 A 'Bolshevik' racist white labour strike was launched on the town. One of its prime targets was *The Star*. The paper's own staff were issued with rifles and called upon to defend lives, while two reporters filed the story of aerial bombing, tank warfare in the streets and ground battles in the central city. They did so by simply standing on the newspaper building's roof to observe what turned out to be the biggest case of civil unrest ever recorded within South Africa's current borders.

The combined efforts of the army, police and air force were called into the city to put down the 'Red' anti-black miners' strike.

1939 *The Star* resorted to skeleton staffing in the war years as its journalists and printers signed up to fight Hitler in North Africa and Europe. The paper received numbers of threats from local, militant Nazi sympathisers.

1977 Closure of *The World* newspaper, leading to a prolonged struggle by its sister paper, *The Star* to save the beleaguered 'Black' press. (Described in the previous chapter.)

For almost half a century – from the year apartheid took over South Africa in **1948**, until President de Klerk made peace with President Mandela in **1994** – *The Star* resisted threats of closure and fought against 98 laws that were promulgated to curb free speech or bypass the courts. With other newspapers it circumvented three waves of 'Emergency Regulations' aiming for total censorship, and opposed apartheid on a daily basis for all those years.

None of the above experiences proves the existence of editorial independence within *The Star*, except by inference of its willingness to stand up for justice rather than mere profit. But there are other historic indications of genuine editorial independence, expressed in written statements and historic actions.

However, *The Star* in the 21st century has lost its independence; lost its exclusive international news sources, lost two-thirds of its circulation and cosmopolitan readership, and lost its international reputation as a leading newspaper. None of that is the fault of its journalists. It has been caused in times of peace by successive 21st-century owners abusing or commandeering the paper's resources.

There is another admonitory tale of this newspaper's past that needs to be told before examining its lack of independence in its new stable of owners of 'Independent Newspapers'. ☐

* Early history of the afternoon newspaper is recorded in *Today's News Today*, by Eric Rosenthal and L.E. Neame, 1956.

23.
Beware the disguised enemy within.

But man, proud man
Drest in a little brief authority ...
Plays such fantastic tricks before high heaven,
As make the angels weep.

Shakespeare's 'Measure for Measure'

The most effective way I can illustrate the finely balanced complex of sensitive conditions that make up the rare embrace of *editorial independence* is to tell you how my newspaper silently lost some of it for a period of nearly 20 years.

In the hundred years between 1887 and 1997 *The Star* was edited independently by 19 editors, each averaging about three years at the helm (all but two of them, I and another, who together spent 40 years in the chair). It was the culture of its founder and first editor, Dormer, which future editors so insistently inculcated over the years to maintain a seemingly constant editorial independence.

A fine example was WF Monypenny, recruited from *The Times* in London to be editor of *The Star* in Johannesburg. He soon became the sole and total opposition to the gold-mining industry's proposal to replace African labour with even cheaper labour imported from China. As editor he campaigned strongly on this issue, without support of, and to the discomfort of, his employers and most of his readers. *The Star* reported all relevant information on the "cheap labour" issue – and the editor criticised the mine-owners' proposal repeatedly in his editorials – despite the fact that mining interests held most shares and were a majority on the Argus Co. board, chaired by his CEO, Dormer.

Dormer never once intervened in Monypenny's campaign. When the mining industry went ahead with its short-lived plan, Monypenny resigned from *The Star* – after printing his protests again (and an open letter of appreciation of the tolerance of Dormer's Argus Board) – and set off, with a presentation company gold watch, to walk the length of Africa. He arrived in Cairo in tatters. His inscribed gold watch established his identity in Cairo and helped him reach London where he took up a senior position again on *The Times*.

Chinese labour was not imported to the mines. The issue – and victory – once more reinforced palpably the newspaper company's culture of editorial independence. Yet even this was not, in the long run, sufficient to maintain such a vulnerable culture.

The darker side

There were periods between the two World Wars and immediate post-war years, when the ideal of editorial independence corrupted and almost died in Argus Printing & Publishing Company's newspapers. It came when a newly elected board chairman dominated the newspaper managers – and later, when powerful managers dominated the editors and the passive company boards.

A balanced history illustrates not only how hard it is to achieve *editorial* independence – but how easily it is lost.

The period between the two World Wars saw conditions and personalities in The Argus newspaper group change – with managers taking full control. It led to a number of newspaper acquisitions which established the power of Argus papers – but it also led to the worst in the Argus Company's history to that point, and it damaged their newspapers' reputations.

Change for the sake of acquisition – with worse consequences – came in the shape of John Martin, a brash, footloose young Scotsman who, at the age of 23, sent the company a merited criticism of *The Star's* unwarranted dedication to the ultra-conservative page layouts of *The Times* in London. He sent his criticisms, not to the editor, but to management; apparently in the hopes of being hired.

At 25 Martin was manager of a short-lived small newspaper named the *Bloemfontein Post*, but soon returned to Britain from where he again sent a report to Argus management on the efficacy of the Argus Company's editorial office at 85 Fleet Street. In the wartime years of 1914-18, all offices were short-staffed, so he was granted the temporary post of managing the journalists in London whom he had criticised. He impressed Head Office so much that he was invited to return to South Africa and, by the age of 31, became General Manager of the company!

Martin was an extraordinary entrepreneur. Virtually single-handedly, he coaxed or browbeat rivals owning five different newspapers to sell them to the Argus Group at 'bargain prices'. The 'bargain-priced' additions were the *Natal Advertiser*, which he grew into the *Natal Daily News* and *Sunday Tribune; The Friend* in Bloemfontein; the *Diamond Fields Advertiser* in Kimberley and the *Pretoria News*. He even bought a newspaper in Mozambique, partly because it was of interest to the gold-mines, but sold it because it lost money. He also saved *The Argus* newspaper in Cape Town from mismanagement and penury.

Soon he was not only head of the Argus Group, but through his company board's connections and other interests, became chairman of Rand Mines and other mining posts – a situation that should have been publicly condemned as intolerable.

By 1938, however, he was also chairman of the South African Chamber of Mines and, soon, an important personage within the Bank of England.

From London he sent advice, or rather instructions to Argus editors. One instruction was that editors should *ignore* news from the rest of the world about the future King Edward VIII's romance with a divorced woman and a likely abdication from the throne. South Africa should accept the regal censorship of the matter, simply because this censorship existed in Britain.

Argus's London Office had no option but to accept his order, telegraphed as 'advice' ... but so did all Argus newspapers apparently, much to their shame afterwards.

Then Martin sent another long, self-important, inside-knowledge instruction: Editors need to be very careful about discussing the issue of whether Britain might go to war with Hitler. Speculation might upset things and cause unwarranted difficulties as Prime Minister Chamberlain negotiated with Herr Hitler.

One editor, ex-Advocate Dominic McCausland of *The Argus*, wrote two telling and richly informed leaders on the subject: one on 24 September 1938 (a year before inevitable outbreak of war) correctly predicting that "the only thing that can now prevent the forcible Nazi seizure of Czech territory is the surrender of the new Czech government to the Chamberlain plan."

McCausland, who had been a well-known barrister in Cape Town (and a leader-writer for *The Argus*) before accepting the offer of editorship, was forced to resign. The incident caused considerable publicity overseas. Martin got out of it by ensuring McCausland departed on the most generous terms possible. CEO Martin did more than make a mistake and insist on an unjust firing. He damaged a healthy editorial culture in his organisation that had lasted for 40 years and would not recuperate for another generation.

A second editor of *The Argus* newspaper was dismissed in the 1950s, unfairly, I believe, by one of Martin's 'gang' of managerial followers.

The victim was Morris Broughton, an erudite British journalist well-known for his South African weekly broadcasts summing up events of War World II, whom I identified in a previous book* as "personifying the values of independent mainstream newspapers".

During Prime Minister Verwoerd's emotional referendum seeking to dump British connections and take South Africa out of the Commonwealth, Broughton had chosen to champion the Afrikaner (but *not* the apartheid Nationalist government) for seeking independence of the British Crown.

His arguments showed deep understanding of a people "who have never enjoyed the security of together governing their own country". However, racism and injustice clouded the political constitutional issue and, when Verwoerd won his anti-British Republican referendum, Broughton was ready, after anxious visits from Head Office, to 'retire early'. He moved gratefully to Spain, retaining even his office car. The banishment was unjust, even if his judgement was considered by his employers and English-speaking 'racists' as wrong, but – regardless of the irrelevant issue – his assisted early departure to Elysian fields was a fate some of us often came to envy in the extremist apartheid years.

Argus Head Office lost face, yet failed unfortunately to shed itself of arrogance for many years. It took nearly two decades for the principle of editorial independence to be reintroduced and reinforced again.

It was only when Layton Slater, one of the company's administrative staff, took the helm in the 1960s that pride was restored to the editorial departments of half a dozen newspapers. And editorial independence was restored, thrice over, in Slater's statement of policy. Total editorial independence lasted right through the apartheid era. The more the apartheid government threatened the English-language press, the more onerous became the responsibility of the company's independent newspaper editors.

When courage wavers …

Fortunately, throughout its existence, the management of the Argus Company was recruited *mainly* from the ranks of journalism. But my faith in this practice was shaken when the sudden death on duty of my friend and editor, John Jordi, left me suddenly as the un-appointed Acting Editor of *The Star*.

The company's General Manager, who was once many years before a copy editor on our newspaper, phoned me one day. I knew him to be as cold, unbending and as uncommunicative as a rod of steel.

"I have to tell you that I thought the political cartoon you published today was in bad taste," he said.

I thanked him for his interest and put down the phone before he could suggest a remedy. Nothing untoward occurred during the drawn-out months while *The Star* awaited the CEO's announcement of its new editor. When, months after it turned out to be me, I received another call at the editor's desk from the managing director of the company. He had a complaint about editorial content in *The Star*.

"Thank you for your view," I said in long-rehearsed, long-remembered words. "I assume you are expressing your views as a reader, not as an employed MD and executive member of the Board. I shall take your views into account as we do with all readers ..." then slowly put down the phone.

I had not heard the start of his telephonic response, but to guard against any wavering independence, I told my deputy – a former newspaper editor of great talent and intense ambition: "Please remind me: if I ever receive one more call from Head Office like that, I shall resign."

It was one way of abiding by the principle we sought.

Elsewhere in this and a previous book* I have listed several other editorial decisions which entailed risk to the entire newspaper group and which might have been vetoed if ever put to a company board to consider – but which on the editor's judgement alone was accepted by the Managing Director, Layton Slater, and his management team. The risk of immense legal costs and possible imprisonment being the least of their worries. There is a much longer, very thin line – which my predecessor John Jordi once mused – might easily be crossed. It could lead to sinking the flagship, possibly other newspapers in the Group, and the loss of *several thousand* industrial and editorial jobs – possibly even the majority of the newspapers making up the 'Opposition Press'.

Guaranteeing an ideal in writing

The first concrete evidence of our newspapers' commitment to editorial independence when I was appointed to the post, was the 'Acceptance of Editor's Appointment' letter I was called upon to sign. Its terms were as enlightened as one could wish them to be, reminiscent of – but more relevant and more precise – than Dormer's statement as editor of *The Argus* newspaper a century previously.

Slater's letter of appointment – back in the 'modern times' of the 1970s and applying I assume to editors of all colours and cultures – stipulated only that the editor should abide by the following code:

"To place South Africa's advancement and well-being before all else. To this end to adhere to independent, honest and responsible standards of journalism that do not pander to personal or sectional interests but are concerned solely with the public interest.

"To further the cause of racial cooperation and pursue a balanced policy calculated to enhance the welfare and progress of all sections of the population.

"To ensure that no one interest is served or policy followed, to the detriment of others."

Could one ask for more?

Well, yes, because many years later when Hal Miller became MD and proposed a revision of the Company's 'mission statement', ('mission statements' were suddenly popular in 'big business' at that time), he arranged what he called a 'thunk' session involving all editors and managers across the country. It required consideration of a statement that read "... the company will produce newspapers of the best possible quality in order to ensure good profits ..."

The accepted version, after serious debate among newspaper managers and editors, was directly opposite and affirmed: "... the company will *make profits in order to produce newspapers of the best possible quality.*"

This revised emphasis became the morale-building golden rule of independent journalism for at least a decade. But when Harry Oppenheimer of Anglo-American Corp sold Argus Newspapers after the collapse of apartheid, many of the company's declared ethics disappeared, and its former mission statement became a Holy Grail which turned into mythology the moment new owners touched it.

Suddenly an ambitious new manager on *The Star* named John Featherstone, tried to assume power – in the name of improving company profits – by proposing that the editor report to an unspecified 'publisher'.

Editor-in-chief, Richard Steyn, immediately resigned in protest. It was a major self-sacrifice made purely on principle.

But the sorry fate of *The Star* is another story, to be told after we have met much bigger destroyers of editorial independence in the world's free press. □

* *Editors Under Fire*, Harvey Tyson (Random House, 1993).

24.
Murdoch the mighty media manager ... Mmmm.

... it was the worst of times ...

Charles Dickens

Rupert Murdoch makes all the other famous and infamous press barons of the past and the present look like pygmies. By any standards and in his own right, and without any recognised official title or office, he was one of the most powerful men in the Western world in the early 21st century.

His chameleon-like media forces, both press and TV, still operate mainly within three English-language political cultures, American, British and Australasian – and also cooperate easily with the authoritarian censorship inside present-day China. His only rival and direct threat has been the worldwide web which his organisations have infiltrated – but failed fortunately to exploit very profitably; let alone dominate worldwide.

The secret of his power lay within the man himself: a mixture of cunning and courage; and a social style not pretty to observe. Yet how else could anyone achieve what he did in creating Fox TV, a fourth nationwide network in the USA when legal statutes specifically forbade its form; where his funds were pitifully inadequate and where no foreigner was allowed to operate?

It was a deft, questionable miracle of dubious financial and political manipulation, brought off by a single individual who believed nothing was impossible ... if one brushed aside tiresome legalities and found and pressed the right buttons.

Murdoch used the same manipulative political tactics in his take-over of more TV stations in Britain, and in acquiring ownership of *The Times* whose editorial independence was thought to be protected from a full-scale take-over by an established Trust and a Westminster statute.

Many see his astonishing coups as a matter of 'doing business', but there is no doubt that they also involve manipulating power by playing politics, and have caused considerable harm to the proper role and ethics of journalism in newspapers and TV. (Journalism's role in society is the very antithesis of 'doing business' – as it ought to be of 'playing – instead of reporting on– politics'. In a democracy the free press is supposed to be the watchdog and live outside the comfort or goings-on in the main house.)

Murdoch has been the subject of hagiographies as well as heavy criticism. One of the latter is investigative journalist Bruce Page's *The Murdoch Archipelago* containing nearly 600 pages of fact and analysis. It concludes that from the beginning, Murdoch the ex-newspaperman, practised the very opposite of what journalism, or rather independent journalism, stands for.

For instance, John Thadeus Delane, editor of *The Times,* back in 1851, proclaimed that "the Press lives by exposure", while Murdoch in the late 20th century was said to live by 'cover-up'. He engineered political tricks in which he or his newspapers had information, but stayed silent in his interests.

Investigative author Bruce Page quotes several instances, beginning with the downfall of Labour's powerful Prime Minister, Gough Whitlam, in Australia where information – including big news – was suppressed. And in Britain, where Murdoch's relationship with British PM Blair involved the use of News Corp's avid attempts to influence public electoral support at all levels of society, but especially the voters usually supporting the Labour Party.

EARLIER, WHEN MURDOCH bought New York's oldest and ailing newspaper, *The New York Post,* and rebuilt its influence and circulation on sleaze, the respected, independent *Columbia Journalism Review*, called it "a social problem; a force for evil".

Murdoch ignored this wounding criticism and claimed that his *Post*'s success in mobilising the workers' vote had put Mayor Koch into power. Koch dutifully agreed, mollifying his benefactor by saying: "You are the real mayor."

Gratified, Murdoch moved on to buy *The Sun* in London and re-launch it with a stridently patriotic voice and a touch of soft porn. Media commentator Raymond Snoddy said, not altogether inaccurately in 1990, that *The Sun* had become "a bigoted, foul-mouth fantasy factory".

Murdoch, however, was more interested in *The Sun*'s allegiance from Labour to Conservative, he claimed that he had won the 1992 British election and made Margaret Thatcher prime minister. It was an over-claim – and not just because in reality newspapers seem unable to change individual political opinions on such a scale. Yet the perception remains. Soon the entire Conservative Cabinet felt it necessary to pay visits to the print factory of *News of the World* and *The Sun*.

The new newspaper owner sought, and was granted by the new government, what he craved most: Britain's TV satellite rights, and permission to launch Sky TV. He felt he had earned these rewards, for he and ex-*Daily Mirror* man Larry Lamb, whom he hired to edit *The Sun*, had bombarded the tabloid's Labour-leaning readership with political pro-Tory propaganda.

The campaigning *Sun* saved for the eve of the election its most powerful and persuasive weapon – the famous bare-breasted 'Page Three Girl'. The daily dish of semi-nudity failed to appear on Election

Day. In her place was a 58-year-old, fat lady in her full underwear, putting her threatening hand on her bra strap. The caption shouted: HERE'S WHAT YOU WILL GET ON PAGE THREE WITH KINNOCK (Labour's leader).

Brash and tasteless as ever, but with a good enough belly-laugh to encourage a last-minute swing of some election votes.

John Simpson, veteran reporter, war correspondent and once BBC's foremost news commentator, wrote in his book, *Unreliable Sources* (Macmillan 2010): "Rupert Murdoch changed the character of every single newspaper he bought ..."

Yes, he may nearly have done that, and all for the worse, but his devaluing and down-marketing of journalism were not the greatest dangers he has inflicted on the world's free press. It is his blatant use of propaganda and press and his TV influences in his pursuit of profit and power that are the most harmful. That aspect is even more a threat to good journalism than his meddling and poisoning of editorial content.

What many of us believe is that he sought out and supported the most favourable candidate for political power, and offered to that party absolute backing ... he was willing to hide harmful news if necessary. It seemed to help him with his media acquisitions in the United States.

It certainly helped in his purchase of *The Times,* London.

When loyalty dies

The Times was a financial burden which Lord Thomson had born gladly in order to preserve its old-fashioned high standards, but which he wished to dispose of when he sold off all his other media and retired. Rupert Murdoch, before he purchased *The Sun,* seemed to be the only likely buyer.

It was made easy for him by his political allies in Westminster, so that there was no need to refer it to the Monopolies Commission. A legally-required independent Trust to ensure editorial independence was also easily agreed to by all interested parties.

All of them underestimated Murdoch.

It appeared impossible for him to refrain from dictating editorial decisions, even minor inconsequential ones. Murdoch's other forms of media across the world were already notorious for ruthless interference from 'the Boss' and his minions. One newspaper editor complained that Murdoch not only telephoned often, sometimes he enforced consciousness of his presence by simply breathing loudly into the heavy instrument during long, inexplicable pauses.

One of Murdoch's first moves in taking over *The Times* was to oust the editor and replace him with Britain's very best journalist. He promoted Harold Evans, editor of the award-winning London *Sunday Times*, to editor of *The Times*. The new proprietor did so, it seems in hindsight, on the understanding that the 'middle-lower-class' Evans would be eager to please.

If so, it was a major miscalculation, as anyone who read his *Sunday Times* would have known.

Evans was made of true steel, as his courageous exposures in *The Sunday Times* have shown. His *Sunday Times* teams of highly skilled and motivated investigators uncovered the scandal of Thalidomide's deformed babies and the scandals of other mighty corporations and 'evil doers'.

He was a match for his new boss and ignored Murdoch's editorial 'advice', after Evans had accepted, in 1980, editorship on the terms of *The Times* Trust. However, the famous, campaigning editor quit, in anger, after one year.

Evans found he was unable to deal with a cadre of his own senior editorial staff, urged by Murdoch, it seemed, to undermine their editor's authority.

I happen to know this story directly from witnesses who were leaving 'The *Thunderer*', but Evans sums it up best in his own book with an account of the Letters Page incident.

Reviewing his first book*, I described the event in the early 1980s:
Evans is fired by Murdoch, despite the newspaper board's previous assurances of editorial independence. Evans refuses to leave, and the battle becomes the focus of international attention.

The editor asks his Letters Page editor: "Have we received any letters on the subject?"

The editor is shown one letter, proofed for printing. It is an eloquent defence by Lord Shawcross of a proprietor's right to dismiss an editor. (Shawcross is a legal adviser to the paper).

Well and good.

"No other letters?" asks the editor. And to the embarrassment of his staff and to the discredit of the Times' reputation, 40 or so other letters and telegrams are produced. All are in support of Evans who is still editor. All have been 'spiked' as unworthy of publication (a sin reflecting a Murdoch-provoked schism over editorship within the editorial department itself).

Suddenly one of the cardinal rules of a balanced, independent newspaper has been broken. Nonetheless, the editor, being an interested party, correctly leaves the problem in the lap of the individual senior journalist normally delegated to do 'Letters' – possibly the ambitious candidate to be the next editor. The 'letters editor' decides (but only after the editor's query) to publish nothing at all on a crisis which the entire world is watching.

How mixed up can any 'independent' newspaper become?

And there lies the problem of the Times and all of us who admire it.

The battle for 'The Thunderer' is over. Its reputation is lessened and its base of operations – so carefully guarded over the decades – is changed. And what of its reputation, that precious commodity which belongs neither to the current proprietors nor editors?

However, in declaring here my bias as a friend as well as colleague of Harold Evans, let me report on 'the other side of the story':

'On the other hand', what Murdoch did do for journalism – though for his own ends – was to save all of Britain's lamely managed newspapers from suffocating and dying under the grotesque and unwieldy weight of the British editorial and print unions in the 1980s. Shop stewards and their leaders were dictating to and over-ruling managements; were over-staffing print shops and were forbidding any attempt at the computerisation that was invigorating and making profitable again the rest of the world's free press. Instead, the trade unions used their unbridled power to feather-bed their exclusive membership – in a phrase, "turn each job into three jobs, each at double pay".

Murdoch protected the very existence of Fleet Street's newspapers by being the only proprietor to take the unions head-on. (Except for one provincial newspaper, *The Nottingham Post*, which had already defied the unions in a fight from its building's rooftop, storing water and electricity generators up there in order to survive any siege; then increasing staff salaries and shareholdings and banning "over-greedy" union labour from its premises.)

Murdoch fought the unions on a grand, ruthless scale. He did so by transferring *The Times* and his other papers down the Thames to Wapping in 1986, directly into utilitarian but modern, computerised premises.

It took the unions by surprise and they responded violently. Street battles injured 400 police officers and 100 civilians before Murdoch won. He never once considered giving up. Also, to be fair, I do know from direct personal knowledge that Murdoch did not harass a future independently-minded editor of *The Sunday Times* such as Simon Jenkins.

And, for example, in a much later era, I visited the *Christchurch Press* in New Zealand in pre-earthquake days back in the 1990s, and was so impressed with its facilities, its values as a relatively small daily; its obvious professional standards and its active concern with its local community, that I made a point of going to their offices to learn more and compliment the editor on his publication.

"I'm surprised, though, that asset stripper O'Reilly of *The Independent* supports you so well financially," I remarked.

"No. We're *not* connected to the Irish guys. The only country where Murdoch owns the name *Independent* is here, New Zealand. We are fully supported and encouraged by our managerial team, and Murdoch has never interfered or even paid us a visit."

IT WAS FORTUNATE, however, that the Levin Commission in Britain in 2012 prompted Murdoch to leave newspapers for more important business. The allegations of illegal phone-tapping and bribery were too close for both his and every concerned citizen's comfort. While he was still extricating himself from that newspaper disaster, reports were published that one of Rupert Murdoch's News Corp subsidiaries, NDS, had been allegedly involved in dirty business in the TV industry. Its 'Operational Security Unit' was accused not only of phone-tapping but piracy of rival television companies' material as well.

Before these allegations were tested, NDS was sold by News Corp for $5 billion ... so there's one press baron who may never go bust like most of 'em.

We can hope that never again need *The Times* publish a leader about its owner, or quip as it did: "Mr Murdoch has not invented sex, but he does show a remarkable enthusiasm for its benefits to circulation."
John Simpson's book suggests that Murdoch's objective in journalism was not to win a British peerage (in any case, the Australian had to be American to own his television properties). He was interested solely in profit and what it could buy. It is one of the saddest things I ever came upon in all my years of newspapering.

The good news, however, is that – in his ageing view of his vast media empire – Murdoch lost interest in the petty business of newspapers. He has enough money to sustain loss-leaders like *The Times* without requiring a pound of flesh for his gesture. Indeed, his wealth seems sufficient to finance an international bank on the lines of the five-nation 'Brics' set-up ... if Murdoch really wanted to aid the Third World.

On the other hand, Britain's 'journalist of the year, 2009', Tom Watson, stated correctly, I believe, at the outset of his co-authored book** on Murdoch, that his internationally powerful company exerted "a poisonous, secretive influence on public life in Britain" and "used its huge power to bully, intimidate and cover up ... Its exposure has changed the way we look at our politicians, our police service and our press." Murdoch could be charming when he wished to be, but seldom was. Another would-be press magnate, Tony O'Reilly was *always* charming, and his methods of 'running newspapers' was an entertainment in itself. Yet the results, as we shall now see, are sadly disillusioning. ☐

* Good Times, Bad Times, by Harold Evans, (Weidenfeld and Nicolson, 1983).
** Dial M for Murdoch by Tom Watson and Martin Hickman MP, (Allen Lane of Penguin Books, 2012).

25.
It depends how you use 'Independence'.

Are you the O'Reilly they speaks of so well?
'Cause if you're the O'Reilly they speaks of so highly,
Gor blimey, O'Reilly, just look where you fell.

Adaption of an anonymous ditty.

Charming, witty Tony O'Reilly, we are told, was blessed and invited by Nelson Mandela to buy South Africa's major chain of newspapers.

However, this convenient and accepted version of O'Reilly's spokesmen is wrong.

O'Reilly's purchase of The Argus Publishing and Printing Company (renamed Independent Newspapers) was neither specifically blessed nor especially welcomed by Nelson Mandela ... because Mandela had an inborn gift for embracing people that superseded all O'Reilly's formidable talents in fostering 'contacts.'

O'Reilly, in his hey-day as an industrial multimillionaire in the USA, had sought out Mandela when the African leader arrived in America as a global celebrity and had provided him accommodation in the Irishman's holiday retreat on an island off the American coast, as well as in his famous castle in Ireland.

The Argus Board of trustees, on which I happened to be serving at the time (*after* retiring from newspapers) had a shareholding structure designed to support a policy that encouraged the newspapers to govern themselves – independently of their owners – in a clearly stated and recorded manner which I described earlier.

Thus the Argus Board specifically avoided discussing the affairs of individual newspapers or their content; editorial policies and staff appointments – unless a newspaper or its editor was:
– unable to do the job adequately
– failed to help ensure his newspaper remained commercially independent, or
– failed to live up to its editorially agreed and published standards.

The major shareholders, Anglo American Corporation and Johannesburg Consolidated Investments, were focused on dozens of gold, platinum and coal mines; most of which individually made more profit in a week than the entire chain of newspapers made in a year. Their investment in Argus newspapers was one simply of benign protection against political (specifically *apartheid*) influence. Their policy had one proviso: No board would support a newspaper that failed to pay its own way ... This was, after all, one of the first tests of independence.

When this financial protection was at last judged no longer to be necessary in a free society, the major shareholders named above opted to sell the newspapers. Finding an acceptable buyer, however, even at a ridiculously low price, was not easy during the uncertain yet exciting period of socio-political 'transformation' of South Africa in the early 1990s.

Even so, Rupert Murdoch, for instance was *never* at any time considered as a potential buyer. Conrad Black, at one stage was considered, but he had blotted his financial copybook and been punished in the US for it.

Tony O'Reilly was finally – and in most quarters *reluctantly* – approved as the potential buyer. He sought the seller's peculiar condition of sale – that he be acceptable to President Mandela – and received it, as most supplicants did.

"But why O'Reilly?" some of us on the Board asked, remembering the Board's earlier experiences with him.

A delegation had been sent to meet the proposed buyer. Three Argus Board members flew to London, then in O'Reilly's private jet from London to his castle where a weekend party was in play. Peter McLean, a man well practised in partying, returned to say they had been magnificently entertained at the historic site, amid excellent company, and a good time was had by all. But they would *not* recommend him to us as the new owner of Argus Newspapers.

"Why not?"

"Because we've investigated his investments and judge him to be, by our standards in newspapering, an asset stripper."

It took me some time to understand what this entailed. Further investigation, particularly of his Irish newspaper connections, suggested that 'asset stripper' seemed a good label for O'Reilly's operations, exceedingly rich as he, as well as his wife, each were in those days. So there the matter rested for some time, with no other candidates entering the lists.

My only personal knowledge of what occurred after an unexpected hiatus was an announcement to our Board chairman that Tony O'Reilly was the buyer acceptable to the major shareholders.

"Why? I asked again. "We were informed he was considered to be 'an asset stripper'."

Apparently the majority shareholders, if not The Argus Board's members, thought otherwise. None seem to have visited O'Reilly's under-resourced local Irish papers.

Good sport and Irish blarney

Tony O'Reilly has always been one of those people everybody loves on sight.

In his youth he was an internationally famous rugby wing, a 'good sport' and a great wit, full of Irish good humoured blarney. He could disarm a critic, bring down the house with a humorous speech, or charm a wallet off almost anyone he chose. He was fiercely competitive and, it seems, a man determined to have the best and be the best in everything he did. How else do you account for his ownership of a castle near Dublin filled with rich antiques, famous and priceless paintings, ornate decorations all worth millions of pounds, as well as a separate lodge on his estate for glamorous starlets; for sailing, or for salmon-fishing guests, and international figures seeking silence and rest, such as Nelson Mandela? How else does one account for his constant drive for dominance as a personal figure?

However, O'Reilly had given up his astonishingly successful leadership of an American baked-bean business to enter Irish newspaper ownership and become an investor in one of Britain's finest newspapers – the new *Independent* in London ... as we were reminded, when he came shopping for SA's major press chain. (The London *Independent* was founded in 1985 *'by journalists for journalists'*. The leading founder and first editor was financial journalist Andreas Whittam-Smith, a loyal colleague who had come to South Africa at my request to support *The Star* in its darkest days. Decades later the London *Independent's* journalists guided their paper away from financial death and into the role of one of the first, hopefully successful, online newspapers.)

In the early 1990s, any champion of *The Independent* in London might seem to be a worthy candidate to own the Argus Company's 100-year-old chain of independently edited daily metropolitan papers. But my old friend, Peter McLean, with long service in management and on Argus Boards, who had fully appreciated the legendary O'Reilly hospitality in Ireland, had doubts about the proposed sale. McLean raised the question of the future security of our company's Pension Fund – an excellent fund, based on Anglo American Corps' generous model – but in our case a Trust with newspaper professionals and with newspaper staff properly represented on it. They provided constant and careful attention to staff pensions at all levels and for all race groups, often doing so well that they allayed some of the grievances about the traditional low pay of journalists.

Unfortunately, no one at this moment could foresee anyone being able to harm that investment. The Pension Fund was itself a significant shareholder of the Argus Company.

But McLean's reservations – like my instinctive ones, and our board's uneasiness – were not sufficient to delay matters. The deal with O'Reilly was quickly done, and a new board for Independent Newspapers soon elected. The original chairman, Doug Band, was amused but not mollified when Tony O'Reilly rose to break into song at a formal dinner in the Johannesburg Rand Club, with a well-known ditty and even better-known refrain: "… la-la-la … *And the Band Played On!*"

Not for long. Nor was O'Reilly's claimed blessing from Nelson Mandela taken seriously by anybody as far as the Argus Board and the press at large knew … not even by Mandela who was being nice to everybody; including foreign investors and other capitalists.

The result, in my view, obviously biased, showed that the new owner was not merely a disappointment, but a tragedy causing immense damage. The tragedy arose from the fact that most of the South African press was about to embrace the new non-racial era that Mandela was counting on originally from Argus newspapers and probably all others in the nation. Here was a vast, exciting opportunity. Now it was about to be limited as the newspaper company was deliberately hobbled by huge new ownership demands on its profits.

O'Reilly's actions were a direct cause in 'transforming' (the politically magic word) the newly-acquired and renamed quote *Independent* unquote *Newspapers* into a company of that name. Argus board members were now happy to be out of it, even before his version of so-called 'transformation' began.

'Transformation' within the newspaper company itself soon came in the form of asset stripping, which included the owner's legally-contrived takeover of the proprietor's share of the Pension Fund – an amount that equated almost with the price he had paid for the entire chain of metropolitan newspapers!

'Transformation' in the form of asset stripping proceeded rapidly and increasingly in the form of 'cost savings' (for proprietorial profit) including a rapid reduction in staff. It also included the stripping away of priceless, irreplaceable news services; editing talents and training facilities which had been carefully built up over many decades. The Argus Company had been a proud organisation, founded by journalists and after 100 years was still providing total editorial independence to each editor of every big and small publication in the group.

Within just a few years the newly-named *Independent Newspapers* became the very opposite. O'Reilly turned the company into a centralised, thinned-down, profit-oriented conglomerate, and milked it, desperately, to cover the debts of his overseas projects.

'Transformation' in the newspapers included one thoroughly misguided effort in supporting the ANC by providing President Mbeki with pages of free space – and thereby unquestioned support – of his notoriously mishandled policy in dealing with the HIV-Aids crisis that continued to cause many thousands of deaths.

But things had already changed at the very start of smiling O'Reilly's take-over.

The challenge experienced by the new SA *Independent Newspapers'* top editor, who had just joined *The Star* (the truly editorially independent Argus flagship) from Natal's family-owned *Witness,* was the first indicator of that change.

Richard Steyn was a legally-trained, independent-minded editor, long since pledged to political transformation – and, of course, true editorial independence. Management immediately sought to change his role by insisting that he report directly to some unnamed representative of the new proprietor.

Photo: supplied by Richard Steyn, author of 'Jan Smuts, Unafraid of Greatness'.

As mentioned earlier in this book, Steyn – at considerable personal and financial sacrifice – immediately rejected this seeming promotion by resigning in protest from his current post as editor-in-chief of *The Star's* various newspaper editions. His protest was based purely on a vital principle.

He refused to accept the new conditions of his employment and the implicit threat to editorial independence. A threat to the rights and duty of each editor to exercise independent judgements as each newspaper editor in the newspaper chain had always done. It was hard for any editor to swallow direct instructions from management. And it certainly seemed dishonest to accept the new ownership's new name: *Independent Newspapers.*

O'Reilly, after a pause to take stock, then appointed to the post another *ware* (true) South African with an Irish name: Peter Sullivan. The new group editor accepted the controversial post and, with a Labour lawyer always at hand, Sullivan immediately disregarded the purpose of his appointment.

Instead of listening to the new proprietor's agents, he began a proper transformation by appointing top 'black and brown', fully-trained journalists in the group as chief editors who were made editorially independent of *Independent Newspapers'* proprietor and managers, with editors' traditional rights and responsibilities intact.

Sullivan needed to be neutralised for economic reasons. But whenever he was offered attractive retirement, or threatened with transfer – if not removal – he treated each approach with a demand to have details in writing so that "I can refer to my legal adviser". His own transfer stalled each time at that stage, for Sullivan would never respond to his employer's gambits until he was finally ready for retirement.

Meanwhile, O'Reilly's management was reducing each newspaper's copy editing and reporting staff from their admittedly magnificently abnormal size and competency, to intolerably tiny quotas that required mass-editing of news content from centrally-controlled news desks!

On the other hand, to give the new proprietor his due, the ever-charming, witty, blandishing Tony O'Reilly kept the first promise which he had given to a few of us personally.

He overturned the disputed and recent closure of *The Sunday Star* and resurrected it as *The Sunday Independent*, regardless of cost. (He presumably altered its accounting system in order to reduce its regularly accounted loss – a loss which I had always disputed as an unfair balancing of the books that charged the Sunday paper office space, overtime, air-conditioning and the rest of the items for which the daily newspaper had already been paying in any case.)

And he did allow his editorial staff space to voice independent views.

Ann Crotty, an Irish-born financial analyst and journalist who often disagreed entirely with her new Irish proprietor, wrote what she wished to write, as did anyone who was ready to challenge management.

Crotty finally summed up O'Reilly's era in *Business Report,* one of the titles published by him:

"Local analysts say it is likely that, after making some provision for tax, the bulk of the approximate R4.5bn operating profit that INM South Africa has generated since it was delisted from the JSE in 1999 made its way to Dublin, with minimum amounts invested in South Africa. The R4.5bn represents an extremely attractive return on the approximate R650m that INM initially paid to acquire the operations. Employee numbers since the initial move have been reduced from about 5,000 to 1,700.

"This 66% reduction in the number of employees helps explain why INM has been able to maintain a profit margin of around 20% in its South African operations despite the substantial declines in the circulation of its flagship English-language daily broadsheet titles."

O'Reilly's Irish luck came to his financial rescue when he sold his profits-drained chain of papers to a suspiciously odd amalgam of shareholders entering the industry for the first time. The fact that he had long ago appropriated the proprietor's half of the greatly envied Argus Pension Scheme – though legally, as I've already stressed, and worth almost what he had paid for the entire company and its under-valued, irreplaceable city-centre properties, as well as other hard assets – should have made the business very hard to sell.

In such circumstances, where in the world would one find buyers willing to pay five times what he paid for the company – particularly after he had stripped it?

For some of us, who were following as intermittent readers at a remote distance, O'Reilly's squeeze of resources and his increasing demands evoked sadness; almost despair.

Could anything be worse?

Yes.

When O'Reilly could milk no more from his newspapers, he sold them to "an unknown" buyer at a miraculous multi-billion-rand price; beyond the market's expectations. The 'unknown' proved to be Dr Iqbal Survé, owner of a politically-inspired 'transformation' fishing company with contacts made in the highest places of President Zuma's government in South Africa. The multi-billion rands required for the press takeover came from several sources, including China and, ironically, South Africa's Public Investment Corporation.

But why would anyone – especially an organisation safeguarding assets such as the Government Employees Pension Fund, the Unemployment Insurance Fund and the Compensation Fund – want to provide non-interest-bearing loans and invest in newspapers when circulations were dropping and the newspaper printing industry was staring at its imminent demise? Who else would have such grandiose ideas of stretching the business across the continent of Africa – 'independently'?

China was interested. The SA government was interested. And the guardians of the governmental State Pension Fund were easily persuaded to sink capital into the stripped-down newspaper company. On paper, both state investors seemed disinterested resources, enough surely to guarantee no interference with editorial independence ... an assumption as superficially naive as it was disturbing.

Before we face this particularly nightmarish threat to independent journalism, let us pause to contemplate the different extremes in Tony O'Reilly's own role in newspapering.

For all his exuberant lifestyle and Irish luck, O'Reilly damaged his reputation and that of his Independent Newspapers in Africa, by simply not caring enough about newspaper values.

Having stripped the assets granted him by Argus newspapers and pocketed the cash from the sale of his investment in his renamed Independent Newspapers; he left without seemingly caring a jot about their future.

Instead, he turned his back and concentrated on his association with the universally admired and highly successful London *Independent*. The *cachet* of being at one stage a part-owner and supporter of the London *Independent* would seem to add credence to his nomination to the British peerage. "Sir Anthony O'Reilly" would have congratulated himself on supporting loyally at all stages that shining example of "true independent journalism".

"A Thing of Beauty"

The London *Independent* was a newspaper conceived, designed, launched (1986) and run by journalists – the founders being Andreas Whittham-Smith (referred to in previous chapters) and two other financial reporters of *The Daily Telegraph*.

They chose their newspaper investors carefully and spread the shareholding internationally, with none allowed more than 10% ownership. Journalists were allowed to be the biggest group of shareholders.

"The Indy", as it was soon affectionately known, was a classic broadsheet paper with immaculate reporting, copy-editing, and new ideas. After 17 years it halved its size to a more compact (tabloid) format without losing its classical approach. The following year the 'compact *Indy*' was named "National Newspaper of the Year" at the 2004 British Press Awards.

For most of its life the paper carried, every day, the banner reading "free from party political bias, free from proprietorial influence".

However, the banner disappeared because of the paper's inability to compete with Murdoch's *Times'* price-cutting, which had caused the *Indy* reluctantly to abandon its pattern of financial controls and surrender it to a Russian oligarch who promised not to interfere with editorial independence.

In 2016 the London *Independent* finally gave up printing the paper and moved its journalistic resources online.

Founding editor (now "Sir" Andreas) Whittam-Smith commented: "The technology that enabled us to establish ourselves has, 30 years later, rendered the printed edition unviable."

Readers and critics were dismayed. They loved the *Independent* for its refreshingly different and thoughtful coverage of issues.

One subscriber wrote: "Leafing through the (last edition of the) newspaper I was struck by what the internet generation is losing by the print edition's demise. The founders decreed a paper that would be aesthetically outstanding and so it was with the last edition: an artefact of beauty, elegantly and cleanly laid out, with strong photographs and wonderful typography."

"Coming from a pre-internet generation that was brought up on Eric Gill's typography, I do wonder if the current generation will ever have the opportunity to understand the sheer beauty of type design and its intimate relationship with a page of white paper." □

26.
When 'independence' becomes a fake.

Nothing is more damaging to a free press and to honest journalism than newspapers surrendering their 'watchdog' role to snuggle up to political power.

A credo of independent journalism

Tony O'Reilly had been quick to sell his South African investment in Argus newspapers, which he had renamed Independent Newspapers in line with his newspaper acquisitions at home. But he was interested in the money he desperately needed, not in the new owner's knowledge of newspapers nor in the ethics of journalism.

This lack of care by O'Reilly, his focus on money and the search for financial power and political influence, have brought tragic results for all those interested in the standards of journalism in their daily metro newspapers in South Africa.

The Cape Times, for instance, a member of the nationwide Independent Newspapers' group, seems likely to publish almost anything these days, provided it does not contradict its own peculiar slant on the news. Currently it is regularly publishing so much irrelevant material and 'manufactured' stories that it has the symptoms of a newspaper which cannot find enough local news to fill its marvellously and extraordinarily wide-open pages. The space made available, without visible financial support, together with the apparent lack of copy-tasting skills and news to fill it, is a rare and bewildering sight for veteran newspaper readers.

Clearly it is publishing too many pages (with too few recognised bylines and credible source acknowledgements). And it does so with minimal and apparently unsustainable advertising support.

On the face of it, this is a recipe for disaster, at least for any independent, self-sustaining newspaper. And especially one in a group that flaunts the title: *Independent Newspapers*. The paper's style and news values can be explained only by a lack of editorial and managerial planning skills or – much more likely – an abundance of funding from Chinese and government investors (who may be expecting their 'Independent' newspapers to repay by launching online into Africa for cardinal reasons that may have little to do with *news* reporting).

10th BRICS Summit | by GovernmentZA. Dr Survé pictured centre.

Whatever the circumstances, the profile of lack of full disclosure and power-instilled investment invites both suspicion and internal abuse. As does the peculiar behaviour of the new owner, Dr Iqbal Survé, and his personal, publicly displayed, initial support of a partly corrupt government and the controversial, clearly corrupt Jacob Zuma when at the height of power as President.

As with Murdoch's ambitions, Survé's were initially vastly underestimated. They turned out to be what logic suggested they might be. Despite pious protestations, they became a means to interfere with a free, already rapidly reformed press. Independent journalists were quickly disillusioned.

When Survé exhibited those same delusions of personal power and ambition with which press barons caused so much strife in Britain in a long ago age of 'unenlightenment', South Africa's editors were anguished. And readers were not spared. Some of the best 'transformation' editors in South Africa – leading black and brown journalists as capable as any masters of their craft – resigned within months of the take-over. Rival newspaper *Business Day* summed up events thus:

> "Managing editor Martine Barker was escorted out of the group's Cape Town offices on Friday and that outspoken Cape Times executive editor Tony Weaver has been made redundant. Packages were given to Western Cape circulation manager Graham Shaw and Gauteng counterpart Pierre Joubert.

They have already left. This comes on top of the resignations, and immediate departures of The Star Editor Makhudu Sefara and of The Mercury Editor Philani Mgwaba late last month. Former Cape Times editor Alide Dasnois was dismissed last week after being found guilty in a company internal disciplinary hearing. She has taken her case to the Labour Court.

In Weaver, Independent will lose an award-winning journalist. Sefara was crowned editor of the year in the Standard Bank Sikuvile Awards in May, when Weaver won the prize for his Man Friday columns in support of Dasnois, who won the South African National Editors' Forum Nat Nakasa award for courageous journalism last month - after her suspension.

These editors and senior management departures followed the resignations of a number of senior journalists within six months.

It also lost almost all of its independent political columnists ranging from the late internationally-known journalist, Allister Sparks, to award-winning Max du Preez."

Some of the reasons for all of these editorial losses were quickly obvious. The new owner of Independent Newspapers was soon 'persuading' his editors to interview him in articles splashed across many columns and dominating pages in each of his chain of newspapers. His pronouncements on newspapers, though understandably and forgivably naive, were puzzling to say the least. But his many photos blazoned in 'his' press; his personal and proud public association with President Zuma's government – and the sight of newspaper editors pretending within vast space within their own papers to ask their boss questions for which he wanted self-publicity, was nauseating for any independent journalist or editor ... though some cynical newspaper readers found it to be novel and entertaining.

Survé encouraged the departure of – or he purged – many of his best-trained, independent-minded staff and columnists. At first he relied instead on the support of his personally appointed new 'Independent' top executives: the 'Group Executive Editor' and the ominously named 'Group Opinion Editor' – a title Orwell might have enjoyed satirising.

The executives were quickly adjusting their stances after the dismissal and resignations in protest by a number of staff and columnists. And the owner – to the relief of all 'his' journalists, surely – began using his own name as the byline on the lengthy articles published with his pictures. These now began briefly to focus, not so much on himself, as on his views of Africa's sad history and the need for 'his' newspapers to ensure that Africa takes it rightful place on the global stage.

Therein lies a suitable form of transition in coverage which journalists on local metro papers might happily adopt … if it were not for Survé's published assumption that this "re-positioning of the African story" should be the responsibility of *his* (partly China-sponsored) media.

This self-important announcement might also resemble the political megalomania of two of the Harmsworth family of press barons previously mentioned – except that the 'barons' were all self-made, fully trained and experienced *newspaper* people. And except that instead of haranguing the government as press barons were inclined to do, the new owner in South Africa publicly sought the government's approbation.

The dubious, sometimes comic, but always sad results of the owner's efforts, appeared daily in the *Cape Times'* pages, careless texts and layouts. Readers might miss much of this – but not any trained journalist, one of whom was so outraged that he ran a daily online column featuring – sometimes with humour, but mostly with professionally disillusioned bitterness – the constantly repeated daily mistakes for which any average copy editor might formerly have been fired.

All my remarks concern only the *Cape Times*. I would like to believe that they are not justified in relation to *The Star, The Daily News, The Pretoria News, The Argus* and the *Diamond Fields Advertiser* – all of which were once *Argus* newspapers; all of which I once worked on and all of which I have deliberately not read in ten or twenty years. The judgements, though, which I receive from retired contemporaries reading those newspapers are depressing.

The *Cape Times* – a venerable newspaper that opposed apartheid throughout its existence and honoured *editorial* independence throughout most of its history, as the Argus Group of papers did – had been transforming into a multi-cultural paper more easily than most, long before the new owner's self-proclaimed 'achievements'.

Soon managerial interference in editorial matters was causing serious concern for all journalists interested in the ethics and freedom of the press. Especially because the new CEO of Independent Newspapers describes this most dangerous fault in his own words – when he boasts of *mobilising* 'his' entire group of newspapers to carry out his goals, however charitable, patriotic, public-spirited or ambitious they might be.

The new boss of Independent Newspapers has been so transparent in his own papers' columns that he has left no space for editorial independence. He and his advisers, if they still exist, appear ignorant of the credo of all independent-minded journalists which is quoted at the head of this chapter.

According to reports in Dr Survé's newspapers, he and his cohorts even dressed up in *government party colours* to meet President Zuma who was himself a threat to honest government and a free press!

And within weeks of the appointment of new President Cyril Ramaphosa, the *Cape Times* was able to publish a photo (covering the top half of the front page!) of Dr Survé's face near that of the new President's. The giant picture in Survé's press was made possible because the media tycoon ensured a meeting with the new President at a newspaper-sponsored jazz festival which the national leader had been scheduled to attend.

These are mere examples of an owner using his newspapers for his own gratification, but there are many occurrences so complicated by the newspaper owner's published opinions and vehement reactions that they are difficult to believe.

For instance, the proprietorship, it appears, early on in the take-over of ownership, used an anonymous "Investigative Unit" to create a disturbing, if risible error of judgement in publishing an editorial "*expos*é" of all Dr Survé's critics.

The article reported that dedicated research had identified "364 derogatory items" about Dr Survé and that this proved the existence of a concerted plot to defame him. Some public figures were named as plotters (though without opportunity to respond to the strange accusations). This apparently sensational news was rushed to every 'Independent' newspaper in the country and published, word for word under the same headline; with no proper sub-editing and no proper byline, and probably to the subsequent embarrassment of every editor of an Independent Newspaper.

In another instance, when a Survé company sought shareholders to increase its value several hundred times, but failed to meet the strictly-detailed regulations of the Johannesburg Stock Exchange, the newspaper owner himself raged about it in full-page displays in all cities, accusing his critics of lying; of undeclared self-interest; of disloyalty to their country and of racism. One such accused critic apologised for mistakes made in his financial critique ... but said some of the false information had come from the Independent Newspapers' nationally published *Business Report*.

The editor of *Business Report* had previously puzzled its readers, and embarrassed journalists, by using the entire top of a page – across nine columns – to picture the newspapers' owner and to wish him a happy birthday!

She now publicly excused her boss's failure to manage an acceptable launch of his ambitious scheme to win shareholders. She did so, in emotional terms by publishing a full page of personal support for his project. It included accusations of financial critics' "dirty tricks" and accusations of dishonesty of "hundreds" of journalists. Speaking proudly "as a white Afrikaner woman" she also accused her fellow financial writers of being racist.

It is difficult to summarise these bizarre events, let alone explain them. But what they do provide is a dramatic case for editors to insist on their own independence.

'ON THE OTHER HAND' (a format providing both sides of the story as independent coverage demands) it should be said that Survé's deft takeover and blatant interventions provide one possibility: a much-needed and rapid if uneven, often dubious switch of news coverage from the concerns of Cape Town's relatively well-off and wealthy patrons to the deep and genuine frustrated concerns of Cape Town's poorer, darker-skinned majority. These are now vociferously vented, though usually one-sidedly and without accountability. Coverage is excellent in depicting the social changes and other activities of the city's upward-moving brown community.

While its political approach is crude and one-sided, the *Cape Times* also offers wide-open broadsheet pages providing an extraordinary amount of space for excellent reporting on the arts; on book reviews and multiple pages of sport.

It should also be recorded that suspicions of Dr Survé's deft takeover are not *all* justified. Newspaper readers' dreams might lie in the wistful possibility of restoring some balance in a changing society and readership. It is a change which had already happened in chief-editor Sullivan's era under owner O'Reilly, and would surely have continued under any proprietor ... more effectively with an owner avoiding personal and aggravating interference. But at least change continues at good speed. The question remains: What kind of change will it become, if blighted by lack of trust, skewed reporting, falling standards of journalism, and the highly visible interference of the "owner"?

Time will tell.

Lamentably, it already has.

Even without these spectacular examples of amateur mal-purposed misreporting, there are days, sadly, when some of the *Cape Times'* more emotional, skewed reportage is inclined to remind one of Dr Verwoerd's *Transvaler* in early apartheid days.

Publication of narrow views and suppression of facts are, of course, entirely permissible and legal in any free country. But the perpetrators, flying under a piratical flag of independence, must expect strong criticism, and hopefully effective opposition. □

27.
How the Past could affect the world's Future.

If you want a picture of the future, imagine a boot stamping on a human face – forever.

George Orwell, '1984'

Before we consider how the press, or rather new forms of accountable digital media, can protect freedom of the individual in the world's future societies we should try to determine what that future holds. A glance at where it will be coming from during this first quarter of the 21st century is not reassuring.

Today, crazy ideology is rampant from North Korea to Syria; from the Sudan to Iraq and Yemen.

China has changed its ideological forms of communism from totalitarianism to single dictatorship to neo-democracy at different times in a single century; depending always on which leader was practising what ideology. Africa, seething with superstition and old but unfamiliar beliefs, may be following South America in a habit of seemingly ceaseless revolutionary patterns which Latin-American ideologists practised so unpredictably and violently in so many countries throughout the 19th and 20th centuries.

Ideology was at its worst internationally during the past century when the most highly educated, phlegmatic nation on Earth was hypnotised by a mad little man named Hitler, who ranted on about socio-political prejudices and policies that didn't make sense in terms of economics, humanitarianism or justice. Germany had *hundreds* of regional newspapers (but no strong national ones). Under Hitler's ideological rhetoric freedom of the press died almost instantly.

In Russia, under self-confessed mass-murderer Stalin, neither theoretical communism nor a free press had a chance.

In the light of the modern world situation, we need to ask ourselves: how restricted is the global role of the media today – the would-be watchdog of justice and freedom? What happens when a huge section of the United States of America – part of the largest democracy on Earth – follows the inexplicable ideology of a man who convinces his followers that his strange theories are all sound and that the media, from top to bottom, are not to be trusted with the truth? What effective role can the media play in this atmosphere of suspicion, prejudice and 'virtual reality', 'fake news' and 'alternative facts'?

What *is* real? And what *is* true in our frantically changing world today? "In a time of deceit, telling the truth is a revolutionary act" George Orwell said during an era in which communistic ideology threatened to subvert the world's free press.

"Political language", he said, as quoted earlier in this book, "is designed to make lies sound truthful and murder respectable, and to give an appearance of solidity to pure wind." (We remember Orwell as the world's champion slayer of dangerous ideological nonsense. Yet ironically he delivered his powerful messages about reality without using his real name.)

Ideologies, of course, with their emotional pollutions of truth and logic and honesty, work effectively, even when the press is relatively strong and able to expose the lies, and point to the truth. For instance: a claimed majority of the followers of presidential candidate Donald Trump reached a stage where they truly believed the media were lying. They were persuaded that the media were a single entity bent on robbing them of their democratic rights. "It's all rigged ... nothing more to say," Trump told his believers.

Such behaviour not only encourages suspicion and prejudice, and hides truth, it also causes the accused media to campaign against these lies until the media themselves appear one-sided and therefore unbalanced.

And "alternative facts" signal the first stages of public irrationality.

Drawing on my own experience, I recall once a newspaper investigation in which – after prolonged investigation and effort – we were able to expose the chairman of a large public business from which he was diverting dubious funds into his wife's accounts. There was a brief and telling public silence after the headlines appeared concerning his dishonest actions ... but soon afterwards he called a meeting of his colleagues and his supporters and stated publicly:

"No, there's nothing to apologise for. No, everything in my business is now open and above-board. There's nothing to hide ... You've now seen everything published in the newspaper."

His supporters, normal citizens in a twisted and very abnormal society in white South Africa in the 1980s, welcomed this 'declaration of openness'.

Of course, even the thin theories of apartheid ignored logic. The system was built on a strange and cruelly dangerous ideology. Yet when its evils could no longer be sustained, and its leaders were secretly seeking peace with the victims who were fighting back – the party's last act, before formal reconciliation could be reached, was to introduce extreme 'Emergency Regulations' designed to gag the press. At the same time a secret section of the armed forces was penetrating civil society and hiring assassins to eliminate innocent civilians who opposed them.

On 1 May 1989, just nine months before Mandela was released and peace negotiations began, a quiet but active academic, David Webster, was gunned down on the pavement outside his home. It happened in broad daylight in a peaceful, high-density suburb not far from where he worked as an anthropologist at the then world-renowned Witwatersrand University. It was a blatant, shotgun-style murder of a model citizen that should have produced witnesses and swift justice, but nothing of any consequence could be found.

A motive was easily apparent. Webster was a founder member of the Detainees' Parents Support Committee, and of the Five Freedoms Forum and of the End Conscription Campaign (opposing compulsory drafting of white youth into the illegal war in Angola). The latter was motive enough for a covert military security group – but these three active civic organisations, and several others to which David Webster belonged, were all legal movements supporting the rights of citizens. His activities were those of a very caring citizen.

In fact, for the first and last time in my professional life, I could no longer resist personally joining ("but as a private citizen") one of the organisations whose goals were close to my heart: the Five Freedoms Forum in which several of the freedoms were those championed by our newspaper and attacked illegally by the State.

It was not until nearly ten years later – in a time of normalcy and early non-racial and universal democracy in South Africa – that Webster's assassin, a hired-gun named Ferdi Barnard – was finally arrested, tried, and sentenced to two lifetimes of imprisonment plus another 63 years for other heinous crimes ... many of them committed on behalf of the military's ironically named Civil Cooperation Bureau (CCB).

Back in the crazy apartheid era, however, our senior investigative team, led by my colleague Rex Gibson, former editor of *The Rand Daily Mail* and of the *Sunday Express,* worked day and night to expose the machinations of the CCB which we found was operating within the City Hall complex itself.

Through a 'Deep Throat' we cultivated in the Mayor's office and, with sufficient corroborating evidence, *The Star* was able to expose a

> "SPY RING IN THE CITY COUNCIL: A sinister spy network deep inside the city council, using ratepayers' money to spy on ratepayers – so secret that its existence is unknown to most – if not all – elected councillors ... The spy ring has gathered personal information to give, not to the City Council, but to supply secretly and directly to Military Intelligence, the Security Police and the SA Police."

The network, we reported, was spying on people like former leader of the Opposition, Van Zyl Slabbert; on Cyril Ramaphosa (now President of South Africa, who at that time led the National Mine Workers Union) and on several other well-known South Africans. Soon we had enough evidence to run page-one stories for days on end. When the most powerful bureaucrat in the city tried to deny some of the newspaper's charges, we were able to confront City-Mayor Venter.

Our frontpage headlines featured some deeply suspicious municipal actions and discredited explanations of many more. The top subheads read: "Wrong! Wrong! Wrong!" The main headline read: 'OFF-CENTRE MR VENTER' and described his suspicious relationships with the suspected murder squad.

The mayor was forced to resign, and the Opposition took power in the city, but Johannesburg's general public, which had been reading reports of bloody violence for months, hardly reacted to this. We were never able to break the Webster assassination case. It transpired later that the hired assassin had been flown out of the country and was hidden in out-of-touch Namibia.

Meanwhile we kept digging. Circumstances were so taut by this stage (and we had proof that *The Star's* offices were bugged) that we found ourselves acting like characters in a B-Grade movie. We needed to walk the city block's distance inside our own building to discuss in semi-whispers the details of our ongoing investigation.

"What's new today?" I asked the team.

"Well, we have the names of the people the Bureau has put on their hit-list," they said.

"Such as whom?"

"The leaders of the Five Freedoms Forum."

"Oh no! They're such nice guys … none of them would turn to violence. I can vouch for it."

"That won't help. You're on the death-list too."

THIS, I BELIEVE, illustrates well the frustrating role of the press when civil life has become so distorted; so unresponsive to dissuasion; so *unreal* that exposure of evil, use of logic and reason and appeals to good civic sense and public honesty threaten to become irrelevant.

Ideological fanatics are immune to the media, and the sad phenomenon may never change in the half-century ahead. The 20th century's soothsayer, George Orwell, suggested: "The very concept of objective truth is fading out of the world. Lies will pass into history."

That is the threat I believe the media – *not* the social media, but the equivalent of an established, accountable internet media of 2030 – will have to prevent.

But before we look at the future, we need to appreciate how hazardous ideology can become, even in the best of times; even in a democracy with a fine constitution, strong judiciary and free press. This time it isn't the USA, but next time it just might be if democratic Europe hasn't produced an awful example first.

The example I have in mind happened among a wide-awake, enthusiastic voting community whose governing party had too many votes to feel challenged. The next chapter reminds us how the media's investigative journalists picked up a trail of multi-million dollar thefts of public money – and saved their country. □

28.
Online investigators bring down the President.

Corrupt influence ... is in itself the spring of all disorder. It loads us more than millions of debt ... takes away vigour from our arms, wisdom from our councils and every shadow of authority from our constitution.

Edmund Burke circa 1780s

While the rumbustious era of Donald Trump was still rising, amid strident tweets and media disbelief, another president in another world was bravely challenged ... and astonishingly struck down.

It signalled the first victory of a handful of online investigators exposing the corruption, not only of a president, but of his entire South African democratic government – as well as dishonest agents and unethical private enterprises from Moscow to London; from New Delhi to Dubai; from Berlin to New York and Washington.

The independent-minded journalists, national investigators and online commentators, who successfully exposed the crooked "capture of a nation", would hardly fill the reporters' room of your local paper. Yet they had the necessary will, the skill, the tenacity – *and the help of countless web-leaked emails* – to overcome all the denials of President Jacob Zuma's office and every South African Government Department; as well as the threats of their police and their Public Prosecutor.

The journalists also had to overcome, sadly, the passivity of many of the nation's daily *"Independent"* metro newspapers not campaigning to expose the corruption of a president; a man who was desperately clinging to power, having already faced a rape charge and with 783 charges of corruption, money-laundering and racketeering still to come.

These charges were made during Zuma's time as Deputy President, when he was fired by Mandela's successor, President Mbeki. The disgraced deputy leader had allegedly associated with Schabir Shaik, a local shady dealer, in selling armaments to their new democratic state. Schabir was tried and sent to jail in 2005. Against all political odds, Zuma won the presidential election three years later. Shaik then impatiently awaited a presidential pardon. He was finally released from prison on grounds of "fatally critical ill-health" or some such, and may still be playing golf to celebrate that long ago dubious ill-health ticket which he knew the new president owed him.

Unchallenged, President Zuma easily dealt with his own dubious standing. He assumed the power to appoint all top government officials, including, of course, the Commissioner of the South African Police, the head of the National Prosecuting Authority and later, the head of the Department of Revenue. The only noticeable threat to the new President in his first few years was the *Sunday Times,* and its associate daily and business newspapers which exposed the very first single, simple act of what grew to become known as 'State Capture'.

The Sunday Times ran weekly frontpage headlines on a tip-off that a plane-load of civilians from India had been allowed to land a charter flight at South Africa's major military, carefully-guarded airport outside Pretoria. The unknown visitors were met with a convoy of cars and set off to spend time in the country without producing any identifying documentation whatever. It transpired that the party were the guests of a little-known businessman named Gupta. The unknown foreigners had arrived, 'like official royalty' of a major state, to celebrate a private family wedding.

The reaction of the Presidency and his government to the insolent break in military security was a blunt and total denial of responsibility. However, it transpired, much later (as an appropriate full-circle story towards the end of President Zuma's tenure) that the mysterious and splendiferous wedding celebration was unknowingly paid for by money due to buy a farm for poor African would-be tenants.

The funds meant for these intended farmers and their families were instead confiscated by a Zuma-government official who secretly appropriated the funds from a provincial agricultural budget and donated about a R30m for the actual Gupta wedding-day festivities.

The Leader of the Opposition in Parliament was able to announce – years later – that he had been handed 200 pages of evidence which showed that the official, now a Cabinet Minister, and Gupta family members: Atul; Ajay and Rajesh, "through an intricate web of companies and actors, stole about R200 million" from the small community in the Free State province.

A gift of R30 million (valued at 2.2. million US dollars at the time) spent on a few hours of Gupta celebration, must have seemed well worth it. After all, what are brilliantly fraudulent friends for?

The stolen agricultural budget was quickly dispensed.

Investigative reporters found fraudulent invoices that noted

Demonstrators in Cape Town protest against the involvement of the Guptas in Jacob Zuma's presidency.

payments of R13,086 for chocolate truffles to R2.3-million for scarves, R247, 848 for fireworks and R13.9-million for wedding "event services". The total bill for the wedding festivities amounted to R30,000,000. However, the rest of the stolen agricultural budget was used thus:
- R30,000,000 as a deposit on a private jet-plane
- R10,000,000 deposited in Atul Gupta's personal bank account, and, oh yes, more than *a hundred million* SA rands spread between several new Gupta-linked companies.

The deprived African would-be farming families would have had an interesting view on this ... if they could read, or – less likely– if they could find an *honest* representative of Government.

Though President Zuma's government did nothing about this corruption – even after full public exposure – the event graphically illustrates the fraud, dishonesty and greed occurring in ever-upward spiralling circles. This story has already reached its climax as I write, though its prosecutions and punishments will proceed in several directions no doubt for the rest of the ex-President's life.

It is a tragic tale with a thousand complicated dark shades. It contains several morals, some of which need emphasis, for they are elements which epitomise honesty and justice and are represented in the pillars of every secure democratic state ... the pillars that were concisely enunciated by former Attorney-General of India, Sorabjee, in his address to the world's free press (see Chapter 16).

In South Africa's 'capture of the state', *Government,* represented by the President and Parliament, failed. The other elements – *public awareness* through *a free press,* and *an independent judiciary* – ultimately saved a nation.

EARLY ON IN its search for clues of mass corruption, South Africa's *Sunday Times* was subtly trapped by what U.S. President Trump – looking up the wrong end of a telescope – might define as 'fake news'. On at least two occasions the Sunday paper's enthusiastic exposures of corruption turned out to be built on false premises, fed to them by a corrupt government as cunningly pretended 'government leaks'.

Fortunately, while the duped Sunday paper took time to sort itself out (and return to lead the battle) the exposure of the outrageous manipulations of "the Gupta brothers" in milking state funds, were now driven mainly by small, independent, online investigative journalists ...

although *Business Day,* and the Afrikaans Press through its new online wing, *News24,* actively joined in.

Those who led the chase included two investigative teams of journalists, the online a*maBhungane* (named after a famous beetle that 'seeks out shit'); the Centre for Investigative Journalism, and another team calling itself Scorpio, with the implied sting in every tale (*sic)* it unearthed.

Laborious checking of vast lists of countless emails, cellphone messages and other anonymous digital leaks provided names, places, appointments, proposals and instructions which – put together – exposed plots and personalities involved in mass defrauding of the state. The leaked emails, and the mass of thinly disguised information they contained, were soon strong enough to face down the usual official public denials. The Gupta brothers and their luxury estate offices in the Johannesburg suburb of Saxonwold were suddenly made notorious through unwanted publicity – so much so that one visitor to the Gupta spiderweb chose to point out that there was *no proof* he had ever visited the Guptas of Saxonwold.

Their address was not the only notable place in Saxonwold, he cautiously pointed out. For instance, he knew of a shebeen (illegal tavern) in that suburb ... a claim that made him notorious and made Saxonwold popularly infamous.

The targets of the financial scams linking the Guptas with corrupt government leaders include:

- **Transnet** (a state-owned enterprise in charge of SA railways) which overpaid *billions* of rands for locomotives from Chinese and other foreign railway companies.
- **Eskom** the national electricity supplier, from which tens of millions of rands were milked ... and *billions* of dollars pledged to Russia for future nuclear power stations not yet designed. Fortunately the pledges for the vague distant future could not be sustained, because SA simply could not afford to start paying such ambitious sums for unknown products for an unknown era. Fortunately too, as President Zuma's political hold was wrestled open, Eskom's chairman and board were fired overnight – literally!– before the public corporation reached formal bankruptcy. However,
- **Coal Mines**, which the Guptas bought to feed the nation's electricity supply, were illegally stripped by Gupta agents to provide the new

owners with R1.75 billion extra, which they deposited in the SA branch of India's Bank of Baroda. The scam was finally revealed by investigative journalists; the funds were eventually frozen by order of the High Court in Pretoria.
- **International Consultancies, such as McKinsey and KPMG** which, when their extraordinary profits were revealed, were criticised across the world as unacceptable. KPMG was criticised for failing to 'blow the whistle' while earning R40m over 14 years for doing the dubious books of the Gupta companies. However, McKinsey earned every eight days what KPMG earned in 14 years. After six months' work, McKinsey walked away with R1.03bn. An ambitious new local advisory group named Trillian, belonging to the Guptas, appeared nowhere in the relevant contracts, yet also managed to siphon off government funding amounting to R565m before being found out.

However: "Apparent efforts of the Hawks (South Africa's priority crime-combating unit) to investigate voluminous allegations made against the Guptas have been minimal to non-existent," announced amaBhungane and Scorpio investigative journalists. They revealed that **over US$1-million paid by Swiss crane manufacturer Liebherr** ultimately ended up in a US company, Brookfield Consulting, owned by apparent US-citizen relatives of the Guptas. Roughly another US$9-million – originating from China South Rail's 'consulting' contract – was also wired to Brookfield in the United States.

"Individuals comfortably sitting in South Africa or Dubai might be unaware of the US legal risks created by the actions of merely one member of a broader conspiracy" wrote the amaBhungane Centre for Investigative Journalism. "But what if the huge movements of illegal US dollars involved were to be investigated by US authorities?"

A good question, when so little was being done by South Africa's own authorities.

The amounts cited above are only samples of the corruption that occurred under President Zuma's reign. It is explicable only because in his near-ten-year term he assumed the power to appoint personally as many Cabinet Ministers and Heads of Government departments as he wished; starting as noted, with dubious and fast-changing Commissioners of Police, heads of Intelligence Agencies and Public Protectors. Chaos might have resulted very early on had not the rest of South Africa's socio-political structure tried to keep watch and alert law-abiding civil society.

The Auditor-General's department, for instance, rebuffed all attempts of crooked invasion and succeeded probably because the President's criminal associates did not possess the auditing skills required. Nor could they invade democratic South Africa's constitutional and civic structures ... including the free press, and newspapers such as the *Sunday Times*, *Business Day*, the *Mail and Guardian* and several other alert publications.

It is important to remember again the many other civic bulwarks, the greatest being *the independent judiciary* whose judges acted decisively in the interests of justice and honesty wherever they could do so without impinging on the constitutional rights of a power-obsessed Parliament dominated by the President's political party, the ANC, which was self-guarding its own monetary interests.

The nation's first official Public Protector (a new role filled by an amazingly multi-skilled, but hitherto little-known woman, Thuli Madonsela) played a major role in exposing the alleged crimes of President Zuma, despite attempts by State Security Minister David Mahlobo who announced an inquiry into claims that Madonsela was a CIA spy! Tellingly, the press quickly uncovered evidence that Atul Gupta knew of the government's proposed "inquiry" long before Cabinet Minister Mahlobo made his public announcement. Thuli Madonsela's parliamentary-appointed successor demonstrated just how valuable Thuli Madonsela had been. An effective, active and courageous Public Protector is a rare thing.

A list of other statutory or voluntary civic organisations *trying to bring back honest government in the new democracy* would fill several pages. Instances that come to mind include:
- **The Helen Suzman Foundation**, a privately funded research group guarding the late, famous anti-apartheid politician's values.
- **OUTA**, an acronym of the 'Organisation Undoing Tax Abuse', formed to investigate specific accusations made by journalists against the 'Hawks' (the government's special investigative unit); alleged SA Airways' frauds; nuclear deals ... and "Who's Next? Our aim is to challenge the rationality of government decisions", says OUTA.
- **Afriforum,** a right-wing all-white counter-ANC organisation employing a private prosecutor to approach the courts when no one else would. Action, even from an extreme minority, is hugely valuable.

- **Corruption Watch,** a body set up by private initiative. It received in the five years 2012-2017 nearly 15,000 complaints of governmental maladministration as well as theft and bribery, ranging from school principals "abusing school funds" to Cabinet Ministers tolerating administrative theft and bribery.
- **CASAC**, the Council for the Advancement of the South African Constitution, which remains vigilant on all constitutional matters, including the dubiously passive role of two successive National Directors in the National Prosecuting Authority appointed by Zuma's Parliament failing to deal with state corruption.
- **Business and Human Rights Resource Centre**, seeking justice; protection of human rights and freedom of information.
- **Accountability,** now under the direction of Paul Hoffman, a senior counsellor in the South African legal system.
- **Centre for Applied Legal Studies,**
- **Public Affairs Research Institute,**
- **Right2Know, Open Secrets** and numerous individuals who also spoke up through the free press against specific cases of corruption.

These and other such independent bodies in South Africa remain dedicated to upholding the nation's three basic structures of democracy:
- public awareness
- a democratic (not government-controlled) parliament
- And all of these mutually supportive elements supported by the free press.

Then why did it all go wrong?
Commentators throughout the South African media have ranted angrily and analysed sadly the reasons for the new nation falling into a self-destructive and deep pit of illegality and corruption, dug by 'official' greed.

There *are* established causes for such widespread behaviour where the majority of the population has gained full freedom, yet found few rewards and much tension in living their lives in overcrowded Western-style metropolitan settlements. But there also seem to be much stronger more obvious causes; the major one being that the style of government had slipped into unaccountability, while the newly born *social media* sprayed the national consciousness with images of a small percentage of newly affluent Africans drinking the most expensive champagnes when not bending down to consume sushi off the naked waists of waitresses in luxurious night-clubs.

The constant examples of unethical and unbridled high-living, set by President Zuma himself, and the accusations against him of fraud and dishonesty are surely major influences on the style of public life ... especially for those who rise fast in presidential favour, and fall so quickly when favouritism fades.

The media's braking role has already been mentioned. Most of the newspapers' blogs and TV news programmes remain steadily concerned about unaccountability of government. Their tone, including the voices of state broadcasters, is usually mildly liberal and strictly non-racist.

Freedom of information, of course, means that a new national TV broadcaster and a new daily paper titled *New Age* were tolerated. Both skated enthrallingly close to self-made corruption, and were illegally subsidised by the Guptas and patronised by Zuma's government through state advertising, and staged breakfast functions at which R100,000 and more provided a 'meal-ticket' for each. It was an occasion at which a prominent government politician would make a speech and sign serviettes and so on for audiences eager to be associated with the new 'get-rich-quick' political racketeers.

Meanwhile, *The Daily Maverick*, an independent online news service deserving far more funding, and the *Businesslive* and *Sunday Times* stable as well as *News24* in the China-rich Afrikaans sector, were all determinedly unfolding the tale of 'State Capture' amid a thousand official denials. The media staying silent were the Gupta-sponsored TV station ANN7 and newspaper *New Age* ... and Independent Newspapers, the national chain of daily newspapers which maintained a strange and intense reticence.

All on his own, Jacques Pauw, a former journalist of *Vrye Weekblad* (later a special assignment TV director turned restaurant chef) set out in his book *President's Keepers* (Tafelberg: four rapid-release editions in late 2017) to tell the entire story of a tribal President's capture of the state.

Pauw's return to journalism was an extraordinary effort in which he was swiftly crowned an international prize-winner while he faced physical and legal dangers, jail or harassment. His wisest step was to persuade the *Sunday Times* to carry book passages as a verbatim frontpage lead, with whole pages inside, revealing details of blatant and massive corruption of the state. That in itself protected him from total censorship and oblivion. That, and a government threat to censor his book, drove its sales far beyond the capacity of the publishers to print enough even in the following month. The book, with its truth-tested melodramatic content, instantly became one of the most successful publications in South Africa's history, even while Zuma's government stooges were trying to censor it and prosecute the author.

Some of the books sensational claims include:

President Zuma, while already in office, received early on in his reign, *a private, employee's salary* of R1,000,000 a month! The employer of the newly appointed President, according to the tax-receipts deducted in advance of payment, was a business tycoon named Chockalingam "Roy" Moodley whose son once told an audience in the President's presence:

"My father is *the* most powerful man in South Africa". The President seemed to acquiesce, but of course no explanations were given for Moodley's boast.

Was it a private joke? Or a moment of unwise hubris on the part of young Moodley? This, despite the likely event of some kind of cross-examination and possible prosecution of the President himself?

What the President thought about it we do not know. Perhaps he chuckled, confident in his power.

What we do know is that countless people were trying to raid South Africa's deliberately unguarded coffers ... some wanting not merely a few million rand, but a few *billion*. That was the sum of tax fees not paid on years' of a single individual's dealings.

Here are two samples:

SCORPIO: THE CURIOUS CASE OF ANC BENEFACTOR
ROBERT HUANG,
A NEVER-ENDING INVESTIGATION AND
BILLIONS OWED TO THE TAX-MAN

Under these headlines is the account of panicked SARS officials who compiled a confidential internal report to their managers on the status of one of the biggest tax evasion investigations, just days after journalist Jacques Pauw's blockbuster book hit stores around the country. The report's focus, according to "Scorpio" investigative journalist Pauli van Wyk involved the curious multibillion-rand and decade-old tax case of the Taiwanese national and Zuma-linked businessman, Jen Chih (Robert) Huang, his company Mpisi Trading 74 and an estimated R3-billion owed to the State Revenue office. Based on leaked tax information, "Scorpio can reveal that Huang attempted to settle his tax affairs for R20-million, that the finalisation of Huang's case, code-named 'Project Nightfury', seems to have ground to a halt, and that Pauw's revelations about Huang were spot-on", Van Wyk reported.

One of the more entertaining passages in Jacques Pauw's disturbing best-seller, *The President's Keepers – Those Keeping Zuma in Power and Out of Prison,* is his account of how internal State Security auditors arrived at the headquarters of the Principal Agent Network at the end of 2009 to investigate the covert unit's finances.

There had been little accountability over the years. An estimated R1.5-billion had been blown on various projects and the grandly excessive purchase of properties and cars. Agent handlers themselves also withdrew huge amounts of cash, for which they did not have to account. They flew economy class carrying large amounts of cash in briefcases. They were masters of their own little tawdry universe.

Eventually, when at last their own (clean) auditors arrived to check them, the guilty security agents set up cameras to watch, secretly, what their auditors were doing.

Pauw recounts that the professional spies, "in a supreme dumb and dumber moment," slipped up when the auditors began perusing the stack of documents in the boardroom of an office on Route 21 in Irene near Pretoria. The *security agents* and their *secret service* managers lingered in a room next door, eavesdropping on the auditors and filming them going through invoices they had faked the night before.

Problem was, the agent who had rigged up the cameras had forgotten to stop their filming when the auditors left. What the camera then captured for all to see was the government agents' own frantic attempt at destroying evidence and manufacturing invoices. In the process they had also accidentally shredded some of their own forgeries, leaving the real invoices behind.

Then one of them turned informer and produced the filmed evidence.

But even such a rich diet of mystery, crime, human greed, misery and farce is not sufficient coverage in such extraordinary circumstances;

not when democracy pretends to rule a country with *millions* of adults out of work and *millions* of young people lacking proper schooling. The issues involve a national government's greatest monetary crime ... though it is not as big as South Africa's previous 50-year-story of apartheid racism, governmental murders and crimes against humanity.

Nonetheless, the ongoing revelations of Zuma's 'State Capture' required democratic debate, follow-ups and comment. In the absence of adequate parliamentary or public leaders' debates and comment by private citizens, the people and the press were essential at all stages. It came online, finally and sufficiently and in full, familiar editorial shape. As the revelations kept coming, several of the nation's best columnists started commenting online on almost every unfolding insight into bribery and corruption.

Bear this in mind while reading the following descriptive, informal commentary piece on one of the first, very belated parliamentary inquiries into state corruption. This 'news commentary' on the event, by Marianne Thamm, was published nationally online by the *Daily Maverick* after the first day's hearing. It is published here for general readers everywhere, so I have deleted references to locally accused police and South African political activists whose identities are not relevant outside of the investigative hearings.

The Turning Point
By MARIANNE THAMM

Where to begin?
Perhaps at the start of proceedings when a high-level SA Police delegation, including newly minted National Police Commissioner, General Khehla Sitole, and other top brass in police Supply Chain Management, Strategic Management and Forensic Auditing, filed quietly into Parliament's Scopa committee room V454 at 09:00 on Wednesday ... Also present were Independent Police Investigative Directorate Executive Director, Robert McBride, and head investigator, Matthews Sesoko. Sesoko is currently probing former acting National Commissioner Khomotso Phahlane on charges of fraud and corruption which relate to his alleged acceptances of kickbacks paid via a Pretoria car dealer to himself, his wife, Brigadier Beauty Phahlane, as well as his sister Josephine during his time

as head of Police Forensics and while head of the entire South African Police Force (SAPS).

McBride and his investigators were in turn being hounded by a posse of North West province-based cops, led by Major-General Jan Mabula ...

And then there was the surprise guest, who must have slipped in when no one was looking – the man in the centre of IPID's investigations and a separate State Info investigation involving evergreen contracts worth around R6.1-billion and awarded to three of his companies between 2010 and 2017, Keith Keating himself.

Keating strategically seated himself on the periphery of the room facing Police and State Info officials. He had a clear line of sight of Police officers as they prepared to deliver an 11-page document.

They needn't have bothered printing it. In the end, as the temperature – literally, physically and metaphorically – rose in the room, the document was turned into hand-held fans.

If it were not all so utterly tragic, one might have been able to charge for the spectacle of the great unravelling that began to take place:

What was clear was that the multiparty Parliamentary committee members, as well as the deceptively affable chair Themba Godi, must have agreed beforehand to allow the DA's Tim Brauteseth – himself a former forensic investigator – to lead what turned into a deep and unexpected interrogation of the Police Force and State Info officials and how both these institutions have been corroded by wide-scale corruption and malfeasance.

Police Command did not even have time to suggest that their presentation be made as Brauteseth went straight for the jugular shortly after Godi's welcomes. Brauteseth zoned in on one component of a network of potential irregular procurements – that of Rofin forensic lights for the Police – which Keating's Forensic Data Analysts (FDA) had engaged State Info to maintain at the cost of around R9-million per month.

While State Info had sent a wad of documents to the Parliamentary committee members ahead of Wednesday's meeting, the Police had simply handed in a quarter of a page. Brauteseth began by asking State Info where the procurement documents for the 3,573 items it serviced for the Police might be found.

No one had an answer.

"Who had bought these items?" Brauteseth continued.

By then the Police delegation knew they had been ambushed with nowhere to hide as current Deputy National Commissioner for resource management, Lieutenant-General Stefan Schutte, battled to answer questions.

Then came the bombshell.

Brauteseth asked State Info whether Keating had signed a declaration in August 2017 that FDA had not been involved in any corrupt or collusive activities with State Info, its employees, customers or their staff, suppliers or "any organ of the state".

Yes, yes, he had.

Could anyone explain then a trip in October 2011 to the UK by Police Supply Chain Management members supposedly to attend an RFID (Radio Frequency Identification Process) conference?

Nope.

Neither could anyone in the delegation explain how the members travelled, who had paid for the trip, expenses or any entertainment (including a visit to a brothel called Babylon in Vienna) that the members might have enjoyed.

And then Brauteseth pulled out enlarged photographs of two Police members posing in the trophy room of Old Trafford, the home of English Premier Soccer League team Manchester United, with Keating and Jerenique Bayard. Bayard is the project director at Unisys and who has supplied millions of rand worth of cameras to the Police.

Was it a coincidence, asked Brauteseth, that Keating had taken the Police Supply Chain members on the jaunt six months after an order for equipment had been placed for millions of rand worth of forensic cameras and other equipment?

Keating appeared to sink deep into the vinyl chair, possibly regretting that he had opted to attend ...

Eventually the Police and State Info executives murmured that yes, the trip could be regarded as suspicious and irregular.

From that point onwards it was like watching a pit latrine collapse on itself ...

At some point everyone in the room became aware of the portly man in the white shirt.

Keith Keating ...

Why was he there, committee members demanded to know. How did he get in? Was he there trying to psyche out Police and State Info officials? He should move to the other side of the venue where he could not stare down officials.

No one on Wednesday could answer why Keating had been appointed as a sole supplier of a variety of goods and services to the Police and State Info Agency from 2010 to 2017 and amounting to R6.1-billion while the Public Finance Management Act made it quite clear there needed to be compelling reasons for the contracting of sole suppliers. There had also been no competitive bidding for any of the products and services Keating's companies offered to the Police and State Info Agency.

Some of the work Keating rendered, the committee heard, also related to the entire Police Intelligence infrastructure, the location of which, the delegation admitted, was presently unknown. What this means is that the country's criminal justice system could be in the hands of one person who might be able to press a button and make it all disappear.

Khehla, towards the end of the meeting, admitted this posed a threat to national security after Brauteseth reminded officials that the Auditor General had stated that the Police's intangible asset register could not be located.

The more committee members learned of the scale of the alleged corruption surrounding the procurement of business with Keating's companies, the angrier they grew.

Police were colluding with criminals!

Keating has captured the Police Department and the State InfoAgency!

Put him in jail! Arrest him now!

This was a repeat of early corruption when colonists traded mirrors for land, said one member.

"Why aren't the Police 'Hawks' division here? This love of money is criminal, it is an embarrassment to our country," said another.

Keating remained seated, betraying nothing, laughing occasionally, sometimes shaking his head in disagreement.

Committee member Vincent Smith suggested that Khehla immediately terminate all contracts with Keating's companies.

"We're coming for Keith Keating," McBride later told committee members ...

Wednesday's parliamentary committee meeting was a sterling example of the power of the oversight role Parliament can and should play in demanding accountability from government officials. The gargantuan extent of the alleged corruption, as revealed at the hearing, is now public knowledge. But in order for this deep root of criminality to be thwarted the country needs an NPA and Hawks capable of protecting the state and taxpayers' money from predators from within its own ranks and in the private sector.

The tide is turning.

It is time now for law enforcement agencies to step up ...

Leaving the Scopa committee room this writer accidentally found herself alone in the lift with Keith Keating.

After a rather awkward silence I asked: "So, how was that for you?"

He seemed surprised and mumbled: "I plan to fight back. It's not true".

Daily Maverick

Thamm's article covers all bases. She appreciates that this was one of the first, almost reluctant, hearings agreed to be heard by a parliamentary committee.

She wrote it only months before President Jacob Zuma appeared before nearly 6,000 people to bid goodbye at the sudden end of his term of office. Zuma lashed out at the media; he lashed out at the courts. He stopped for applause, almost begged for it from the masses of ANC party supporters. In the silence he then sang, expertly, a famous song in his chosen vernacular. The response from inveterate party congress singers was lukewarm.

An ANC majority finally turned its back on him ... though it was a close call.

Zuma and the raiders of the state coffers still have huge support in the ruling party. They may soon be back, unless disciplinary action is taken. And unless the new online free press remains strong, independent and on its toes.

Democratic South Africa is back on track. The only foreseeable threat it faces, as I write, is the unbridled monster of racism. It is a beast still easily baited by anyone seeking or holding power.

As a reminder of such racism, let us go back now for a glimpse of a beautiful unspoilt piece of southern Africa ... □

29.
In search of a place to talk freely.

But then the lion roared. I looked up and saw on the ridge of hills in front of us a scene that would be imprinted on my mind for the rest of my life. In the soft, late-afternoon light walked a long line of tall, magnificent black Sable antelopes, their horns arcing over their backs in sharp, curling waves.

I t was way back in the 1980s and we were sitting in a broken-down, roofless 4×4 on the edge of a swamp in Botswana; not far from the Caprivi Strip and the borders of Zambia and Zimbabwe. Our guide had set off on foot to fetch help. He'd left us with a flask of gin and instructions to keep the lioness away – and her cubs from chewing on our vehicle's tyres. Which was exactly what they were now doing.

Zapiro, South Africa's internationally-known cartoonist, has depicted with searing accuracy the last years of apartheid and the first decades of South African democracy. Here he pictured the struggle against state secrecy, one of the themes of this book. It is an insidious and dangerous secrecy that continues to threaten, long after full democracy was attained.

"Shoo", said Adele, waving her glass of gin ineffectually at a lion cub gnawing away at the left-front wheel just below her.

A bit cheesy, I thought. Not that I'm against gin cocktails, but it felt inappropriate as another wildlife experience in deepest Africa; more suitable to a moment in a game park in Bedfordshire, England or in a Bronx zoo.

But then the lion roared. I looked up and saw on the ridge of hills in front of us a scene that would be imprinted on my mind for the rest of my life. In the soft, late-afternoon light walked a long line of tall, magnificent black Sable antelopes, their horns arcing over their backs in sharp, curling waves. They halted, heads up, and posed on the ridge in a magnificently elegant frieze silhouetted against a vast African sky. Such moments are rare, unplanned, and as priceless as they are unexpected – yet any active veteran journalist comes to expect astonishing surprises in his working day – and as I happened to be working that day, I was impatient with any form of game viewing at so critical a time.

Okavango River. Courtesy of Botswana Tourism.

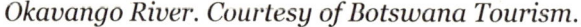

But, after being 'rescued' and flown to inspect several unoccupied camps across the vast, forested Okavango delta that spills itself into the desert, a second rare experience occurred. Our small plane headed north, to the Chobe Reserve where we had no trouble landing on a makeshift landing strip. The camp's accommodation and its situation looked promising for the purpose we had in mind.

"Did you see the leopard as you came in?" asked the excited owner. We didn't, but later in the dark we heard the scream of a terrified tourist, and saw a flash of movement, which her party claimed was a leopard.

"It's gone," they said as I rushed out to see it. During the night, however, the whole width of my tent bulged inwardly. The canvas pushed against my pillow as I heard sighing and rumbling noises that sounded like a hungry elephant's stomach.

It *was* an elephant's stomach.

It was just above my head, as the elephant in a drought-induced, desperate search for a drink, ripped out the water pipe beside my tent.

You wouldn't choose that as a great moment of exhilaration. The exhilaration was in the thought that this was one of the camps that Adele Lucas, a crazy PR company owner, and I were planning to use as an alternative venue for a meeting of the world's top media. On behalf of the Johannesburg *Star,* I was inviting the heads of great newspapers, as well as TV and radio, from Washington to London, from Madrid to Stockholm, from Israel to Australasia, and from India and beyond, to an *indaba* on the plight of the media in many countries, especially my own.

The late 1980s were critical times for SA's press.

It was a time when an apartheid government was attempting to censor SA newspapers out of existence – and Russia and China, with similar motives, were seeking to impose on the UN a controlled "new international Information Order". Because of the stark threats of censorship to my own newspaper, I was attempting to rally the world's free media to our own particular cause. In fact, two of the 'tent-poles' of this great marquee of a proposed conference had already expressed willingness to come. One was Katherine Graham, head of *Washington Post* and *Newsweek,* the courageous newspaperwoman who was crudely disparaged by the US president's men for "getting her tit caught in the (political) wringer".

As a young mother, once a secretary and suddenly a widow, Katherine Graham was called upon to head Washington Post and Newsweek and to seek truth until she and her journalists finally caused the downfall of a US president.

Undaunted, her newspaper continued to publish the heatedly denied findings of a journalistic investigation which finally brought down President Nixon. The decision to publish was finally hers alone, and Watergate was just one of several of her brave acts which bolstered reporting standards and the right to publish.

The other 'tent-pole' on whom I was relying to attract the world's press to southern Africa was Lord McGregor of Durris, independent trustee of Reuters, chairman of a British Royal Press Commission and adviser to press councils, in the East, the West, and elsewhere.

However, I had not yet told either of them the details of our possible venue. It might be on the edge of the Okavango 'swamp' close to Chobe, or in one large, well-established camp overlooking a broad expanse of savannah and dried-up river bed which we gazed upon on our final day.

"What if there's no water?" we asked our potential host anxiously. "It'll come," he assured us. "The swamp's late this year because of this exceptional drought, but its waters will come."

Sure enough, the first trickle arrived even before our departure. It came winding down a dry incline, though it never actually reached us. We could see elephants celebrating as they stamped on a tiny, snaking rivulet and rolled in its newly made mud. The elephants greeted the long-awaited arrival of life-giving water with so much joy that the inconsiderate beasts were temporarily impeding its flow.

We clambered into our small plane to be airlifted back to The Duck Inn at Maun, the nearest 'outpost of civilisation'. In 1987, The Duck Inn – we called it The Sitting Duck, I seem to remember, or The Effing Duck during its earlier days – was the transport depot for the through traffic of bush pilots, trackers, truck drivers, hunters and a pioneering breed of amateur 4×4 'explorers' who spent the night standing in the bar until sufficiently desensitised to noise and local conditions in order to fall asleep in their allotted accommodation.

Adele immediately set about tying up the detailed but unconfirmed arrangements of our seemingly impossible venture. She organised eight or ten pilots to be ready to fly small aircraft into all of the accessible semi-permanent Okavango Delta camps then in existence, ferrying more than a hundred city-dressed delegates to their lodgings under mosquito netting and canvas. They were then to be transported daily, in forest-hopping relays, to and from their island camps to the proposed venue which would require imported marquees and catering facilities. There were other minor details to consider, including the fact that Lord McGregor, for health reasons, could fly only first class. There were also political issues including sanctions and bannings in apartheid South Africa. And there were intricate border problems. Also there were problems with some essential delegates who normally would not be seen alive or dead with each other in any tent, cathedral, mosque or on any platform whatever.

Yes, there was a great deal of exhilaration as we downed our fifth beer in the old 'Duck' dive.

But it didn't last.

AS AN UNAVOIDABLY reckless Plan B, the holding of a press convention in Africa's greatest blind river swamp, was a wild idea with hippo-sized traps. But it might cause our State President, known to his inner circle as the Great Crocodile, to blink or shed a pretended tear or two, and shut his eyes. If he didn't, we would have to turn away most of the media, men and women who accepted invitations to our Johannesburg press congress, and invite only the top 100 delegates, hoping perhaps 80 of the best among them would pack their mosquito nets and join the planned adventure beyond our country's stifling borders.

Even though President Botha didn't give a damn any more for hostile world opinion, he would appreciate that a wild walk of metropolitan news people in a park in deepest Africa would attract more world attention than a joint press protest in Paris and Pretoria; or a mass cry for press freedom at the UN and in the Albert Hall.

At least Foreign Minister 'Pik' Botha would understand that instantly. He quickly got Cabinet permission (or rather President PW Botha's permission) to let it be known to us that no delegate would be refused entry to South Africa for a stipulated, very brief period. This guaranteed that the issues of *Conflict and the Press** would be examined and discussed freely, and by nearly three times as many delegates, at a luxury hotel in the City of Gold, Jo'burg. It would deal with global questions as relevant in today's instant internet environments as they were in the time of the Cold War and the age of apartheid.

Zapiro's message

Zapiro's cartoon shown earlier, is, I believe, directly relevant to every voter – and to every resident non-citizen and every person who can read or is learning to read. For if you do not have freedom of information you can trust nothing. And then what's the point of voting or reading anything?

Freedom of information is an ideal that has been fought for throughout the past 100 years. It is no safer today than it was in America in the 1950s ... when even freedom of speech was in danger of being lost in the world's truest democracy! Neither is it any safer today in South Africa or in many other 'democracies' around the world. Zapiro's donated illustration is a reminder that all of us should act the moment we see a snake trying to devour our precariously established rights. □

* *Conflict and the Press* – The Star Centennial Conference. The role of the Press in a divided society, edited by Harvey Tyson (The Argus Printing & Publishing Co., 1987).

30.
Conflict and the Press.

*We blacks have learned how to
mask our feelings and disguise our hate ...
I love communism – don't know what it means,
but I love it because just the word
causes whites to panic.*

Famous African actor, John Kani.

Shakespearean actor John Kani was taking time off from filming *Othello* in Johannesburg to jolt *The Star*'s conference guests, and the world media, reminding them of how critical relationships were in South Africa.

"The pain in this country is that we're going down very fast. Bloody confrontation is going to be unavoidable unless we do something *now*," he said.

Yes. Something had to be done – by many people at many levels, reaching across to each other. That very day, 18 October 1987, the editor of *New Nation,* Zwelakhe Sisulu, was counting his 282nd day in detention

"Suffer little children ... I forget the rest."

in terms of the first of several waves of government-declared Emergency Regulations. Three other journalists, Mxolisi Fuzile (472 days), Phil Ngqumbva (461 days) and Brian Sokutu (463 days) were also languishing in prison without any charge laid against them. They did not know when, or if, they would ever be released.

We knew only that 22 other journalists, who had been arrested in the past month, were back in business. The press had managed to establish their whereabouts and publish their names. That was a newspapers' obvious, but increasingly difficult job. It meant that at least those identified and still in prison would probably be safe. But what about scores of other political prisoners still unknown?

"What about the *children* held in jail?" asked my colleague Joe Latakgomo.

"Even if we knew, we would not be able to publish the facts," he told the world's media in the presence of an apartheid Cabinet Minister.

"Society generally would therefore never be able to comprehend the horrors that these children in particular have faced. Our ignorance will be used in judgment against us. It is the government that has decreed that this is so ..."

Yes. Something had to be done. But it needed something much more than just editors lamenting or shouting objections in the 'Opposition Press'. We had been doing that for more than *forty years* already. To little effect. Or so we thought, in those despairing 1980s. Events would later prove otherwise.

For the moment, however (the moment being the 100th anniversary of the birth of *The Star* – born many years before South Africa itself), some prospective delegates were looking for another way to save our country.

First I had approached the CEOs of South Africa's 17 top companies and business corporations and asked them to help sponsor an international meeting of the world's media with all relevant local political interests – banned and unbanned; government and anti-government, Far Left and Far Right movements – to discuss the vital role of a free press in a non-democracy.

It doesn't sound much, but business leaders appreciated it was a radical concept for a semi-police state. Every one of the 17 business leaders immediately donated a five-figure sum for our campaign "in support of freedom of information and equal opportunity". It was an unaccustomed political risk for them – as it was soon to be for the government. And for my newspaper. And for every participant, each of whom, whether from some distant nation or from some banned local organisation, would be accused of giving a platform to the apartheid regime. There were, of course, numerous last-minute crises. We lived on the edge of all of them from day to day.

Finally I was able to inform delegates as they met safely at last in Johannesburg: "In the next few hours there could be some changes, but representative organisations ranging from the United Democratic Front (UDF) to Inkatha (Zulu Conservative wing); from Azapo to Cosatu; from the South African government's Security Forces to the 'Release Mandela' campaign, are here tonight. They – and all of you who are delegates from the world's media, including a representative from behind the Iron Curtain – are gathering under one roof for the first time ever."

Leaders of the international news agencies, the BBC and US television and radio heads as well as global professional free press organisations based in London, Paris, Washington and New York were also there. Ironically, the only delegate noticeably missing was the third of the planned 'tent poles', Cushrow Irani, chairman of the World Press Freedom Committee and editor of *The Statesman* in India. The obtuse but politically correct Prime Minister of that country had banned him from visiting South Africa to discuss press freedom!

Instead, Cushrow sent a recorded message supporting our cause and criticising his Prime Minister, with whom he was already in dispute on the same matter. Cushrow's stirring message ended:

"As you debate these issues, my thoughts are with you. I wish you fulfilment in your task …"

"To South Africa's father figure, imprisoned on a lonely island, my homage on bended knee …"

The SA government, with little option but to acquiesce to the gathering of such a powerful audience, had sent two Cabinet Ministers to persuade the world's media that freedom of the press had to give way to "a real (communist) threat to a nation's existence". The Cabinet Ministers' argument, even in the still existing – still hotly intense – Cold War between free nations and communist totalitarianism, was so palpably irrelevant in the case of apartheid's minority domination that delegates spent little time on the well-explored debate of Security vs Freedom of Information.

Instead, our conference, I believe, provided us with vital support in a very real battle against censorship. And it seemed to do much more than that.

It examined the codes of the independent free press, and the threats to its freedom around the world. Also, at a minor and personal level, it convinced journalists like me not to quit our jobs or our country during its worst thousand days. Those worst days were still to come, for while the government was already talking by proxy and in utter secrecy to Mandela, and later to Oliver Tambo and a future African National Congress government, the threat of communist totalitarianism still existed ... and the Cabinet was at that same moment quietly handing over power to a cabal of secret police and militia that bypassed parliament and waged a mysterious, yet at times, a murderously blatant war of terrorism on all who questioned the hated apartheid state.

Our major task was obviously going to be to attempt to report to the country and the world on every suspected political murder and every heatedly denied political assassination. As the state refused to provide relevant information, rumour would be a vicious handicap yet never an impossible hurdle. The real, formidable hurdle was made up of successive censorship decrees and 'Emergency' statutes piling up on each other that might make our job futile – if not a charade. That was always our fear. There seemed to be no place left for moderation and honest journalism in South Africa.

However, the views of the major players in the press freedom debate persuaded me otherwise. They also reminded all of us of the media's obligations to their societies.

Many 'press freedom fighters' in many countries embraced and extravagantly praised the project. The editor of *Index on Censorship*, the international journal known as champion of all the world's gagged writers and reporters, described it as: "One of the most exhilarating and useful experiences of my life".

Drawing the line

The questions examined by leaders of the international media at that event are as relevant in today's instant internet environment as they were in the time of the Cold War and the age of apartheid.

Questions such as:
• *Do the media encourage violence through their constant coverage of*

rioting, revolt and political murder on all sides?
- *Does constant reporting of unrest and general 'bad news' distort reality and threaten security?*
- *Is the 'Right to Know' a threat to privacy and an excuse for sensationalism?*
- *Should there be effective control of the 'free' press?*

Under any authoritarian government the answer to each is 'YES'.

Indeed, these four questions became Government accusations against the SA 'Opposition Press' for almost three decades following 'the Sharpeville Massacre' in 1960. Without the South African press, the Sharpeville massacre was in danger of becoming just another 'accidental incident' in a silent, uncaring, secretive era.

It's astonishing to remember that the 'Opposition Press' was the only effective public medium in Africa at that time. South Africa had to wait another 16 years before the first television sets began sending out government approved 'test signals', and people had little option other than to listen to two national radio stations – both strictly controlled by the state. No wonder the state was desperate to muzzle the press. It staged, in the first decade of apartheid rule, half a dozen official Press Commissions which were tuned to shut down newspapers. They failed because government-supporting fanatics were the only people to support such a thing. Unquestioning government supporters were always in the minority ... unlike in our democracy today.

Our instant, internationally-spread Sharpeville coverage had provided a big 'No' to questioners seeking curbs on the free press. As were the Soweto 1976 youth riots to which the South African 'Opposition Press' alerted Africa and all the world to its significant context. But the other questions above *still* had to be answered by looking at them from all angles and divergent interests. This was what the 'Conflict and the Press' conference set out to do. Unsurprisingly, in the open debate among the majority of reasonable delegates of many political persuasions across the world, the answer to each of the above questions asked in 1987 was again 'NO'.

The verbatim debates and the accompanying 'workshop' reports on the often conflicting views of more than 250 delegates were published at the time*, but some succinct answers are worth repeating, even after more than 20 years of democracy, with its dubious assumption that freedom is protected by Parliament and the web with its unrestricted twittering and tweeting.

Does media coverage increase unrest?
Delegate David Steward's view, as a spokesman for the SA government Bureau for Information, had already stated at our conference: "Many contend that the media may have become more than observers of modern history, they have become participants."

Stephen Claypole, Director of BBC External News Services, responsible for programmes reaching 120 million people in 36 different language services responded to this, and more vociferous criticism, with: "We have been blamed for much. 'The Evil Eye' ... The 'medium which has dislocated the social order and set community against community' ... 'The vultures of the media who have gathered when passion is aroused and blood is spilt' ... 'If only we would put away our cameras and microphones and lights, all would be well'."

He sighed and added: "As if the times *before* television were noted for peace and tranquillity!"

Richard Hardwood, representing the American Society of Newspaper Editors, said: "The journalist, we like to believe, seeks to describe the events and forces of history. The advocate seeks to manipulate them." (He was referring to partisan, 'advocacy journalism', which a free nation rightly tolerates ... as it does 'irresponsible' journalism in all those magazines catering to all kinds of unfashionable views.) All had a place in a society that treasured free speech, he reminded the audience.

Why do the media emphasise negative news rather than positive news?

Responding to this, Prof Gavin Stewart of Rhodes University Journalism School referred to the South African government's use at that moment of its own devised 'scientific method' of measuring newspaper reports for 'positivity' or 'negativity'. The state was testing newspaper coverage on its own strange measurement scale ranging from Plus 7 to Minus 7. Mock scientific judgments of this kind, made after the government had suspended law and declared a National Emergency, threatened all newspapers and the very existence of some, he pointed out.

No one needed to repeat the tired maxim that "one man's positively rave 'freedom fighter' is another man's negatively despicable 'terrorist'."

Dana Bullen of the World Press Freedom Committee said independent journalists believed governments who imposed regulations on the press usually did so to hide official embarrassment, or corruption or as a pretext to stifle legitimate public debate. He was familiar with the criticism of publishing only the 'bad news', for it had been voiced by many authoritarian governments.

He rejected the entire concept of either 'positive' or 'negative' reporting. The 'either/or' could not exist. Even the result of a football match was both positive and negative – good news for the winners; bad news for the losers. His own experience was that credible journalists worked hard to retain their reputations for independent and unbiased reporting, so much so that as a reporter he had ensured his neutrality by not even voting in a political election at home.

"... like Robespierre, a sea-green

incorruptible", beamed a conference workshop convener, Michael Green, when reporting back the debate to the full congress.

Timothy Balding of the International Federation of Newspapers in Paris made the point that anybody should be able to publish a newspaper, and its existence should be determined by its readers who were the final arbiters. When Casper Venter of the SA Department of Information argued that a reporter should at least cover both sides, the pros and cons, of a story, Balding asked: "Then what about the ANC's side of events? Both the organisation and its spokesmen are banned and the press may not even quote their public statements."

A good point, said the same discussion group's convenor, Michael Green of the *Daily News*, Durban. He summed up by deciding that the criticism of 'negative' news – reporting in place of 'positive' news was so subjective, and the debaters so divided, that he could only suggest that if a clear definition of positive and negative were needed one should ask someone in a press photographer's [pre-digital] darkroom.

Reporting in a tense and divided society
Editors and journalists invited from countries in conflict like my own were asked to share their experiences with us. Their responses were on these lines:

'The Basque problem'. "Only intellectual honesty and personal courage allow a journalist to survive under the social and political conditions of the Basques ... (but) the high level of freedom of expression existing in newly-democratic Spain allows even the radical newspaper acting as ETA's ('terrorist') organ to continue operating, although its editors have had to appear in court on more than one occasion accused of justifying terrorism." – Dr Vincente Verdu of *El Pais,* Madrid.

Israel. "(The problem is) people avoid the complications and stress of living in a society in conflict by resorting to a process of psychological repression of the realities. And they hate those who constantly remind them of the bad news. Their attitude to facts is selective." – Yehudi Litani, Middle East Editor, *Jerusalem Post.*

Sri Lanka. "Despite widespread violence, division and terrorism, my company published papers in English, Singhalese and Tamil. Readers of all three complained their newspaper carried too much depressing news." – Mdsandhya Gunasena, Editorial Executive, Independent Newspapers, Colombo.

Northern Ireland. "The truth matters whether you are in government or against the government ... In a conflict situation – and I speak only of direct experience in Ireland – what an embattled community requires and deserves is a maximum of old-fashioned reporting (without hindrance)." – Douglas Gageby, ex-editor of *Irish Times*; and Director of National Newspapers of Dublin, Ireland.

Protecting your Right to Information

The most urgent need of any citizen for information arises during times of political crisis or instability. How can this balance with the need for security?

The reply came in one sentence. It was the key point, in my view, of the key universal debate on freedom of speech and freedom of information. It came from Andreas Whittam-Smith, at that time founder, owner, editor and chief executive of *The Independent,* London. In answer to my request to join us, he had opted to leave the vital first-birthday celebrations of his challenging, brand new newspaper to assist me in the critical times of *The Star*'s 100th anniversary conference on a free press.

He said: "The key considerations for a balance of security and freedom of information are that there should exist:

No prior restraint on publishing (pre-censorship)

A right of the press to a public trial

A right to plead 'public interest'."

There it is. Let the people decide.

'Letting the people decide', however, can lead to many arguments. I had invited a member of my own staff on *The Star* to express his own views, and to start an argument if he wished. He did much more than I hoped – waving a red flag at his colleagues and creating a delightful furore.

Defying the Law

My greatest fear, a ceaseless one, was that my newspaper would end up, willy-nilly, as a front for the apartheid government; a toothless, gagged critic going through the motions – like the vast South African Broadcasting Corporation did – of publishing to all the people, but honestly serving none. We were already being accused by the refugee wing of the ANC and its local agents of being a government puppet ...

which we were not, and would never be. Nor were we, as the government often alleged, in cahoots with the ANC, trying to bring communism to 'the nation'.

We had no option at that stage, but to defy the law blatantly and to challenge the government to close us down. It would be a grand gesture. But that is all it could be. At least once a month, as we purposely broke government laws and decrees, I began asking my senior colleagues: "If we do make a grand gesture in defiance, now, and invite being closed down – what could we ever do for an encore?"

"And at what stage then should we quit?" I asked myself later.

Of course that's an editorial 'we'. This latter question could only be a personal one for every journalist. Some editors might ask it in the tempting knowledge that they could, and perhaps should, leave their country to find satisfaction in a meaningful, prosperous job in some fine democratic paper in some other land. The temptation was always there. Now I was relying on three important guests, three foreign ladies at our conference, to guide us – without being asked; without being briefed; and without them knowing our precise problems.

Three Guiding Angels

It is a delicious irony that, after hundreds of years in which no female was allowed to play any executive part in the world of newspapers, three courageous heads of internationally famous newspapers – all women – had come to South Africa to attempt a rescue of the South African press. They unknowingly gave us the answers I sought.

The 'gracious ladies' were:

Countess Marion Donhoff, publisher and 'senior editor' of *Die Zeit* in Germany. She had witnessed Hitler's crushing of the *Reich*'s vast press, which rapidly withered because it consisted in the 1930s of about 3,000 (*!*) independent papers ... but all of them were regional, the vast majority relatively small. The press had no strong voices. Thus, after nationalising the film industry and radio (there was, in that era, no TV to speak of) Hitler quickly found it easy to pick off the fragmented press.

Countess Donhoff, who had also witnessed the censorship by the post-war Allied occupation forces in the 1940s, said: "There is a distinct difference between a totalitarian dictatorship and an authoritarian regime. If a dictatorship has been established it is too late to fight it ... The main thing, I think, is not to give up trying to persuade and convince

public opinion, in spite of all inhibitions ... The South African press has not been silenced yet ... I have been admiring *The Star* and some others for how they have managed to keep their reporting standards ..."

That, surely, was enough to settle most qualms. "You draw the line when they tell you what to write," she said.

The Star had not reached that point. It should fight on, and look forward to 100 years of freedom, she advised.

But then came **Helen Vlachos**, publisher and editor of the *Kathimerini* in Athens, who opposed the military dictatorship in Greece in the 1960s, and closed down her newspapers rather than submit to their censorship. "Where to draw the line?" she asked. "I could accept a certain amount of negative censorship – that is what *not* to publish. After all, it happens during many situations of war and (extreme cases) of national security. Respectable newspapers accept that. But what is not acceptable, is to be *told* what to write. To force-feed your readers with lies, slander, poisonous propaganda.

"I never worked throughout the regime. I never published again during the seven years."

None of us, I was certain, would ever have accepted such terms either. To the very end no newspaper in South Africa would allow an official censor – as distinct from a policeman bringing threats or warrants – onto its premises, let alone allow any outsider to tell him or her what to write and what not to write. Most editors, Afrikaans as well as English-speaking, had already threatened to quit journalism if the apartheid government ever succeeded in licensing us, or taking control of our newspapers' Press Council. We were a long way; it appeared, from 'crossing the line' where total submission to authority began.

Katherine Graham, publisher of *The Washington Post* and *Newsweek,* said:"Our only hope for continued progress in our countries is through an open dialogue, deeper knowledge of the facts and a clear understanding of the hopes and fears of blacks and whites." She assured us this was no time for the independent press to falter in South Africa.

The gift these three women gave us, without being asked, was that we could regain our determination, hold our heads high and ignore the carping and threats of the propagandists on our left as well as on our right.

Finally, the man who had witnessed Russian tanks grinding through his home town in former Czechoslovakia back in 1960 – and seen the invaders head straight for the small nation's Writers' Union – was ready to give advice (after studying for a quarter of a century similar cases around the globe).

George Theiner quoted South African novelist Nadine Gordimer whom his organisation, Index on Censorship, had defended in the past, and who had said some months back that "the heat was not so much on South African writers anymore, but on the press".

Theiner told the conference: "Journalists are no strangers to 'the heat'. Far worse is the situation in many countries in the world (Central and Eastern Europe, China, Vietnam, Africa, Asia, South America and the Middle East) where *no* heat is applied to the media. There is no heat for the simple reason that no such drastic action is necessary. Journalists working in such conditions are required to be propagandists ..."

So there we were. A recommendation to enjoy the heat.

A thousand days

Every month the heat would come closer and closer with every new censorship rule; every 'Emergency' decree. It would last three long years more. But the biggest concern remained the frustration that creeping censorship caused. Every time you outwitted censorship decrees, new decrees came into force. We would need to measure our effectiveness – every day for a thousand days.

Our international mutual assessment of censorship in 1987 has some practical lessons for every journalist and every part of the media in the technology revolution now in midstream. □

* *Conflict and the Press* – The Star Centennial Conference.
  The role of the Press in a divided society, edited by Harvey Tyson
  (The Argus Printing & Publishing Co., 1987)

31.
The end of mainstream newspapers.

*The indefatigable pursuit of an
unattainable Perfection ...
is what alone gives meaning to our lives
on this unavailing star.*

Logan Pearsall Smith 1865-1946

At the end of the first decade of the 21st century, many senior business executives in many fields did not believe that the days of the newspaper were almost over. They failed, 'just the other day' in 2010, even to see the obvious economics of it. Or they overlooked the fact that no large independent newspaper was likely ever again to be able to afford to replace its modern presses, even at current costs. And in half a lifetime from now, the world population will have increased by more than 30%, with nearly ten billion mouths to feed. It will never be able to tolerate using land for forests to produce newsprint. Pulp will be recycled ... and used mainly to replace certain plastics perhaps, in the small ways that it can.

Whatever the future may be, we have no option but to research its ramifications and prepare for it. The problem is that mankind's knowledge is increasing *exponentially,* not in a linear process which is the way most of us instinctively think and calculate today. The difference between the two goes beyond the difference between, say, compound interest and 'normal' interest. Ray Kurzwell, one of the chief exponents of the theory, told *Time* magazine: "*If I take 30 steps linearly, I get to 30. If I take 30 steps exponentially, I get to a billion.*"

Most of us cannot even accurately visualise a billion, let alone the immense power of exponential growth.

The scientists who subscribe to the theory of mankind's *exponential growth of knowledge* predict that mankind will reach a 'singularity' soon after the year 2040 – when the computers we invented will be more intelligent than we are.

What will that entail? A university was established relatively recently in California in which scientists of many disciplines around the world are today studying this predicted 'singularity'. The nearest date they can agree on is that robots will be more intelligent than people in about 2047 ... when today's children will be at the height of their adult careers! For the majority of aware people this is already being seen as a major threat to life itself. Others among the scientific futurologists see it as a breakthrough into a world of opportunity. Recently IBM, once known as the biggest supplier in the world of computers, produced a list of foreseen changes coming in the next few years.

Loss of jobs. Computers forecast that 70-80% of jobs will disappear in the next 20 years. There will be a lot of *new* jobs, but it is not clear if there will be enough new forms of work and enough skills in so short a time.

For instance, one prediction today is that there will be 90% fewer lawyers in the future. Only the top specialists will continue in the general legal profession, it seems. The same may apply in many other professions. The optimistic, and I believe, correctly grounded prediction is that highly efficient specialised robots will do all routine work in a future world, leaving time for humans to take charge of how that work capacity is used; how it is 'humanised' by human supervisors with sufficient time to do very thoughtful, productive managing.

Renewable energy sources have been developing for decades, but this industry is experiencing exponential change. The 'Big Bang' for energy – hydrogen fusion – will occur sooner than expected, claim some scientists.

Electricity will, in any case, become incredibly cheap and clean. Last year, more solar energy was installed worldwide than generators powered by fossil fuels.

The price for solar will drop so much that coal companies should be out of business by 2025 ... to the benefit of the entire world.

Key issue is water. With cheap electricity comes cheap and abundant water. Desalination now only needs 2kWh per cubic metre.

The threat of scarce water on Earth is not seen as prevalent. What is scarce is drinkable water ... Imagine what will be possible when everyone can have as much clean water as they want, at very little communal cost.

The IBM list is long and filled with surprises.

The usual disagreement arising over major change is magnified when one faces the statistics. But now let us focus on just one issue here:

How in the next decade, do we keep up *independent* standards of journalism that will ensure better human communications during the rest of this century?

Do we need to?

I am reminded that the founder of Facebook, Mark Zuckerberg, who is already part of the future change, told *The Daily Telegraph* in July 2015 that he believed "the ultimate communication technology" would enable people to send thoughts directly to each other using technology.

"You'll just be able to think of something and your friends will immediately be able to experience it too, if you like." (Well, I believed that would be possible when I was a young man 70 years ago. I witnessed a family member reluctantly demonstrate proven telepathic transference of messages – from him in Cairo to his wife and to his sister, my mother, in Cape Town – using only intense mental concentration.)

Zuckerberg's predicted path starts at the concept of video transmission of news and mass communication of knowledge to the moment when virtual reality techniques become the norm. "And after that we'll have the power to share our full sensory and emotional experience with people ... "

This development will make true the threat that *writing* will disappear as a form of mass communication; that writing will be reduced to the esoteric art it was 400 years ago; after Shakespeare, but before mass education and the invention of the flatbed press.

But that's a long leap, beginning with very tiny steps such as the changing language of internet users and the use of *emoticons* – so many invented in just a few months recently that they have their own *hug-u, lov-u, f-u* dictionary.

They represent a human need for expression of feelings that Artificial Intelligence will have to acquire at an early stage – long before it achieves global communication across all intellectual, cultural, ideological and literary barriers.

However, I suggest many other things are going to happen before mental messaging becomes 'a norm', or replaces hieroglyphic icons and abbreviated writing as a means of communication. There are already many other threats looming for ethical and independent (and accountable) journalists. Here is a short list of just some of the immediate threats society will face if or when serious newspapers are no more.

Threat to the internet. "The US and the EU are on the verge of giving rich corporations the right to control what we all see on the Internet. It's the apocalypse of the internet as we know it. But free speech advocates and web companies are fighting back." So said public campaigner Avaaz and other watchful organisations gearing for worldwide protests at threats to freedom of expression (I nearly said 'press' freedom). And this is before one takes into account the threat of illegal national intervention by countries such as Russia.

Public Relations replaces the Press. The trend became apparent, wrote columnists, when the Gulf oil spill became the 'biggest story' of 2010.

"You would go into these hearings and there would be more PR people representing these big players than there were reporters, sometimes by a factor of two or three, investigative reporter for *The New York Times*, David Barstow, wrote recently. In another article he wrote: "The muscles of journalism are weakening and the muscles of public relations are bulking up, as if they were on steroids."

In their recent book, *The Death and Life of American Journalism*, Robert McChesney and John Nichols tracked the number of people working in journalism since 1980 and compared it to the numbers for public relations. Using data from the US Bureau of Labour Statistics, they found that in 1980, there were about .45 PR workers per 100,000 population compared with .36 journalists. In 2008, there were .90 PR people per 100,000 compared to .25 journalists. That's a ratio of more than three-to-one, better equipped, better financed ... from PR agency revenues that had jumped from $3.5 billion to $8.75 billion in the 10 years 1997-2007 when newspapers started folding or cutting costs.

Collapse of Press Advertising. The advertising industry has provided the economic backbone of the world's free press for 400 years. However, it is playing an extraordinarily passive, wait-and-see role during the exponential changes taking place ... except in bullying weakening newspapers into giving their advertisers the best positions in the paper. Advertising today is allowed to ride roughshod over editorial rules. The typographical blending of adverts with editorial may confuse or upset readers, and thus damage both parties.

Major typographical and layout messes imposed by advertising agencies on a press industry can be seen in almost every publication in the free world today. Even *Time* magazine recently caused an international uproar when it published a tiny advert on its front cover, next to the title's bar code.

Though relatively discreet at present, in online advertising, where no rules apply, *some* advertisements are already becoming unacceptable in recent cases by producing intense noise and/or movements that seriously interfere with online content. The balance between advertising and editorial in online news channels is a long way from becoming a practical reality.

But the main role of advertising, which I'm told is happening already, will probably be through digital communication – addressing customers *individually* – knowing in advance their preferences, their prejudices, their needs and their wants, all analysed from global research of consumer usage patterns.

It's another nightmare that Orwell referred to decades ago in less technical terms.

Rise of digital censorship. Digital media have enabled writers to reach new audiences around the globe; but the promise of these technologies can come at a terrible cost, says PEN International.

"Governments are increasingly imprisoning and persecuting writers for what they write, blog, and post online."

PEN's case-lists over 12 years show that attacks on writers have risen, yes, exponentially, "including trials in the Americas and Europe ... Subversion, sometimes called 'using propaganda against the State', is the most commonly used charge to imprison writers using digital media."

The danger of bloggers. While there are some great individual commentators who share or occupy news websites, there are also newspapermen in the United States and Europe who are suggesting that the proliferating individual news bloggers are in danger of becoming "echo chambers of their own digital world." And that they are confusing readers into believing their opinionated blogs are providing reliable *reporting* of news ... a confusion, which, sadly we see in many newspapers, too. The line between news and comment appears to be disappearing fast among all providers of news, let alone the bias that a single cellphone picture or a tweet may bring.

Oliver Kamm wrote in *The Guardian*, a blistering piece about political blogging when it was 'all the rage', back in 2015.

"To its admirers, the fact that anyone can publish their views 'for free' (to quote the new English tongue) without the intervention of any editor or proprietor, is a boon for democracy and the cause of independent, fearless debate. It sounds great in theory, but the reality of web-based commentary falls well short of those noble ideals.

> "Far from leading debate or adding to the stock of ideas, blogs invariably act more as a predictable 'echo chamber' for commentary in the traditional media. Were mainstream columnists such as Polly Toynbee and Nick Cohen to disappear, for instance, a significant part of the blogosphere would have no purpose and nothing to react to.
>
> "What's more, since political blogs are always aimed at like-minded readers, balance and persuasion all too often fall by the wayside, replaced by smug insularity and biliousness. The blogosphere, in short, is a vehicle for the coagulation of opinion and the poisoning of debate ... . It is changing the tone of political discourse overwhelmingly for the worse, and with no one accountable for the decline."

Accountability is a word that should be written on banners and used as a battle-cry bringing all editorially independent, working journalists together in the new age that faces us. As I write, countless displaced journalists are searching for support and help in order to carry out their professional calling. They are the ones who should be creating, now, the bases for skilled teams that will need to work together in online news-media at all levels; all *accountable* to their local, regional or global readers.

This is already happening in various forms. Publishers – big newspapers from *The New York Times* to little local weeklies – are negotiating to join up with 'platforms' ranging from Google to Facebook sites. These moves are causing furious debates. A random instance is a quote from journalist Matt Carroll, posted in Mediashift on the web: "One of the single biggest defining issues for journalism over the next few years is the evolving – and uneasy – relationship between social media platforms and newsrooms. It's a complicated issue," he says.

Nevertheless, newsrooms and publishers are tempted to risk independence and join the giant social network services in search of new audiences and new sources of revenue.

But it is an uneasy pairing, with potential consequences unheard of today.

"The budding relationship between journalists and social chatter is not between equals," argues Carroll. "Social media are enjoying explosive growth. Newsrooms are struggling with a loss of influence and profitability. The two have vastly different cultures and goals. (i.e. a generalization: 'Muckraking vs keeping stockholders happy'.)

"Journalists see high risks. They worry that a growing dependence on platforms they don't control could lead to a loss of editorial independence."

Whither investigative journalism?

In the current state of flux, in which newspaper revenues are shrinking and journalist jobs are declining, journalists not only need to band together to support each other and widen their skills, they need also to find time and money for costly research and investigative journalism.

Platforms for this and organised aid are already appearing. At random at this moment one can find several options by scanning the web. My elderly, inexpert digital research instantly brings up MuckRock and Alaveteli – two organisations I'd never heard of until I set off on a hunt for something else.

Between them they offer a *global* service, it seems, to help journalists find the evidence they require in endless governmental files – providing valuable information which many public organisations prefer to shelve, quietly.

Recently three different news organisations used MuckRock to search for countless documents concerning a dubious bid to host the Olympics in 2024. The information that was discovered ended the bid.

MuckRock now offers a programme to gather specific information requested by clients, then charges for the results. But which reporter, which newsroom, can afford such 21st-century luxury? Well, MuckRock has already used 'crowdfunding' to retrieve documents in perhaps 100 cases by now.

The investigative platform was created with newsrooms in mind. Crowdfunding, stimulated by public interest, made costly investigation possible.

SO, AMIDST ALL the threats sampled above, and many more among the practical changes that loom over our lives and our jobs – what have we to fear from the future?

Nothing really – least of all intelligent, supportive and sympathetic robots – provided we willingly accept change, *and work with it* to ensure that we perceive the threats correctly, and work together to drive away the real possible threats. (It will help also if you are open-minded enough to read the views of the future of journalism expressed in the next chapter by an interested 90-year-old newspaper person.)

Provided, too, that journalists hold fast to their professional ethics – and support viable *digital newspaper* organisations that can continue to operate as responsible, accountable, entities that protect reputations and editorial independence. They will do so, surely, for the sake of their pride as well as the public interest. □

32.
The future of journalism.

You want a seat? Then boldly sate your itch;
Be very radical, and very rich.

Alfred Austin, 1913

"Sating your itch," even figuratively, is an instinctive and compelling urge. In the digital age it is making some people very rich, even though few seem to quite know why. All that professional newspaper journalists are sure of at this stage is that their jobs are changing and their status is directly threatened. Yet their role, already examined and stressed here, is vital in the coming years.

While corporates – and governments – in this new era seek ownership and/or control of new media, it is essential in the name of democracy that the future of journalism must be led by skilled journalists who usually prefer independence to riches.

What their role can be is still unclear, however, for the digital revolution is moving in several directions at speed. Let us remember that it was first noticeable just over a decade ago when information technology made its greatest leap in 400 years, with the arrival of Facebook (2004); YouTube (2005); Twitter (2006) and the rest.

News on radio, TV and in the press suddenly encountered a new medium which linked the cellphone to the web and 'published' news and information in a newly organised fashion. Almost overnight a flood of dramatic news-event cellphone photos and videos were splashed across the world.

The phenomenon brought back the words of Prof Marshall Mcluhan, the whiz-kid of my day whose theories were discounted for nearly half a century. In the 1960s Mcluhan famously invented the term *"The medium is the message,"* a phrase meaning that the form of a news medium embeds itself in the message, creating a symbiotic relationship by which the medium influences how the message is perceived.

Mcluhan's rejected theory is suddenly true. For instance, *"I read it in the newspaper,"* gave a message some kind of authenticity which differs from the reaction to an excited *"I saw it on Twitter",* etc.

The London *Independent*, commenting a decade ago when cell-phoned, private-sourced news pictures and news flashes were breaking out all around the world, said: "These are incidents with enormous implications for the conduct of modern life. It is growing ever harder to cover up public acts, either by 'spinning' them or pretending they never happened, for the simple reason that at any moment those acts might be recorded and disseminated with little more required than a USB plug-in and a few clicks of a camera."

Now, with 4 and 5G connectivity available on the go you don't need to plug-in anymore. The speed of change in human communications – not to mention independent machine-to-machine communication with the commercial roll-out of Artificial Intelligence – is so fast right now the next step is almost unimaginable. Yet, for journalists and newspaper readers today it is no longer the technical developments but their consequences which are relevant.

In practice, the reshaped media may be made up of several different small and big moves. The answer may come from Tokyo where one of the world's biggest circulation newspapers is produced in a well-educated, inventive society; or from Silicon Valley where 'digital' is mother's milk; or from Shanghai, or wherever commercial innovation is currently king. We can only hope this is not so, for news sources controlled by website billionaires, or 'big business' or vague NGOs, or unaccountable foreign funding, are likely to be bad news for readers globally.

Fortunately there are innovators in the daily *accountable* and independent free press who are also trying to adapt to the coming change. Unfortunately they are finding it difficult to anticipate the effects of all kinds of inventions such as the 'watch' on the wrist that will receive news messages; headpieces designed to capture virtual reality transmissions, and the banks of steadily improving all-media communication-receivers (smart phones) which everyone is already carrying in their pockets.

Instead, the press is simply trying to find ways to carry its current readers into new formats of digitally imaged words and pictures and its growing collections of sound-video.

One non-profit group, NewAssignment.net hopes to combine the work of amateurs and professionals to produce 'investigative stories' on the internet. Craig Newmark, of Craigslist provided a token $10,000 for a project emanating from a group of free classified-advertisement websites. Ironically, however, the free-ads movement has probably done more than anything else to threaten the income of journalists and newspapers.

Perhaps SA's own amaBhunghane, the centre for investigative journalism mentioned earlier, through its non-profit and accountable journalistic status, provides a useful model for the dissemination of credible news, whatever the platform. Their website states that they serve the public interest through:
- "The best practice of investigations;
- Helping others to do the same; and
- Helping to secure the information rights investigative journalists need to do their work.

Through these activities, we hope to promote a free media, and open accountable and just democracy."

But, despite the commendable non-profit example above, to ensure a future balance of independently reported news on a grand and universal scale, an economically viable mix of adverts and independent news is desperately required on whatever new medium there may be – online, or something else.

Already, a few respected news organisations sustain themselves independently online –including *The Guardian*; *The Christian Science Monitor*; the London *Independent,* most U.S. major papers and National Public Radio. They form an elite group of serious news providers available everywhere online, offering independent journalism backed by trusts, charities, thousands of fired-up bloggers and well-informed citizen journalists. Yet, even as the movement grows, giants in the digital world such as Google are already being accused of trying to take over, rather than assist trusted news organisations and smaller news sources.

Local papers and the community press believe they will be around for a long time ... if they can adapt to changing 'readership patterns'. Knight newspapers (formally the highly ethical and education-oriented Knight de Ridder chain of papers mentioned in an earlier chapter) is already spending large amounts of Knight trust funds on training cadets in new ways – including video-reporting – to meet what Knight newspapers see as the future needs of their local community readerships.

Video-reporting is already making great leaps and bounds in the long-established TV news services.

CNN and Al Jazeera, for instance, have since 2016 dramatically advanced world television coverage by devoting 24-hour coverage, to the exclusion of almost everything else, when major world stories break. In the past this happened only selectively – such as the 2003 US coverage of the fast advance and victory of US forces fighting in Iraq – at a time when news analysis was poor. Today, video wrap-ups and running video analyses of an issue featured on the TV stations mentioned above often go far beyond what even the best newspaper or online print report can achieve. Video-journalism is about to explode in the media in many guises.

A 'NEW WAY' was developed by Circa News, a mobile app (a website portal was added later) which has been trumpeted by journalists and media industry-watchers as a glimpse into what the future of mobile media publishing might look like. When it was launched, Circa's main strategy was to take complex stories published by other organisations and break them down into bite-sized news updates (something they called "Atomization") for consumption on mobile phones.

This 'new way' also envisages updating these 'news stories' via bullet-like 'points', linked to previously circulated items that result in 'running stories' for those news items an app subscriber chooses to follow. But, after a hiatus in operations during mid-2015, following some difficulties finding a new backer, Circa re-launched its initial product-offering while adding short and long video presentations optimised for social media usage.

THE UNPREDICTABLE future strikes again, at this moment as I write.

My intention was to remind you of what some of the leading newspapers are currently doing to meet that future. My samples included:

The New York Times, for instance has introduced *NYTNow* (originally a paid-service based on Circa News that is now free). And Middle East-based Al Jazeera's *AJPlus* has tried the same experiment.

The Sydney Morning Herald decided early and all by itself, to change as quickly as possible into an online 'newspaper'. It is already nearly there, but some of its journalists have complained that the resulting reductions in editorial staff are lowering standards and creating instability. (Journalists love to complain about any change that directly affects our work. When computers were first introduced to news rooms back in the 1980s, newspaper people and their unions demanded 'cover' against eyesight damage and, as mentioned earlier, the threat which personal computers might present to pregnant workers and – worse – mortal danger to male scribes: impotence. Change is never easy for the nay-sayer.)

The Guardian (for most of its long history it was the famous *Manchester Guardian*) migrated to America in its search for a suitable global base. It also has links with the transforming *Sydney Morning Herald*.

How are the surviving great newspapers going to make enough money to carry on?

The Washington Post, bought a few years ago by Jeff Bizos, founder of Amazon, was spending hundreds of millions of his dollars in the search of a news system that would use every form of media and become an international voice, communicating with the planet from the US capital. Bizos – having already created arguably the world's biggest e-commerce company – may still be searching for the newspaper's best answer.

Asking consumers to pay for content isn't a model he is sold on.

"These things can change, but I don't see evidence yet that consumers are amenable to those kinds of micro-payments," Bizos once said. He wanted to move *The Washington Post* from "making a relatively large amount of money per reader, having a relatively small number of readers – that was the traditional *Post* model for decades, [a] very successful model by the way," ... to a model "where we make a very small amount of money per reader on a much, much larger number of readers."

The *Post* has already experimented with a number of new advertising products that fit Bizos' philosophy.

There are countless other newspapers around the world planning their moves into the future, but all may have to rethink their current strategy ... because Google seemed to be pointing to the next big move: amalgamation of news providers.

After abandoning Circa News, Google received sharp criticism from the European Union and from newspapers in Germany and Spain for taking shortcuts and abusing its powers on the web. Google has made some public apologies, but re-launched its rebuffed plans.

Google re-launched its direct entry into journalism in 2015 by announcing "a new partnership with several publishers." The company sought to create a €150m (£107m) fund "to support innovation in journalism and product development in Europe."

Another announcement said: "The Digital News Initiative (DNI) is a partnership between Google and news publishers in Europe to support high quality journalism through technology and innovation."

"The goal is to encourage a more sustainable news ecosystem – and promote innovation in digital journalism – through ongoing collaboration and dialogue between the tech and news sectors."

So, years ago, Google spent $5m on an experiment with Knight Newspapers in the US. Later it tried teaming up with eight European newspapers: *Les Echos, FAZ, The Financial Times, The Guardian, NRC Media, El Pais, La Stampa* and *Die Zeit*.

On this project, Google carefully explained its course of action. The money would not be spent at those titles. Rather, Google would advise on the spending of a €150m fund to help news organisations "demonstrate new thinking in digital journalism." Google said it intended to invest in training and research for journalists, including staff in London, Paris, and Hamburg. It would train newsrooms in digital skills. It would "invest in training partnerships, as well as funding research into digital journalism."

The online giant also published an endorsement of this plan, by Matt McAlister, GM of new digital businesses at Guardian Media Group and co-founder and chief executive of *Contributoria*, who said that a healthy publishing market was "good for business on the Internet." He added: "I'm always a fan of finding ways to create opportunity in the face of adversity. Given the challenges journalism is up against in the world, investing in new ideas is going to do a lot more for the trade than ... re-inventing your own core activities and supporting failures."

The immediate counter-reaction (also provided by Google research) was typified by the view that organisations receiving direct funds from Google ... "will have to tread a careful line, with their news coverage. They won't want their users to think they're sugar-coating the coverage to favour their benefactor."

It is hard to find criticism of the plan, especially if one has personal knowledge of the ethics of the majority of those mainly independent news sources. During my last days in full-time journalism a long time ago I would have unhesitatingly stated that the editors of *The Financial Times, The Guardian, El Pais* and *Die Zeit* were dedicated to independent journalism, and would be the very first to raise the alarm if outside forces tried to interfere with that independence.

However, I doubt that any corporation would retreat from its prime, long-term, monetary goals. Circumstances within any benevolent digital programme might alter sometime in the short future of this rapidly and unpredictable era of change. And what if future editors of the above-named newspapers were, say in five years' time, to quit in protest at some attempt at direct influence on news-reporting, or a takeover? Would *editorial* independence be upheld online?

Google might allay such fears by focusing only on training of journalists for the new era, guided by the independent journals with which it has allied itself. But I cannot see such beneficence happening for independent news sources elsewhere. Not in Africa, where signs of Chinese funding of media are already evident, or South America, or China, or Russia.

In great, big, democratic India, while at this moment under Prime Minister Narendra Modi's 'Digital India' initiative, plans are being rolled out for expenditure of the equivalent of $71 *billion* on creating online communications; designed to change the entire canvas of the country.

But the news media will be a mere leaf trying to float on the national digital tide. Thus, the goal of independent news media is suddenly and everywhere under threat, not only from governments – the obvious and most persistent ogre – but from corporates and even from the digital skills of revolutionaries such as IS terrorists and from anti-democratic forces wherever they arise.

Beware the Big Boys

The backlash against the seemingly benign big boys on the democratic internet is also growing. There are two major themes of criticism growing louder and louder. The first criticism was voiced publicly again very recently in a talk at Harvard's Shorenstein Centre where Jeffrey Rosen argued that "Twitter, Facebook, and Google are facing increased pressure to moderate content in a way that is inconsistent with First Amendment protections – in the name of promoting civility rather than democracy."

This threat of insidious, self-inflicted, self-monitoring is scary. It could become a greater threat, in the long term, than any cyber-damage by IS or Russia's Putin regime, or any other enemy of democracy.

But the second threat – the sudden growth of a dominant corporate empire taking control of the media and the web – is even worse. One angry author, Tim Wu, in his well-informed book *The Attention Merchants: The Epic Scramble to Get Inside Our Heads* suggested that Google and Facebook's moves to 'rescue' the printed press would result in making "the printed word mere collateral damage in the relentless expansion of the most powerful 'attention capture' machines ever built."

Instant videos, it seems, will be the future form of communication – driven by advertising sold by the combined merchants controlling the web.

Jacob Weisberg, a reviewer for *New York Review of Books*, explains it all. To summarise his views:

The research scientists who designed the World Wide Web intended it to be free from commercial exploitation. The company that decisively fastened it to an advertising model was America Online (AOL), which by the mid-1990s did this in notoriously unscrupulous fashion – including revving up business with 'sex chats' yes – but more significantly booking phony revenue, exploiting its users, and engaging in other dishonest practices that caused it to implode after swallowing Time Warner in a $164 billion merger that took place in January 2001.

Google originally rejected the attention model too, only to succumb to it in turn. Tim Wu writes that Larry Page and Sergey Brin, the company's co-founders, were concerned about the corrupting potential of advertising, believing that it would bias their search engine in favour of sellers and against consumers. But because search is so closely allied with consumption, selling advertising became irresistible to them. With its Ad Words product – the text ads that appear above and alongside search results – Google became "the most profitable attention merchant in the history of the world." When Google sells ads accompanying the results of searches people make, it uses a real-time bidding exchange. This electronic auction process remains its central cash machine, generating most of the company's $75 billion a year revenue.

"You begin with idealistic hauteur and visions of engineering purity, proceed to exponential growth, and belatedly open the spigot to fill buckets with revenue." This sequence describes the growth of tech-media companies including YouTube, Twitter, Pinterest, Instagram, and Snapchat, their success underpinned by kinds of user data that television and radio have never had. Many younger start-ups pursuing this trajectory are focused on the next attention-mining frontier: wearable technology, including virtual reality headsets that will send marketing messages even more directly to the human body.

Netflix has pursued a free-standing subscription model that, in the words of its founder Reed Hastings, doesn't "cram advertisements down people's throats." Under its CEO Tim Cook, Apple rejected the prevailing model of gathering private information and selling it to marketers to subsidise free services. From Cook's perspective, advertising didn't merely harm privacy, it depleted battery life, ate up mobile data plans, and created a less pleasing experience on Apple's beautiful devices. To the chagrin of publishers, the company offered ad-blocking apps on the iPhone that allow users to gain access to the Internet without any ads at all.

"To be fair," says New York reviewer Jacob Weisberg, "there's no reason to think that people in ad tech are greedier than anyone else. Their work is simply more obscure. Some 2,500 companies are part of the technical supply chain for digital advertising. What many of them do to create and transmit ads is largely incomprehensible and uninteresting to outsiders. The simplest explanation is that they interpose themselves between buyers and sellers in an attempt to capture a cut of the revenue."

He might have added: Regardless of people's rights, their freedoms and their cultures.

So what should the press-scribes do?

Although current changes are occurring so fast that it is impossible to know what will happen next, it remains essential that today's global digital trends be carefully watched and, if necessary, opposed by every democrat in every country. Ethical journalists and journalism schools scattered across too few nations – and universities and honest democrats wherever they exist – need to be not only vigilant as usual, but to embrace specific issues and opportunities that foster, rather than threaten, the standards and ethics of journalism.

'Specific' in the sense that the issues are aimed at youth – but the goals need to be broad, including such things as campaigning for education for every child in the world. And 'idealistic' in the aim of abolishing the nationalism and patriotism fostered in schools, in democracies as well as in under-developed societies, where the next generation needs to be reminded – specifically – of their human rights and the dangers of censorship.

The whole world needs to be reminded by independent journalists in all media that news has no real value when it is published by the state, or by employees who are accountable to their employers instead of their readers, the public.

But worse things may affect a digital 'press'. Where news 'deadlines' are vanishing or gone, so has the framework for measuring news *accuracy*. When the mixed flow of news, information and comment never pauses, then standards fall in terms of *professional review*. In such circumstances, when tradition and reputation no longer exist, nor does *accountability*.

Thus, if 'news' is to maintain its value and the intrinsic veracity readers expect, today's journalists must assume a huge role in the future. They and their successors need to make their voices heard, their skills appreciated, their standards upheld in the rush to rebuild the media at local, national and international levels.

Fortunately, there are already fine examples of independent journalism at work on the web – even in South Africa which ranks currently with the world's best. But independent-minded journalists will need to influence a looming digital commercial revolution and they must lead the change in the way some online media users currently consume all online news, regardless of its source, as if it were all factual. Credible news organisations and like-minded independent journalists will need to promote themselves, their brands, as such and in that way establish islands of credibility and accountability in the sea of largely unchecked information available online.

Those of us on the far side of newspapering will not be around when the opportunities and problems of the developed digital age become clear. That is the only regret I have in the challenges ahead for those believing in independent journalism and freedom. But, if good journalists decide to act together more often – instead of individually – there is reason for hope. There is reason for welcoming the challenges ahead. Journalists need to combine actively with any of the powerful forces that will listen and treat them as partners in launching news feeds in the new age. It should be an age of instant imagery, messages and tight, hard commentary.

An imaginative advertising director, a famous print publisher, or more likely a digital multi-millionaire or even multi-billionaire whiz-kid with a Space Age mind might still be able to blast the right mixture of journalistic and digital skills into the planet's brightest future for 'the Press'.

Meanwhile, the world's press flagship, *The New York Times,* has been announcing record statistics of profit ... but this reflects online sales mainly, I hear, and its printed editions are no longer all profitable. Where, one wonders, will the *NYT*'s beacon of hope be in the year 2030?

Whatever the future will be, it will always need tens of thousands of men and women to practise accurate and ethical journalism and to fight for *editorial* independence in whatever media exist. □

Index

Accountability Now, 280
Advertising World, 190
Adviser (Colorado), 88
Afriforum, 279
Aitken, William Maxwell (Lord Beaverbrook), 4, 189, 198
Al Jazeera, 325, 326
Alaveteli, 319
Alphon, Peter, 169, 170
amaBhungane, 277, 325
Amazon, 327
American Society of Newspaper Editors, 305
ANC (African National Congress), 144, 146, 148, 157, 215, 251, 279, 282, 289, 302, 306, 307, 308
Anglo–Boer War, 31, 78, 223
Angolan War, 122–33
ANN7, 281
AOL (America Online), 330
Apple, 331
Argus Group, 48, 204, 206, 213, 215, 218, 224, 225, 229, 230, 231, 232, 234, 247, 248, 249, 250, 251, 254, 255, 259, 262, 297, 310
Argus, The, 48, 206, 225, 231, 232, 234, 262
Artificial Intelligence, vii, 315, 324
Astor, David, 171
Astor, Gavin, 171
Astor, John Jacob, 171, 172–76, 189
Atlee, Clement, 198
Austin, Alfred, 322
Avaaz, 315
Azapo, 301

Bacon, Francis, 3
Balding, Timothy, 306
Baldwin, Stanley, 3, 4, 198
Band, Doug, 250
Baneshik, Percy, 25
Bantu World, The, 217
Barker, Martine, 260
Barnard, Ferdi, 269
Barstow, David, 316
Bartholomew, Guy, 196–97, 198
Bayard, Jerenique, 287

BBC (British Broadcasting Corporation), 18, 36, 37, 40, 104, 126, 146, 174, 205, 240, 301, 304
Beaverbrook, Lord – see Aitken, William Maxwell
Benchley, Robert, 58
Belfast Telegraph, 64, 66, 69, 70, 71
Berlin Wall, 97–109, 110, 111, 133, 134
Berry, Gomer, 189–191, 199
Berry, Seymour, 190–191
Berry, William, 189–191, 199
Bierce, Ambrose, 182
Bizos, Jeff, 209, 327
Black Sash, 56
Black, Conrad, 189, 248
'Black Dahlia' murder, 187
Blair, Eric Arthur (George Orwell), 38, 109, 171, 261, 266, 268, 271, 317
Blair, Tony, 239
Bloemfontein Post, The, 230
Bly, Nellie – see Cochran, Elizabeth Jane
Bosman, Herman Charles, 38
BOSS (South African Bureau of State Security), 139, 140, 141, 144, 145, 147, 148, 149
Boston Globe The, 187
Botha, Pik, 296
Botha, PW, 56, 127, 148, 296
Bradlee, Ben, 201, 202
Brauteseth, Tim, 285, 286, 287
Brezhnev, Leonid, 157
Bridgland, Fred, 128, 129
Brin, Sergey, 330
British Education Act (1870), 3, 192
Brookfield Consulting, 278
Broughton, Morris, 232
Buffalo News, The, 210
Buffet, Warren, 209–211
Bullen, Dana, 305
Bureau for Information, 304
Burke, Edmund, 2, 3, 272
Business and Human Rights Resource Centre, 280
Business Day, 260, 277, 279
Business Report, 253, 264
Businesslive, 281

Calcutta Times, The, 202
Canete, Ricardo, 139
Cape Times, The, 66, 141, 206, 259, 260, 261, 262, 263, 264, 265
Caprivi Strip, 291
Carey, John, 62, 82
Carlyle, Thomas, 2, 3
Carolus, Johann, 9–10
Carroll, Matt, 318–19
CASAC (Council for the Advancement of the South African Constitution), 280
Castro, Fidel, 157
Catledge, Turner, 203
Centre for Applied Legal Studies, 280
Chamberlain, Neville, 41, 231
Chaplin, Charlie, 184
Chicago Tribune, The, 179, 187
Christchurch Press, The, 100, 243
Christian Science Monitor, 325
Christiansen, Arthur, 199
Churchill, Winston, 31–32, 33, 99, 143
CIA (Criminal Intelligence Agency), 127, 129, 138, 139, 140, 146, 147, 153, 279
Circa News, 326, 327
Citizen, The (Johannesburg), 142, 147, 148
City Press, 53
Civil Cooperation Bureau (CCB), 149, 269, 270
Claypole, Stephen, 304
Clemens, Samuel (Mark Twain), 32–33, 182
Clinton, Bill, 29
CNN (Cable News Network), 104, 325
Cochran, Elizabeth Jane, 39
Cohen, Nick, 318
Cold War, 36, 93–95, 100, 102, 104, 108, 110, 111, 123, 128, 134, 135, 137, 145, 146, 148, 173, 296, 301, 302
Coleman, Max, 53, 56, 57
Collier's Weekly Magazine, 43, 84
Columbia Journalism Review, 239
Comet, The, 216, 226
Connor, William, 160
Contributoria, 328
Cook, Tim, 331
Cooke, Alastair, 34, 36–37, 205
Corruption Watch, 280
Cosatu, 301
Coward, Noel, 119
Craigslist, 324

Crane, Stephen, 37, 182
Crimean War 75–77
Crotty, Ann, 253
Cudlipp, Hugh, 197, 198, 199
Cuito Cuanavale, 132, 133
Curtis, Charlotte, 207
Curvin, Robert, 207

Dahl, Roald, 183
Daily Express, 199
Daily Herald, 198
Daily Mail (London), 100, 170, 193, 194
Daily Maverick, The, 281, 284, 289
Daily Mirror, 8, 18, 20, 193–94, 195, 196, 197, 198, 199, 239
Daily Nebraskan, The, 210
Daily News, 49, 262, 306
Daily Telegraph, 41, 189, 190, 191, 199, 255, 315
Daily Universal Register, The, 161
Dartford Chronicle, The, 113, 118, 119, 120
Dasnois, Alide, 261
Davenport, Lindsay, 79–80
Davies, Marion, 182, 184
Davis, Richard Harding, 182
Dawson, Geoffrey, 194, 199, 225
De Klerk, FW, 56, 227
Defoe, Daniel, 33
Delane, John Thadeus, 238
Delmer, Sefton, 35
Detainees' Parents Support Committee, 53, 54, 56, 269
Detroit News, The, 187
Diamond Fields Advertiser, 11, 230, 262
Dickens, Charles, vii, 33, 114, 115, 200, 236
Diederichs, Nico, 144
DINA (Chilean Secret Service), 139, 140
Donhoff, Marion, 308–309
Dormer, Francis Joseph, 224–25, 226, 229, 234
Drum, 216
Dryfoos, Orvil, 203
Du Preez, Max, 261
Dube, John Langalibalele, 215

Eastern Star, The, 224
Eisenhower, Dwight D, 36, 37, 94, 122
El Pais, 306, 328
European, The, 19

335

Evans, Harold, 171, 199, 205, 241, 242, 244
Evening Star, The, 210

Facebook, 315, 318, 323, 329, 330
Fawcett, Millicent, 78
FAZ, 328
FBI (Federal Bureau of Investigation), 21, 137, 138, 139, 140
Featherstone, John, 234
Fechter, Peter, 106
Ferris, Paul, 199
FIEJ – see World Association of Newspapers
Financial Times, The, 189, 190, 328
Fisk, Robert, 90
Five Freedoms Forum, 269, 271
Flather, Horace, 155, 156
Fleet Street, 18, 34, 35, 116, 117, 118, 167, 171, 197, 230, 243
Fox TV, 238
Frenkel, Max, 207
Friend, The, 230
Fugard, Athol, 38
Funder, Anna, 108
Fuzile, Mxolisi, 300

Gageby, Douglas, 71, 307
Gellhorn, Martha, 42–43
Gibson, Rex, 56, 142, 148, 269
Godi, Themba, 285
Golden City Post, 216
Google, 114, 318, 325, 327, 328, 329, 330
Gorbachev, Mikhail, 20, 155, 156, 157
Gordimer, Nadine, 310
Graham, Katherine, 201, 202, 203, 205, 222, 294, 309
Graham, Margaret, 180
Graves, Robert, 37
Greeley, Horace, 24
Green, Michael, 306
Guardian, The, 36, 37, 42, 174, 199, 317, 325, 327, 328, 325, 327, 328
Gunasena, Mdsandhya, 306
Gupta family, 274, 275, 276, 277, 278, 279, 281

Haley, William, 174–75, 199
Hanratty, James, 169–70
Hardwood, Richard, 305
Hari, Mata – see Zelle, Gertrude Margarete
Harmsworth, Alfred (Lord Northcliffe), 192–95, 198, 199
Harmsworth, Harold (Lord Rothermere), 4, 193, 195, 198
Hastings, Reed, 331
Hausmannin, Walpurga, 5–7
Hearst, William Randolph, 84, 181–87, 195
Hecht, Ben, 37
Helen Suzman Foundation, 279
Hemingway, Ernest, 34, 37, 42
Herald, The (Harare), 152
Hitler, Adolf, 18, 19, 35, 37, 41, 102, 108, 126, 143, 195, 199, 223, 227, 231, 267, 308
Hobhouse, Emily, 78
Hoffman, David E, 92–97
Hogg, James, 16
Hollingworth, Clare, 34, 41
Huang, Jen Chih (Robert), 283

Ilanga lase Natal (The Natal Sun), 215
Illustrated London News, The, 163
Ince, Thomas, 184
Independent Newspapers, 247, 250, 251, 252, 255, 259, 261, 262, 263, 264, 281
Independent, The (London), 249, 250, 255–56, 307, 323, 325
Index on Censorship, 302
Index on Censorship, 310
Information Scandal (Infogate), 47, 147, 148
Inkatha, 301
Instagram, 330
International Federation of Newspapers, 306
International News Service, 86
International Press Institute, 151
International Publishing Corporation, 197, 198
Irani, Cushrow, 152, 301
Irish News, 66, 69, 70
Irish Times, 71, 307
IS (Islamic State), 329
Isvestia, 155, 156

'Jack the Ripper', 114, 115, 160, 161–67, 176
James, Clive, 34
Jameson Raid, 40

Jenkins, Paul, 54
Jenkins, Simon, 243
Jerusalem Post, 306
Johnson, Lyndon B, 36
Johnson, Martin, 78–79
Jordi, John, 233
Joubert, Pierre, 260

Kamm, Oliver, 317
Kani, John, 298, 299
Kathimerini, 309
Keating, Keith, 285, 286, 287, 288, 289
Keeler, Christine, 172, 173
Kennedy, John F, 36, 94
Kentish Times, The, 113, 119, 120
King, Cecil Harmsworth, 195–97
Kinnock, Neil, 240
Kipling, Rudyard, vii, 4, 26, 33, 198
Kissinger, Henry, 204
Klaaste, Aggrey, 214, 215, 218
Kliem, Heinz, 107
Knight de Ridder (newspapers), 325
Knight Newspapers, 325, 328
Koch, Ed, 239
Koenig, Friedrich, 11
KPMG, 278
Kruger, Paul, 216, 224, 226
Kurtz, Howard, 29
Kurzwell, Ray, 313

La Epoca, 153, 154
La Prensa, 9, 223
La Stampa, 328
Lamb, Larry, 239
Laptev, Ivan, 155, 156
Latakgomo, Joe, 218, 300
Laurence, TE, 37
Les Echos, 328
Levitas, Mitchell, 207
Lincoln Journal, The, 210
Lippmann, Walter, 35–36
Litani, Yehudi, 306
Lloyd George, David, 194
London Independent, 90
London, Jack, 83–85, 182
Los Angeles Examiner, 186, 187
Louw, Raymond, 151
Lucas, Adele, 292, 294, 295

Mabula, Jan, 285
Madonsela, Thuli, 279

Mahlobo, David, 279
Mail and Guardian, 279
Manchester Guardian, The, 40, 199, 205, 221, 327
Mandela, Nelson, v, 56, 146, 227, 247, 248, 249, 250, 269, 274, 301, 302
Martin, John, 230, 231, 232
Maxwell, Robert, 17–20, 189
Mbeki, Thabo, 251, 274
McAlister, Matt, 328
McBride, Robert, 284, 285, 288
McCausland, Dominic, 231
McChesney, Robert, 316
McCurry, Mike, 29
McGoff, John, 148
McGregor, Oliver Ross (Lord McGregor of Durris), 295, 296
McKinsey, 278
McLean, Peter, 248, 250
Mcluhan, Marshall, 323
Mediashift, 318
Mencken, HL, 37
Mercury, The, 261
Meredith, George, 40
Meyer, Karl, 207
Mgwaba, Philani, 261
MI6 (British Secret Intelligence Service), 147
Miami Herald, 187
Miller, Hal, 234
Milton, John, 150
Modi, Narendra, 329
Monypenny, WF, 229
Moodley, Roy, 282
Moorehead, Alan, 37
Morning Post (London), 31, 190
Morris, James, 38–39
Morris, Jan – see Morris, James
Morris, Richard B, 7
Motlana, Nthato, 218
Mozambique civil war, 133–34
MuckRock, 319
Mugabe, Robert, 152, 153
Mulder, Connie, 147, 148
Murdoch, Rupert, 8, 19, 20, 22, 171, 189, 205, 221, 236–44, 248, 255, 260
Murrow, Edward R, 37
Myburgh, Tertius, 130

Nabokov, Vladimir, 183
Natal Advertiser, The, 230

Natal Daily News, 28, 100, 230
National Public Radio, 325
Neame, LE, 227
Netflix, 331
Neuman, Johanna, 29
New Age, 281
New Nation, 299
New York Herald, 187
New York Journal, The, 180, 181
New York Post, The, 239
New York Review of Books, The, 330
New York Sun, The, 180, 181
New York Times, The, 7, 14, 29, 36, 43, 97, 128, 146, 180, 187, 201, 202–206, 207, 222, 316, 318, 326, 333
New Yorker, The, 156, 183
New-York Tribune, 24
NewAssignment.net, 324
Newhouse, Samuel, 208–209
Newmark, Craig, 324
News Corp, 239, 243, 244
News from Moscow, 157
News of the World, 5, 8, 239
News24, 277
Newsweek, 294, 309
Ngqumbva, Phil, 300
Nichols, John, 316
Nightingale, Florence, 76
Nixon, Richard, 139, 201, 295
Nottingham Post, The, 243
Nover, Naomi, 29
Novoe Vremia, 157
NRC Media, 328
O'Hara, John, 183
O'Reilly, Tony, 20, 243, 244, 247–55, 259, 265
Observer, The, 171, 173, 174, 198
Ochs, Adolf, 187, 203
Oppenheimer, Harry, 234
Orwell, George – see Blair, Eric Arthur
OUTA (Organisation Undoing Tax Abuse), 279

Page, Bruce, 238
Page, Larry, 330
Pakeman, RJ, 226
Pall Mall Gazette, 40
Parker, Dorothy, 183, 184
Paton, Alan, 159
Pauw, Jacques, 281–83
Paz, Virgilio, 138, 140

Pearsall Smith, Logan, 220, 312
PEN International, 317
Penny Press, The, 207
Pentagon Papers, The, 204–205
Phahlane, Beauty, 284
Phahlane, Khomotso, 284
Philadelphia Inquirer, 42, 187
Pinochet, Augusto, 139, 153
Pinterest, 330
Post, The, 216, 218
Pravda, 155
Pretoria News, The, 230, 262
Private Eye, 51
Profumo, John, 173–74
Public Affairs Research Institute, 280
Pulitzer Prize, 36, 91, 92, 96, 178, 180, 205
Pulitzer, Joseph, 39, 178–87, 182
Pumpyansky, Alexander, 157
Putin, Vladimir, 156, 157, 329

Qoboza, Percy, 212, 213–16, 217, 218

Ramaphosa, Cyril, 263, 270
Rand Daily Mail, 45, 56, 148, 152, 269
Reagan, Ronald, 21, 29, 94, 95
Remnick, David, 156
Reston, James ('Scotty'), 34, 36, 202, 203, 204, 205, 206
Reynolds, Peter, 54
Rhodes, Cecil John, 40, 225
Rhoodie, Eschel, 47, 48, 142, 147, 148
Right2Know, 280
Rivonia Treason Trial, 144
Roosevelt, Eleanor, 42
Roosevelt, Franklin D, 36, 42
Roosevelt, Theodore, 33
Rosenthal, AM, 207
Rosenthal, Eric, 227
Roth, Philip, 183
Rothermere, Lord – see Harmsworth, Harold
Runyan, Damon, 83, 88–89
Ruskin, John, 40
Russell, William Howard, 75–78

Sachs, Bernard, 38
Salinger, JD, 183
San Francisco Examiner, 182
San Francisco News, 34
Sànchez, Ochoa, 133

Saurez, Jose, 139
Savimbi, Jonas, 124, 127, 129, 130, 131
Schutte, Stefan, 286
Scorpio, 277, 282
Scotsman, The, 128, 171, 198
Scott, CP, 199
Scott, Norman, 147
Scripps, Howard W, 207–208
Scully, Steve, 29
Sefara, Makhudu, 261
Sesoko, Matthews, 284
Shaik, Schabir, 274
Shakespeare, William, 17, 33, 88, 228
Shamir, Yitzhak, 20
Shapiro, Jonathan (Zapiro), 291, 297
Sharapova, Maria, 79–80
Sharpeville massacre, 66, 116, 147, 155, 303
Shaw, Flora, 40–41
Shaw, George Bernard, 136
Shaw, Graham, 260
Shaw, Irwin, 183
Sheffield, George, 224
Sheffield, Tom, 224
Sillitoe, Percy, 147
Simpson, John, 34, 40, 78, 240, 244
Sisulu, Zwelakhe, 299
Sitole, Khehla, 284, 288
Sky TV, 239
Slater, Layton, 213, 214, 215, 216, 218, 232, 233, 234
Smit, Jean-Cora, 138–40, 145
Smit, Robert, 138–40, 145
Smith, Emma, 164
Smith, H Allen, 89–90
Smith, Ian, 152, 214
Smith, Vincent, 288
Smuts, Jan, 38, 144, 252
Snapchat, 330
Snoddy, Raymond, 239
Snyder, Louis L, 7
Sokutu, Brian, 300
Sorabjee, Soli, 157–58, 276
South African Broadcasting Corporation, 307
South African War, 31
Sowetan, The, 216–219
Soweto uprising, 116, 213, 303
Sparks, Allister, 261
Spectator, The, 129
Stalin, Joseph, 35, 99, 108, 267

Stanley, HM, 32
Star, The (Johannesburg), v, 28, 45, 46, 47, 48, 52, 54, 55, 56, 60, 66, 70, 126, 127, 129, 135, 137, 139, 140, 141, 145, 146, 152, 155, 194, 206, 207, 210, 216, 218, 223, 224–35, 250, 251, 252, 261, 262, 270, 294, 297, 299, 300, 307, 308, 309, 310, 340
Stasi (State Security Service – *Staatssicherheitsdienst*), 108, 109, 110
Statesman, The (India), 301
Steel, Robert, 36
Steinbeck, John, 34–35
Steward, David, 304
Stewart, Gavin, 305
Steyn, Richard, 235, 251, 252
Storie, Valerie, 169
Suchet, David, 18–19
Sullivan, John L, 40
Sullivan, Peter, 252, 265
Sulzberger, Arthur Hays, 187
Sulzberger, Arthur Ochs ('Punch'), 203, 205, 206, 207
Sun, The, 8, 22, 198, 239, 240
Sunday Express, The (Johannesburg), 142, 148, 149, 270
Sunday Independent, 253
Sunday News Journal (Delaware), 137, 138, 139, 146
Sunday Star, The, 253
Sunday Telegraph, The, 42
Sunday Times (London), 171, 189, 190, 191, 199, 205, 241, 243
Sunday Times (South Africa), 130, 274, 276, 279, 281
Sunday Tribune, The, 230
Survé, Iqbal, 254, 260, 261, 262, 263, 264
Sydney Morning Herald, 326, 327

Tambo, Oliver, 302
Telegraph, The, 18, 41, 42, 78
Tennyson, Alfred Lord, 74
Thamm, Marianne, 284–85
Thatcher, Margaret, 21, 116, 239
Theiner, George, 310
Thesiger, Wilfred, 37
Thompson, Hunter S, 34
Thomson, Roy, 171, 198, 240
Thorpe, Jeremy, 147
Thurber, James, 183
Time Warner, 330

339

Time, 313, 316
Times of India, The, 100, 152
Times-Herald, The, 210
Times, The (London), 8, 11, 40, 61, 62, 75, 76, 129, 159, 160, 161–76, 191, 193, 194, 198, 199, 204, 205, 221, 225, 229, 230, 238, 240, 241, 242, 243, 244
Tit-Bits (magazine), 192, 193
To the Point, 147
Topping, Seymour, 207
Toronto Star, The, 202
Toynbee, Polly, 318
Trail, George, 96, 134
Transparency International, 158
Transvaler, Die, 45, 265
Trillian, 278
Troubles, The (Northern Ireland), 66–72
Truman, Harry, 36, 94
Trump, Donald, vi, 13, 37, 205, 222, 268, 273, 276
Twain, Mark – see Clemens, Samuel
Twitter, 323, 329, 330
Tyler, Wat, 113, 116–17

United Democratic Front, 301
United Press International, 208
United Press, 89
Updike, John, 183

Van den Bergh, Hendrik, 141–49
Van Wyk, Alec, 147
Van Zyl Slabbert, Frederik, 270
Venter, Casper, 306
Verdu, Vincente, 306
Verne, Jules, 40
Verwoerd, Hendrik, 45, 46, 144, 171, 232, 265
Vietnam war, 36, 42, 89, 204, 205
Virginian Pilot, 85
Vlachos, Helen, 309
Vorster, BJ, 142, 143, 144, 147, 148, 149

Wales, Henry G, 86–87
Wallace, Edgar, 33
Walters, John, 161
Washington Post, 29, 128, 146, 156, 187, 201–202, 203, 209, 210, 222, 294, 309, 327
Watergate, 201, 295

Watson, Tom, 244
Waugh, Evelyn, 27
Weaver, Tony, 260, 261
Webster, David, 269, 270
Weisberg, Jacob, 330, 331
Welles, Orson, 184
West, Rebecca, 30
White, EB, 183
Whitlam, Gough, 239
Whittam-Smith, Andreas, 250, 256, 307
Wickham Steed, Henry, 194, 199
Wierichs, Jeff, 183
Wilde, Oscar, vi
Williams, Francis, 197, 198, 199
Willkie, Wendell, 36
Wilson, Harold, 19, 147, 197–98
Wilson, Woodrow, 35, 36
Witness, The, 251
Wohifahrt, Dieter, 107
Wolfe, Humbert, 27
Wolfe, Tom, 34
World Association of Newspapers (FIEJ), 9, 12, 153, 154, 155, 157
World Free Press Organisation, 155
World Press Freedom Committee, 151, 301, 305
World War I, 35, 93, 196, 223, 230
World War II, 17, 34, 35, 41–42, 93, 99, 101, 119, 126, 195, 223, 225, 227, 230
World-Herald, The, 210
World, The, 9, 179, 180, 213, 215, 216, 218, 227
Wright, Orville, 85–86
Wright, Wilbur, 85–86
Wu, Tim, 330

Yellow Journalism, 22
Yellow Kid, The, 181
Yellow Press, 9, 84, 179, 181–86
Yeltsin, Boris, 156, 157
YouTube, 323, 330

Zeit, Die, 308, 328
Zelle, Gertrude Margarete (Mata Hari), 86–87
Zuckerberg, Mark, 315
Zuma, Jacob, 219, 254, 260, 261, 263, 273, 274, 275, 276, 277, 278, 279, 280, 281, 282, 283, 284, 289

Acknowledgements

AS IS ALWAYS THE CASE, it is almost impossible to thank all the people – not least of which are the fine journalists, friends and authors from whom I've borrowed – involved in putting together a historical work such as The end of the Deadline.

But I would like to name at least some of those who have supported and helped me assemble this book. Particularly in recent months, when I wasn't quite sure what day it was never mind being conscious of the need for the vigorous attention to detail, editing and fact-checking that go towards making what I hope will be, inter alia, a cogent and useful history of the printed press and brought to life by the small part I played in it.

The first person is my patient and ever supportive wife, Arlene, who has consistently nurtured my need to write and protected me from interruptions over too many years to mention. The freedom you have allowed me underlines your generosity and selflessness.

Secondly, there is Vanessa Swanepoel, my talented website designer (Writing Inc.) and book concept layout wizard who has assisted me greatly to remember where I was, what I was writing about and sometimes even who I was over the past few years.

Then to my team of editors, Nick Yell and Craig Tyson backed up by Vanessa, thanks for your invaluable input and helping to make this book the readable and reliable reference work on the printed press I hope it will one day become known as.

Mention must also be made of the sterling design, layout and sales efforts of Robin Stuart-Clark's team at Print Matters (Heritage) without whose expert packaging of this book and sales network it may never have made it onto the shelves of bookstores.

Last, but not least, all my family members and loyal friends who've read and endured all my writing over the years, your bravery and dogged perseverance is the stuff of legend.

Harvey Wood Tyson
Hermanus
South Africa
September 2018